WONDER AND EXILE IN THE NEW WORLD

ALEX NAVA

WONDER

AND EXILE

IN THE

NEW WORLD

The Pennsylvania State University Press

University Park, Pennsylvania

Library of Congress Cataloging-in-Publication Data

Nava, Alexander, 1967–
Wonder and exile in the New World / Alex Nava.
      p.   cm.
Summary: "Explores the language of wonder in the history
of the New World. Traces the preoccupation with this
concept in the history of the Americas from the colonial era
to the twentieth century, with the emergence of so-called
magical realism"—Provided by publisher.
Includes bibliographical references and index.
ISBN 978-0-271-05993-8 (cloth : alk. paper)
1. Spanish American literature—History and criticism.
2. America—Early accounts to 1600—History and criticism.
3. America—Discovery and exploration—Spanish.
4. Baroque literature—History and criticism.
5. Wonder in literature.
6. Wonder—Religious aspects.
7. Magic realism (Literature).
8. Exile (Punishment) in literature.
9. Mysticism and literature.
I. Title.

PQ7081.N2826 2013
860.9'98—dc23
2013003232

TO MY TEACHERS, *especially*
Robert A. Burns and David Tracy, with gratitude

CONTENTS

ACKNOWLEDGMENTS

When trying to express gratitude for a book on wonder, it's tempting to begin with the budding memories of childhood, since the aptitude for wonder seems highly developed in this early stage, only to retreat and diminish in adult years. In some cases, under the pressures and routines of the mundane, it goes into hibernation. In my case, childhood was, indeed, the wonder years, a time of fascination and exploration, when everything around me pulsed with life and seemed so remarkably strange and peculiar. I can recall, in particular, the early fascination I had for books and learning and the equal attraction for matters related to the mysterious question of God. And I came to love the rhymes and rhythms of language, especially in literature, poetry, and music. Though my first attraction to poetry occurred through the words and beats of hip-hop (perhaps a subject for another book), I soon turned to the study of literature and religion at the University of Arizona, where my professors (especially Robert Burns, Robert Gimello, and Heiko A. Oberman) fed my insatiable curiosity. I am very grateful for their formative impact on my life.

Upon graduation, I made my way to the University of Chicago, a place that offered my hunger a great banquet of ideas. Bernard McGinn, Anne Carr, David Tracy, Friedrich Katz, Homi Bhabha, and Jean-Luc Marion, among many others, gave me a wealth of knowledge and a completely new set of questions to entertain and explore. This book would not have been written without their teaching and scholarship.

Beyond my teachers in the classroom, this book is a dialogue with numerous scholars that I cite throughout my study. Hopefully my debt to them is clear, but nevertheless I would like to single out a few of them. Edward Hirsch introduced me to the wonders of poetry in his numerous studies on the subject; Roberto González Echevarría was an engaging and excellent guide to the Baroque traditions in Spain and Latin America; Stephen Greenblatt's work on the marvel of the New World is an obvious influence on this study; and the work of Rolena Adorno, Diana de Armas Wilson, Frederick de Armas, Walter Mignolo, Ilan Stavans, and Lois Parkinson Zamora each contributed significantly to my understanding of Latin

American literary and cultural traditions. In theology, the list of influences and contributors to this study is long, but at the top is David Tracy, Gustavo Gutiérrez, Enrique Dussel, Roberto Goizueta, and Benjamin Valentin.

Richard Rodriguez read an early, abridged version one of my chapters, and I was delightfully surprised by the time and care that he put into reading my work and, of course, for the valuable suggestions he gave me, especially pertaining to the writing style. Thank you.

I had the benefit of some good, tough, anonymous readers who gave me fine suggestions and feedback for improving the manuscript. And, of course, my copyeditor, Nicholas Taylor, read the manuscript with great care and helped me clarify and refine it in many ways.

Numerous friends gave me much needed support throughout the entire, long process of writing this book and deserve thanks: Michael Ferguson and Jim and Mimi Dew for the rare and enduring friendship that we have shared; Rick Duran for his friendship and never-ending wealth of humor; Fr. Bill Dougherty for his wisdom and grace; Eileen Couch for her affection and kindness during my graduate school years in Chicago; and Annie Rhodes for her vitality, craziness, and sweetness.

I am also very grateful to my second family from Somalia. They have given me so many precious gifts that it would be hard to express my gratitude in a few words. What I can say is that I have been enriched for knowing them. And my relationship with them would not be what it is if not for two friends of mine—Isabel Shelton and Brooke Sabia. Thank you Miss Isabel and Miss Brooke for being a part of this family and a part of my life.

Of course, I cannot neglect mentioning my great family for all that they have done to shape my life and career. Beyond their unending love and support, my parents, Eduardo and Alicia, instilled a love of learning in me from the very beginning. My siblings, Andy and Mindy, have always been an important part of my life, and supported and encouraged me in everything I have done. My brother's wife and kids, Bettina, Zeta, Bianca, and Paloma, have also given me the precious gifts of affection and joy and I am grateful that they entered our lives. Finally, my cousin, Robert Robinson, has been like a brother to me since our childhood, something that I cherish greatly and never take for granted.

I would like to dedicate this study to each one of the above names, but for the sake of this book, I would like to mention in particular my teachers, especially my undergraduate teacher, Robert A. Burns, and my graduate school adviser and friend, David Tracy.

ABBREVIATIONS

C   Columbus, Christopher. *The Four Voyages*. Translated by
J. M. Cohen. New York: Penguin, 1969.

CV   Cabeza de Vaca, Álvar Núñez. *Chronicle of the Narvaez
Expedition*. Translated by Harold Augenbraum. New York:
Penguin, 2002.

DQ   Cervantes, Miguel de. *Don Quixote*. Translated by John
Rutherford. New York: Penguin, 2003.

EC   Carpentier, Alejo. *Explosion in a Cathedral*. Translated by
Harriet de Onis. Minneapolis: University of Minnesota Press,
2001.

HS   Carpentier, Alejo. *The Harp and the Shadow*. Translated by
Thomas and Carol Christensen. New York: Mercury House,
2007.

KW   Carpentier, Alejo. *The Kingdom of This World*. Translated by
Harriet de Onis. New York: Farrar, Straus and Giroux, 2006.

LC, *A*   Las Casas, Bartolomé de. *Apologia*. Translated by Frances
Patrick Sullivan. In *Indian Freedom: The Cause of Bartolomé de
Las Casas, 1484–1566: A Reader*. Kansas City, Mo.: Sheed and
Ward, 1995.

LC, *DI*   Las Casas, Bartolomé de. *A Short Account of the Destruction of
the Indies*. Translated by Nigel Griffin. New York: Penguin,
1992.

LC, *HI*   Las Casas, Bartolomé de. *History of the Indies*. Translated by
Francis Patrick Sullivan. In *Indian Freedom: The Cause of
Bartolomé de Las Casas, 1484–1566: A Reader*. Kansas City,
Mo.: Sheed and Ward, 1995.

LD	Calderón de la Barca, Pedro. *Life Is a Dream*. Translated by Gregory Racz. New York: Penguin, 2006.
LS	Carpentier, Alejo. *The Lost Steps*. Translated by Harriet de Onis. Minneapolis: University of Minnesota Press, 2001.
MC	Foucault, Michel. *Madness and Civilization*. Translated by Richard Howard. New York: Vintage Books, 1988.
MM	Asturias, Miguel Ángel. *Men of Maize*. Translated by Gerald Martin. Pittsburgh: University of Pittsburgh Press, 1995.
OHYS	Márquez, Gabriel García. *One Hundred Years of Solitude*. Translated by Gregory Rabassa. New York: Harper and Row, 1970.
OP	Paz, Octavio. *Sor Juana; or, The Traps of Faith*. Translated by Margaret Sayers Peden. Cambridge: Harvard University Press, 1990.
PQ	Quiroga, Pedro. *Coloquios de la Verdad*. Seville: Tip. Zarzuela, 1922.
SJM	Mandeville, Sir John. *The Travels of Sir John Mandeville*. Translated by C. W. R. D. Moseley. New York: Penguin, 2005.
SJ, *PPD*	Inés de la Cruz, Sor Juana. *Poems, Protest, and a Dream*. Translated by Margaret Sayers Peden. New York: Penguin, 1997.
SJ, *SW*	Inés de la Cruz, Sor Juana. *Selected Writings*. Translated and edited by Pamela Kirk Rappaport. New York: Paulist Press, 2005.
SP	Asturias, Miguel Ángel. *El Señor Presidente*. Translated by Frances Partridge. New York: Waveland Press, 1997.
T	Benjamin, Walter. *The Trauerspiel: On the Origins of German Tragic Drama*. Translated by John Osborne. New York: Verso, 1992.
WT	Carpentier, Alejo. *War of Time*. New York: Knopf, 1970.

INTRODUCTION

Were this world an endless plain, and by sailing eastward we could forever

reach new distances, and discover sights more sweet and strange than any

Cyclades or Islands of King Solomon, then there were promise in the

voyage. But in pursuit of those far mysteries we dream of, or in tormented

chase of that demon phantom that, some time or other, swims before all

human hearts; while chasing such over this round globe, they either lead

us on in barren mazes or midway leave us whelmed.

—Herman Melville, *Moby Dick*

Few things enchant the human mind more than tales of travel to faraway lands. Such stories can carry us away and take us to places that are barely imaginable, places that are beyond the borders of what our mind conceives as possible or logical. There is, for this reason, something delightful and wondrous in travel narratives. Perhaps they delight us for giving verbal expression to the infinite impulse and restless craving that make human beings set out in quest of knowledge or wisdom, beauty or love, or else something more indefinable and mysterious. Or perhaps it is for their daring, their willingness to confront danger and trespass familiar limits in the search for some unheard of, fantastic truth that causes us to admire and delight in these stories. Herman Melville, for one, likened the tall tales born from such expeditions to the pleasure of sinning because they were equally seductive and indulgent, wild and romantic. They were sinful for exciting and swelling that dangerous appetite—curiosity (too frequently the path to heresy in the Middle Ages). And they were sinfully delightful in their capacity to stimulate our deepest urges and propel us into new worlds of possibility.

Something like this must have happened to the explorers of the New World, as if sirens cried out to them in an enchanting and curious voice that they could not resist. In flirting with the novelty of a once unknown continent, they would gradually revise older fears of curiosity and transform these fears into noble possibilities for discovery. The modern world would be made of such principles and the Americas, in particular, played an important role in this revolution in values. With the frequency of wonder at a particularly high pitch, the travelers to the Americas would rhapsodize and improvise in trying to name and identify their discoveries. Their preoccupation with wonder was a motif unmistakably related to their efforts to invent a whole new worldview that would capture the sounds and flavors of an American landscape. The language of wonder would come to represent a defining feature of its cultures, literatures and religions.

At the outset of my own story in this book—a book about the distant mysteries that the New World represented—it is important for me to provide a brief map of the journey, lest the reader end up lost in a barren maze as Melville warned. So, let me begin by saying something about the ambiguity and perplexity of this thing called "wonder." At the very least, there are a few entrances to the labyrinths of wonder. For one, the experience of wonder can suggest something pleasurable and attractive, something that can ravish and intoxicate. In this sense, when we are faced with something wondrous, we are stimulated by a beauty or good so inviting and charming that we want to revel and lose ourselves in it. Though wonder represents what the mind cannot fully know or understand—for being so novel and startling to our normative conceptions of knowledge—this very intractability and inscrutability makes it all the more seductive, all the more intriguing. It stimulates curiosity and beckons us to explore its hidden mysteries.

Curiosity, as I have suggested, is an element of this hunger for the unknown, the itch of the human heart for exploration and adventure, for movement into strange and exotic regions of human knowledge. Wonder and curiosity are manifestations of the soul hunger that drove Melville's Ishmael to take to a whaling ship. And it was a similar torment, even before this American wonderer, that brought the ever-expanding mass of European explorers to the unknown shores of the New World.

If this glimpse of wonder's alluring and radiant beauty—the gush of life—is the most pleasing, it is not the only one. We all know that the feast of beauty is often interrupted and spoiled by the unnerving appearance of suffering, as if the stale bread of exile was suddenly the only food available in a once abundant feast. So much for aesthetic abandon—when exile enters the feast, the expression of wonder takes on a different tone, something closer to dread than ecstasy. This face of wonder is tormented and foreboding, and makes the blood freeze, the soul shudder. Wonder takes on something like a blue note in these circumstances, sounding like a scorched voice, a tear in the throat, a melancholic expression of what is both awe-inspiring and awful at once. Under the impact of exile, wonder is dragged through muddy waters and it hollers, screams, shudders, wails, laments. And in this process, wonder emerges more soulful than before.

In speaking of this blues-like shading of wonder, I am looking at wonder in light of the post-lapsarian history of humankind going back to Adam and Eve's expulsion. In fact, wonder would have no meaning in a pre-fallen Edenic world. It has its reason for being only in the tormented history of the human race. Punished for breaching the limits of knowledge, for wanting too much, Adam and Eve would lose the garden for the desert and here they would know fear and shame. Now their lives and loves would be subject to the pains and pangs of a naked, fragile mortal condition. They would have to earn their daily bread by an arduous contest with the parched desert soil. Neither the fruits of the earth nor the fruits of knowledge would ever again be as accessible as in Eden. Like fruit fallen from a tree, worm-eaten and decayed, knowledge tumbled away and suffered dispersion and deferral, making truth into something indeterminate and inaccessible. Wonder had its humble origins here, when Adam and Eve began their nomadic wanderings, far from the tree of the knowledge of good and evil. The human capacity for wonder is born in this distance from Eden, in this desert experience of dispossession.

Or, in philosophical language, a postlapsarian version of wonder has some of the dark, scarred features of the sublime. For many contemporary thinkers, at least, the sublime is a version of wonder in a wounded, fragmented form. It shares with wonder the encounter with something indeterminate or unthinkable, but in this account (an unorthodox reading of Kant's third critique), the sublime fragments and disrupts the harmony of classic aesthetics.[1] It introduces us to something that would make reason cringe and recoil, the presence of an absence or void that has suffering written all over it.

When wonder embodies the sublime, then, it sings the blues and gives tortured voice to the alphabet of suffering. And make no mistake about it: the alphabet of suffering is never like the innocent and thrilling first moments of a child learning his or her letters. It is, instead, a scrambled alphabet, hard to decipher, unintelligible, inscrutable. If something is learned from it, it exacts a heavy price for disclosing its secrets. And this is, perhaps, one of the lessons of both wonder and exile: that for mere mortals, wisdom is always an inexact science, always a kind of knowledge that comprises jumbled letters, half-heard words, stammering expressions. It is, at best, a gift half understood, half comprehended.

Notorious for its inclusive and bountiful imagination, the Baroque, or so my book argues, is one of these gifts, a capacious, beautiful, tragic representation of wonder in a variety of guises, including this trace of the sublime. Anticipating modern and even postmodern themes, the Baroque included doses of both dimensions of wonder noted above, like a brew made with a variety of potions, some charming and delightful, others frightening. The Baroque combined the beautiful, strange, and terrible in an uneasy and disjointed harmony. The result was intoxicating, a Baroque concoction that has something of the dark arts in it. Initiated into these arts by the deeply felt misfortunes and struggles of their age, Baroque artists would give us classic descriptions of the tragic contours of wonder. They would create black magic out of the terrors of their own soul and give us something similar to Rudolph Otto's account of the sacred as the *mysterium tremendum et fascinans*.[2]

The book before the reader is devoted to travelers that knew this ambiguity of the sacred, its allures and terrors. Their capacity for wonder propelled them on quests of the most uncanny and foreign sort, even at the price of great danger and peril, like having to cross the menacing abysses of ocean or desert, having to go farther than anyone has gone before. The course of my book follows the imagination of American explorers, beginning with the figures of the Conquest (Columbus, Cabeza de Vaca, Bartolomé de Las Casas in chapter 2) through the Baroque (Cervantes and Sor Juana Inés de la Cruz in chapters 3–4) and into twentieth-century literature with the genre of so-called magical realism (Miguel Ángel Asturias and Alejo Carpentier in chapter 5). I am interested in how these explorers and artists represented wonder and what this can teach us about the history of the New World, from its great promises to its failures and tragedies. Each of my subjects in this study has something valuable to say in this regard, including the one who never made it to the New World despite numerous attempts to secure a post in the Indies (Cervantes).

Indeed, because Cervantes seems to be the exception to my focus on New World figures, a comment is in order about his inclusion. In addition to the biographical fact that Cervantes had requested on at least two occasions (in the early 1580s and early 1590s) to travel and work in the New World (his petitions were denied by the Council of the Indies), his literary creations seemed to follow in spirit this desire of his and, thus, are imbued with a plethora of New World themes, images, dreams, and aspirations. As Diana de Armas Wilson has shown so well, Cervantes's novels traveled to the Indies in imagination when he was prohibited from going in person.[3] The most notable case of this concerns the intersection of Don Quixote's chivalrous dreams with the imperial and conquering dreams of Columbus and other conquistadors. Traces of this impulse are evident in many instances, but when Don Quixote describes to us the military attributes of the knight in shining armor, resonances with Spanish imperialism are loud and clear. Clearly, and notwithstanding Don Quixote's other lofty and admirable purposes, Don Quixote celebrates the great pleasure of victory in battle: "What greater contentment or pleasure can there be in the world than winning a battle and triumphing over one's enemy?" (*DQ*, part 1, 18). Columbus and other conquistadors may not have described this pleasure in such a candid and blunt manner, but it is impossible to deny that their aspirations were concentrated on conquest and that their lives and chronicles had quixotic traits (hopelessly romantic or wildly delirious, as the term "quixotic" suggests in our own time).[4]

If this is at all true, and if the final purpose of Cervantes's novel is to destroy the illusions and fantasies of the chivalric genre (as the last page of the novel suggests), then *Don Quixote* represents a deconstructive satire of the "real-world discourses connected with the conquest and colonization of the Hispanic Indies," and a criticism of what is insane about Spanish imperialism.[5] In the terms of my study, we can say that *Don Quixote* is a warning and censure of any form of wonder (from fantasy to religious fanaticism) that soars too far from the earthly, historical, mortal nature of the human condition.

In studying Cervantes in this way—in light of the New World—we would also be faithful to Walter Mignolo's insistence on recognizing the "darker side of the Renaissance" by meditating on the Renaissance and Baroque from the perspective of the colonies, vis-à-vis the Atlantic and Pacific.[6] It would enable us to bring greater attention to the part played by the history of conquest and colonialism in the formation of the modern age (and on this matter, Mignolo acknowledges the pioneering work of the theologian Enrique Dussel). And it would force us to reconsider the work of many of the greatest artists of the early modern age, to see how the wounding traces and scars opened up by 1492 altered their conceptual maps and consciousness.

The inclusion of Cervantes in my study, finally, should remind us that we cannot subject the continents of the Old and New Worlds to a "historiographical divorce" (in the words of J. H. Elliott).[7] There are numerous instances in my book where I travel between the two worlds in seeking to understand the pleasures and wounds of wonder and exile. My book follows the same restlessness of Don Quixote's wandering (another metaphor of the impulse for travel and exploration widespread in the sixteenth century), and hopes to shed light on various artists as they grappled with suffering and injustice, with beauty and mystery. It follows in the footsteps of these ancient travelers as they crossed borders of ocean and desert, and as they crossed more mysterious borders.

This latter preoccupation should make clear that my study is interested in the theological inclinations of New World explorers, writers, and poets. In interpreting the language of wonder and exile, therefore, special care is devoted to the matters of the soul among these pioneering American voices. In fact, the theological features of my study are crucial to the particular accent of it, thus distinguishing it from other studies that have influenced my approach (like the work of Stephen Greenblatt, Lois Parkinson Zamora, Roberto González Echevarría, Rolena Adorno, Walter Mignolo, and others). This book could not have been written without their scholarship. I am, however, also leaning on a rich tradition of religious studies in the course of my study. In this case, I am working with an assumption that, I trust, is not too contentious: that religion is a key feature of Latin American cultures and traditions. Indeed, I would echo Cornel West's claim that religion is fundamental to many of the cultures of the oppressed in the Americas. For West, one of the greatest flaws and prejudices among the political left concerns its refusal to appreciate the role of religion among oppressed peoples. "It is," he writes, "the European Enlightenment legacy . . . that stands between contemporary Marxism and oppressed people. And it is the arrogance of this legacy, the snobbery of this tradition, that precludes Marxists from taking seriously religion, a crucial element of the culture of the oppressed."[8] Fortunately, none of the scholars mentioned above suffers from this snobbery, but it is, nevertheless, an active presence in the world of academic scholarship. I hope that my study threatens any form of this presumption, from enlightened contempt for religion to fundamentalist confidences.

In addition to this fidelity to the cultures of the oppressed in the New World, there is another benefit, it seems to me, about a theological approach, and it concerns the wide-ranging scope of my book. As my study unfolds, it should become clear that my primary concern in exploring the history of the New World is the value of the past for present-day problems and issues. Though the historical method is essential to any study of the past and informs every page of my book, theological concerns demand attention to the constructive nature of historical studies, to their relevance in our own time. In my reading of the theological enterprise (in the tradition of Karl Rahner, Paul Tillich, and David Tracy), theology must always be able to demonstrate the relevance and importance of past traditions for our contemporary situation, to correlate the voices of ancestors with the voices of the present.

I am interested, thus, in the ideas of past masters for how they enrich our present and future, how they can elevate our lives. In addition to the theological method, I am following Nietzsche in this way, by insisting that history provide us with the models and incentives to re-create, invent, and discover anew, not to remain fixed and frozen in the remote past.[9] As Nietzsche argued, when the historical method is the sole and determining approach, intolerant to anything other than its dream of "objectivity," it becomes the domain of the "spoiled idler in the garden of knowledge" and, subsequently, withers and degenerates.[10] As he suggests, we must pry history loose from antiquarians and specialists in order to move forward and not stand still, in order to use history not only to preserve but to create life. The broad span of time in my book has this purpose in mind, then, to appropriate the images and monuments of the New World past for the struggles and hopes of our own age.

In fact, even better than Nietzsche's portrait of the uses and abuses of history is the model Cervantes gives us. He reminds us what happens to the mind and spirit of someone who is trapped in the remote past: he loses his mind. Though we admire Don Quixote's defense of ancient values, every reader knows that this comes at the heavy price of his sanity. With his sole concentration on the immediate present, however, Sancho Panza's perspective is not without its problems and shortcomings. In balancing multiple voices and perspectives, Cervantes was able to achieve a brilliant fusion of the past and present. According to Carlos Fuentes, this was Cervantes's major achievement in the creation we know as the novel: "Cervantes was able to go beyond the consecration of the past and the consecration of the present to grapple with the problem of the fusion of past and present. . . .

The past (Don Quixote's illusion of himself as a knight errant of old) illuminates the present (the concrete world of inns and roads, muleteers and scullery maids); and the present (the harsh life of men and women struggling to survive in a cruel, unjust and shabby world) illuminates the past (Don Quixote's ideals of justice, freedom and a Golden Age of abundance and equality)."[11]

This fusion of the past and present in *Don Quixote*, where the narratives of the past meet the conflicts, uncertainties, and disasters of our present, is the model for my own study. In my reading of past masters—from Las Casas, Cervantes, and Sor Juana to twentieth-century "magical realists"— I am following Don Quixote's enchanted imagination in his defense of ancient values, in his devotion to the ideals of justice, freedom, and equality. And with Sancho Panza, on the other hand, my study hopes to remain grounded in the concrete beatings and nightmares that constitute the histories of the New World. Thus, guided by the knight of faith and his squire, this study will explore the histories of wonder and exile in the New World.

In order to understand better the theological approach of my study, I begin in chapter 1 with a preliminary exploration of the language of wonder and exile in light of the mystical and prophetic traditions of Judaism and Christianity. The distinctiveness of my study from strictly literary approaches shines brightest here and should illuminate the interpretive method used throughout the rest of my book.

The central thesis of this study is that wonder and exile are both forms of absence or dispossession: wonder as a form of absence in the order of knowledge, and exile, in place and location. Wonder is defined by an encounter with something we do not and cannot fully understand, or by a recognition, and here I am following Stephen Greenblatt, that our grasp of the world is always incomplete and indeterminate.[12] Wonder marks the radical otherness and impenetrability of a given phenomenon, the ineradicable mystery at the heart of all human knowledge. Given this feature of wonder—its intellectual modesty and learned ignorance—our age would do well to embrace it to resist the self-righteous triumphalism and absolutism of any form of human understanding, from religious fundamentalism to the fundamentalism of some Enlightenment narratives. If human knowledge is frozen in place, definitive and confident, there will be no place for wonder and, thus, nothing will be surprising, nothing remarkable, nothing novel.

Exile, too, is characterized by absence, but with the terrifying face of absence, an absence that is intimate with the terrors of history, with the forced displacement and dispossession of the poor and oppressed of the world. As a tear and cut from house and home, exile is wounding and heavy-handed, born of history's cruel passages. Our own age is reeling from the effects of exile, and there is no greater evidence of this than the desperate exoduses of millions of migrants throughout the world. Whether forced or voluntary, the passage of migrants in our times is the clearest manifestation of our unsettled and unhoused age. Homi Bhabha calls these facts the defining features of our postmodern condition:

> If the jargon of our times—postmodernity, postcoloniality, postfeminism—has any meaning at all, it does not lie in the popular use of the "post" to indicate sequentiality. . . . For instance, if the interest in postmodernism is limited to a celebration of the fragmentation of the "grand narratives" of postenlightenment rationalism then, for all its intellectual excitement, it remains a profoundly parochial enterprise. . . . For the demography of the new internationalism is the history of postcolonial migration, the narratives of cultural and political diaspora, the major social displacements of peasant and aboriginal communities, the poetics of exile, the grim prose of political and economic refugees.[13]

As much as my book is concerned with the portrait of wonder in the New World, then, a central concern is with these great migrations and displacements, past and present. As a Mexican American myself, born close to the U.S.-Mexico border in Tucson, I can testify to the stream, or better, river of migrants walking through the vast and perilous deserts of border territories, dying to live, desperately wanting the opportunity to live and blossom in a context that provides the body and soul oxygen to breathe. Every year, hundreds do not make it so far and end their long sojourns in the middle of the desert, to die, like Moses, before ever making it to the Promised Land. When I speak of exile in this study, even through the lens of older voices and laments, I have in mind the scorched lives of these immigrants and refugees.

Though my study is unabashedly academic and theoretical, I hope that it is also the desert space in which a poetics of wonder encounters a poetics of exile, and each are changed as a result, wonder now mindful of the suffering and trials of history, on the one hand, and exile gaining in imagination. In this case, my book argues that wonder turns ominous and menacing, even grotesque, when the force of exile is felt the most, as in prophetic and apocalyptic literatures. As I read them, these texts are haunting examples of how profoundly wonder is changed under the most disjointed and oppressive conditions of history. Latin American history is a case in point and its classic texts, whether theological or literary, often resemble the apocalyptic imagination with its brood of eccentric wonders.[14] I hope that my study proves this case by exploring some of these classic texts in which wonder and curiosity (a "Baroque curiosity" in the words of José Lezama Lima) coexist with a wrenching bewilderment at the horrors of history.[15]

To return to Melville's Ishmael, we might see in him an allegory of these themes of wonder and exile. Melville tells us that life at sea generates the most astonishing and wildest of all marvels, as if travel on the remotest waters, to the farthest ends of the earth, in such latitudes and longitudes, produces an imagination like no other, one bursting with energy and pregnant with the "wonderfullest" of all fancies.[16] Ishmael, no doubt, is tantalized by these marvels, by the anarchic pleasure of sailing forbidden seas and landing on barbarous coasts, but he soon becomes acquainted with another facet of the sea. The sea is freedom for Ishmael, but it is also terror (Melville is a Calvinist after all). Ishmael may want to drown in the sea of wonder, but his name, too, conjures memories of his ancient ancestor, the biblical Ishmael who is exiled from the Promised Land (with his mother, the slave woman Hagar). So, Melville writes of the marvels of life, but with the warning noted in the epilogue of this introduction: that there are dangerous, destructive wonders that lead to barren mazes and leave us overwhelmed, ones that carry us into the maelstroms of history and leave us capsized and lost, exiles in the abyss.

At the end of *Moby Dick*, when Ishmael's ship (the *Pequod*, piloted by the mad Ahab) is destroyed, Melville invokes another biblical figure, mother Rachel weeping for her exiled and dispossessed children: "By her still halting course and winding, woeful way, you plainly saw that this ship that so wept with spray, still remained without comfort. She was Rachel, weeping for her children because they were not."[17] And Rachel weeps for other American children as well, "because they were not." Much of the literature of the New World exhibits the same tears as mother Rachel, the same hardships as Hagar and Ishmael, the same capacity for wonder as Melville and the other American artists that are the subjects of my story in this book.

ONE

In *One Hundred Years of Solitude*, Colonel Aureliano Buendía is born with his eyes wide open, as the author himself, Gabriel García Márquez, was reported to have come forth from the womb.[1] This image of a wide-eyed child—eyes swollen and enlarged, looking like a full moon—will serve us nicely in considering the theme of wonder in the New World. From the time of the Discovery through the twentieth century, representations of this previously unknown continent would resemble these bulging eyes, pregnant with an extraordinary capacity for wonder. Wonder was on the tongue of explorers and writers of these lands to the point of excess, and they would use its language with Baroque-like extravagance and with a frequency rivaled only by appeals to exile. *One Hundred Years of Solitude* has remained something like scripture in Latin American literature because it captured these wide-ranging moments of life in the New World, wonder and exile alike.

As I see it, then, representations of the New World are often close to the spirit of this great novel, somewhere on the border between wonder and exile, sometimes with one more than the other, but more commonly, with an ambiguous and messy mixture of both. Whatever the case, the language of both wonder and exile is as common to the Americas as the experience of dispossession; in fact, they are one with dispossession, different manifestations of it. In the course of my study, I examine this claim thoroughly, that wonder is an experience of dispossession in the order of knowledge, while exile means dispossession in place and location. Though wonder and exile are universal experiences, my study argues that they reach a point of saturation in the momentous events surrounding the Discovery of the New World and in the bewildering events that follow. The New World, thus, gives us an intense case to study, one that is as profuse and extravagant with its wonders as it is with its agonies.

The focus of the book is with poets and writers of the New World and, more specifically, with their theological inclinations. When exploring these figures, then, my attention will turn to the mystical and prophetic trajectories of these writers to see what they can teach us about the language of wonder and exile. At times, my concentration will be on the space between wonder and exile (e.g., the shared experience of dispossession) and, at other times, my concern is with the distinct accents of wonder and exile, mysticism and prophecy. In this regard, I claim that the mystics have a special fluency when it comes to the language of wonder, and the prophets, an unmistakable and tortured familiarity with exile—and both of them, a proficiency with the strange and wondrous concept of God. As unbelievable or impossible as the idea of God is to some moderns, I find it equally impossible to neglect the question in a study devoted to the wonders of the New World. I am following the lead of Jorge Luis Borges when he insisted that any anthology of fantastic literature must include the theologians: "I compiled at one time an anthology of fantastic literature. I have to admit that the book is one of the few that a second Noah should save from a second flood, but denounce the guilty omission of the major and unexpected masters of the genre: Parmenides, Plato, John Scotus Eriugena, Albertus Magnus, Spinoza, Leibniz, Kant, Francis Bradley. In fact, to what do the prodigies of Wells or Edgar Allan Poe amount . . . confronted by the creation of God?"[2]

The book before the reader owes much to a claim of this kind and, for this reason, is distinct from strictly literary or cultural accounts of the themes of wonder and exile. My book, too, denounces the guilty omission of the name "God" from studies of fantastic, magical literature. There is nothing more uncanny, nothing more unsettling and fantastic than the thought of God, and to banish the theologians from the wonders of this genre equals the wrong done to the poets when Plato exiles them from his republic. So much is lost in this banishment, so many dreams and emotions—and so many wonders. Whatever else it is, wonder owes much to this strange and curious name that cannot be spoken.

Wonder and Mystical Languages of Unknowing

Wonder is a natural bedfellow of mystical language. It comes to mystics with the suddenness and burning passion of a new flame that sets one's heart on fire and reduces the tongue and mind to silence. Like mystical speech, wonder is always a form of communication, but it reaches for what is un-sayable over what can be said, for the unknown over what can be known—in theological terms, for what God is *not* more than what God is. Rather than leaving us self-assured, wonder disrupts our certainties and presump-tions, leaving us mystified and bewildered, lacking in absolute confidences, with more questions than answers. In this way, wonder is an experience of apophasis—literally, a speech of unsaying—because it undoes and negates known and predictable suppositions. It is an experience, instead, of the indeterminate and surprising, of something so novel and strange that it overwhelms and dazzles the most familiar categories of human knowledge and understanding. It has the power to stun and shock and to leave its re-cipient speechless, in awe. It makes its appearance when the mind is faced with the unfathomable and ineffable. When shackled by certain horizons and foreseeable principles of knowledge, wonder cannot emerge, or if it does it is a tired and false version, an idol posing as an icon.

So, for wonder to emerge and thrive, it must disrupt and confuse any system of totality, any version of knowledge that is absolute and smugly cer-tain. Wonder breaks through the hardened shell of definitive and uncon-ditional claims to reveal new queries, new problems, new doubts concealed within a system that once seemed so impregnable to uncertainty. It seems to me that something like this happened to the legacy of the Enlighten-ment, once seemingly secure and certain in what it achieved, now stained with more difficulties and puzzles than answers. What was once a picture of assurance now looks like a tattered picture of misgivings. In a sense, one might say, wonder entered the picture and uncovered a deeper and more ancient image beneath the modern one, an image that was much more at ease with mystery than was the Enlightenment portrait.

If one took a famous figure of the Enlightenment, Descartes, for instance, the natural inclination would be to assume that he fits perfectly within the self-assured version, and that wonder would be hard to find in the pages of his books, so closely aligned is he with the search for absolute and certain foundations of truth. In fact, it's impossible to deny that Descartes is anx-ious in his search for certainty, and that he puts a sacred trust in the power of reason to achieve this. And yet . . . Descartes is never as self-assured as many caricatures might suggest. Indeed, when Descartes takes up the ques-tion of wonder, for instance, he speaks with a different tone and suddenly sounds more modest and reserved about the powers of the human mind.

In Descartes, wonder is described as a "sudden surprise of the soul" in the face of something new, unusual, or strange.[3] As Stephen Greenblatt explains regarding Descartes, this sudden surprise in the experience of wonder is the quintessential response to a "first encounter": "Wonder—thrilling, potentially dangerous, momentary immobilizing, charged at once with desire, ignorance, and fear—is the quintessential human response to what Descartes calls a 'first encounter.'"[4] As a first encounter, wonder has so much force that it causes a momentary paralysis of the intellectual faculties (and, thus, for Descartes, occurs strictly in the brain). At best, the mind will grasp one side of the object of wonder, it will get only a glimpse. "One can perceive of the object," he explains, "only the first side that has presented itself, and consequently one cannot acquire a more particular knowledge of it."[5] One might say that the mind reaches an impasse in wonder because passage to the other side is blocked. Because of this limitation in wonder—an experience of ignorance—there is something unsettling about wonder for Descartes, as if it introduces doubt and equivocation into his most cherished convictions.

No wonder, then, that Descartes is ambiguous about wonder, expressing both fear and delight about it: fear, because it is loaded with ignorance and this philosopher wants to pass through wonder to reach the other side, the Promised Land of certainty; delight, because it provides us with the opportunity to learn about something "of which we were previously ignorant."[6] In the former instance, Descartes warns of the potential perversion of reason in the free play of wonder, especially when it turns extravagant and excessive. In excess, he writes, wonder "prevents or perverts the use of reason" and thwarts the acquisition of knowledge.[7] For this philosopher, wonder has to be a momentary paralysis of the mind, as thrilling as it is, because he is after a solution to the puzzle of human understanding. He wants to pluck the heart out of the mystery of wonder in order to advance scientific knowledge.

As Jean-Luc Marion argues, however, there are numerous moments in Descartes when this project is significantly interrupted by phenomena outside the control of the human mind. When Descartes stops to consider the thought of infinity, for instance, the surprise and thrill of wonder suddenly returns to suggest something enriching. When discussing infinity, his language suddenly sounds a lot like the apophatic language of the mystical traditions. It is this opening in Descartes that gives us his more passionate and soulful side—and his capacity for wonder. Since infinity is strictly incomprehensible for Descartes, human thought can only "touch it," not comprehend it.[8] In the face of infinity, even Descartes's beloved and proud "cogito" appears rather impotent. The gaze of the cogito cannot "take hold of it as much as surrender to it," an experience that is closer to dispossession than possession.[9] And most significant for our purposes, when Descartes describes the human gaze looking toward God, he speaks of the failure of comprehension as an experience of wonder. The gaze is stunned by the appearance of wonder: "I should like to pause here and spend some time in the contemplation of God, to reflect on his attributes, and to gaze with wonder and adoration on the beauty of this immense light, so far as the eye of my darkened intellect can bear it."[10]

These instances when Descartes concedes the weakness and submissiveness of the cogito, when he describes the intellect as darkened and blinded by "this immense light," are the precious cracks in Cartesian philosophy that Jean-Luc Marion wants to expand and deepen. Marion deepens these cracks so that they become gaping chasms, and wonder has a part to play in all of this. Indeed, Marion considers amazement a paradigmatic case of the mind's response to a "saturated phenomenon"—that is, something inescapably inaccessible and incomprehensible, something that forever remains in the dark no matter how much brilliance is brought to the matter. When confronted by an amazing phenomenon, the soul is bedazzled by a phenomenon so saturated with novelty, splendor, and otherness that it is unbearable and overwhelming to the human gaze.[11] The mind is flooded by a tidal wave of meaning, leaving the subject flabbergasted and unsure. The object of wonder is stranger than anything that can be imagined or foreseen and, thus, impossible to possess, like trying to palm the wind or touch the sky. The object of wonder, in this sense, is an impenetrable mystery: it comes in an enigmatic guise, unrecognizable, incommensurable, and unfathomable to all categories of knowledge.[12] Baffled by so much surplus, the mind finds it futile to control and assign it a determinate meaning. The mind is ravished, awed, stupefied, undone.

Because wonder comprises these features—uncertainty, obscurity, inscrutability, alterity—there is something in wonder fundamentally at odds with "Enlightenment" models of knowledge, if only because it dwells in shadowy and foggy conditions instead of the light of the sun. "The eye apperceives," Marion writes, "not so much the appearance of the saturated phenomenon as the blur, the fog, and the overexposure that this phenomenon imposes on its normal conditions of experience."[13] As a saturated phenomenon, wonder steals up in the fog or cloud of unknowing.

In this case, the alliance between wonder and darkness is expressed nicely in the Spanish verb *asombrar*, to wonder, carrying within it the word for shade or shadow, *sombra*. Something wondrous can be seen only through the haze of shadows, as a blur, like the fleeting and vanishing passing of the Lord God before Moses (he is permitted only a glimpse of God's back, not the face as he desired; see Exodus 33:23). Wonder is this partial glimpse, never the fullness of God's face, never the fullness of knowledge. Even as an object of wonder appears and reveals itself, thus it shrouds itself in darkness (*obscuridad*) to remain obscure and hidden, concealed in its beauty, a black beauty of sorts. The truths that hold us spellbound are, in this sense, wondrous because of their lack of transparency and intelligibility. They are shadowy epiphanies.

To be lost in wonder, consequently, would describe the moment when the mind is suddenly lost and confused, when the racing mind is stilled and paralyzed, when something so different and fascinating appears to startle us enough that our habitual and predictable patterns of thought and action are disrupted. The mind is then driven beyond itself into a condition of ecstasy where shadows and their uncertain ghosts dwell in lieu of clear and evident truths.

Many of the classic Jewish and Christian mystics knew these ecstasies of wonder. Their encounters with otherness always carried them outside themselves and beyond—beyond the ordinary, beyond reason, beyond being, beyond God. For them, wonder was a bridge to transcendence, to a larger domain outside the fixed truths and confining borders of reality. It was a bridge across the river, through the fields, and into the vast and infinite ocean. Because it would carry them to the infinite depths of the ocean, mystics were always deep sea divers, exploring the mysteries of life and God in all their most peculiar, odd, and startling manifestations. Though wonder is surely not the sole property of mystics, it is, nevertheless, a particularly intense and concentrated case of it.

Though this elusive term, "mysticism," has been subject to a wide variety of nonsensical and inane interpretations—fueled by the "New Age" movement—it is clear that the early Jewish and Christian sense of this term is synonymous with a strategy of apophasis. In contrast to kataphasis, or positive language about God, apophasis is the undoing of positive predications about the divine, or more precisely, all predications about the divine, positive or negative. Apophasis is a strategy of language that turns on itself, that deconstructs any and all concepts, images, and experiences that presume to capture the totally other and incomprehensible God. Apophasis is our guide in how to remain silent while still speaking, how to use words while saying nothing. Mystical apophasis, then, is speech about God that is a failure of speech, or theology in light of our ignorance of God.[14]

The masters of this genre—Gregory of Nyssa, Pseudo-Dionysius, John the Scot Eriugena, Meister Eckhart, Nicholas of Cusa—one might say, were experts at saying nothing, and they did this in ways that do not fit the simple alternatives of atheism or theism. They would challenge everyone who claims to know God, as Eckhart puts it: "A master says: if anyone thinks that he has known God . . . he does not know God."[15] Or with Aquinas: "The ultimate point of the human knowledge of God is to know that we don't know God."[16] To say the very least, mystical theology is a threat to all who are certain and confident in their understanding. To the dismay of atheists, it remains part of a tradition of religion and spirituality, and to the disappointment of theists, it radically contests and threatens all systems of theology. Nicholas of Cusa calls it "learned ignorance": "According to negative theology, infinity is all we discover in God. . . . In the shadows of our ignorance shines incomprehensibly the truth. . . . That, then, is the learned ignorance for which we have been searching."[17]

In modern times, I love Fernando Pessoa's description of the peculiar position of mystical language in both affirming "God" and denying "God"—or rather, beyond both: "Every sound mind believes in God. No sound mind believes in a definite God. There is some being, both real and impossible, who reigns over all things and whose person (if he has one) cannot be defined, and whose purposes (if he has any) cannot be fathomed. By calling this being God we say everything, since the word God—having no precise meaning—affirms him without saying anything. The attributes of infinite, eternal, omnipotent, all-just or all-loving that we sometimes attach to him fall off by themselves, like all unnecessary adjectives when the noun suffices."[18] For Pessoa, God is this slippery and unfathomable name, on which all adjectives slide off and cannot hold. We embrace the name God the way a bird embraces and gathers the wind beneath its wings, helping it rise, keeping it aloft. And yet the wind falls through and away from the bird's grasp, never settling and confining itself to this one creature. Mystical speech is something like this, a confession of faith in a name without precise meaning, indefinite and impossible, and yet with the power to bear the soul into ethereal heights. For the mystics, faith is this journey to the unfathomable other that we affirm without saying anything.

For its daring and eccentric discourse, mystical theology has proved alluring to a wide variety of contemporary intellectuals. Called one of the "greatest audacities of discourse in Western thought" by Jacques Derrida, apophatic theology is oddly familiar to deconstruction: "This apophatic boldness always consists in going further than is reasonably permitted.

That is one of the essential traits of all negative theology: passing to the limit, then crossing a frontier, including that of a community, thus of a sociopolitical, institutional, ecclesial reason or raison d'être. . . . This thought seems strangely familiar to the experience of what is called deconstruction."[19] In this way, apophasis crosses all kinds of frontiers and behaves like an illegal immigrant in its audacious and transgressive ways, walking across borders with all kinds of wild hopes and dreams. Heedless of human laws, apophasis follows higher, transcendent laws, like justice or God, but whatever the case, we know for sure that it wants to go farther than anyone thought possible.

It is true that mystics must speak and interrupt their preferred condition of silence, but they do so with metaphors suggestive of silence or emptiness—hence, their affection for bare metaphors like the desert, nothingness, the One, and so forth. Whether their language is reticent or profuse, they are indicating the inexpressible the way a nightingale's song indicates the night. Take the case of the desert: for Derrida, the image of the desert illustrates "negative theology," with the absolute aridity of the desert serving as his metaphor for the aridity and barrenness of apophasis. As a perfect image of divine nothingness or emptiness, the desert is an apophatic image par excellence, one that describes the barrenness of all our intellectual and cognitive presuppositions about the unknown. In bare and unadorned beauty, the desert is an icon of anti-iconic art like Islamic calligraphy. Apophasis, in this sense, is a "desertification" of language, a kenosis of discourse. "'God' is the name," Derrida writes, "of this bottomless collapse, of this endless desertification of language."[20] Mystical theology, he tells us, is literature for the desert and for exile: "This literature forever elliptical, taciturn, cryptic, obstinately withdrawing, however, from all literature, inaccessible there even where it seems to go, the exasperation of a jealousy, that passion carried beyond itself; this would seem to be a literature for the desert or for exile."[21]

With a focus on the New World, I will defend this claim throughout this study and insist on the relevance of mystical theology—this cryptic passion carried beyond itself, as Derrida puts it—for the desert and exile. For centuries, Jewish and Christian mystics made the desert their home and went there to retrace the wandering steps of the Israelites. For many of them—Philo of Alexandria, Gregory of Nyssa, and Pseudo-Dionysius, for instance—Moses was their spiritual guide through the vast and perilous lands of the desert; and if they had any hopes of achieving wisdom, they knew it would be nothing more than what Moses got, a glimpse of God hidden by a dark cloud or burning bush. The narratives of exile and divine hiddenness shaped their mystical theologies.

Take the remarkable case of Dante's mysticism of exile, for instance. Though Dante is narrating a mystical journey of the soul to God in *The Divine Comedy*, the poem is also haunted by the personal exigencies and terrors of Dante's own desert experience of exile from his beloved Florence. When Dante writes of the character Romeo, for instance—an infamous wanderer exiled in the thirteenth century from the courts of Provence—he surely has himself in mind:

> Romeo, proudly, old and poor, departed.
> And could the world know what was in his heart
> as he went begging, door to door, his bread.[22]

And when Dante meets his ancestor Cacciaguida, he is told of the agonizing future that will come to him, the heavy weight of exile that he must carry with him until the end of his days:

> While I was still in Virgil's company,
> climbing the mountain where the souls are healed,
> descending through the kingdom of the dead,
> ominous words about my future life
> were said to me—the truth is that I feel
> my soul foursquare against the blows of chance . . .
> As Hippolytus was forced to flee from Athens
> by his devious and merciless stepmother,
> just so you too shall have to leave your Florence.[23]

In *The Divine Comedy* and other writings (the *Convivio, De Eloquentia Vulgaria*), Dante would not only use language to convey silence like a mystic, but also to convey exile like a prophet, as a voice crying out in the desert.[24] It is not surprising, then, that Dante would turn to the biblical narrative of Exodus to make sense of his own refugee condition. Although Dante does not name God with desert language, Israel's bitter exodus through the desert becomes one of the most important narratives that define the *Divine Comedy.*[25]

With this image of the desert before us, we can see why Bernard McGinn insists that the mystics are wrestling with the absence of God as much as presence: "If the modern consciousness of God is often of an absent God (absent though not forgotten for the religious person), many mystics seem almost to have been prophets of this in their intense realization that the 'real God' becomes a possibility only when the many false gods (even the God of religion) have vanished and the frightening abyss of total nothingness is confronted."[26] If mysticism entails a confrontation with the abyss of nothingness, as in this description, then it seems profoundly appropriate to our modern age, as if the mystics had foreseen and divined the desertlike desolation felt by modern man and woman. The mystics knew that one had to face the wastelands before one could enter the gardens of life. They are our guides through the deserts of discourse where all our preconceptions, ideas, and images are consumed in a blaze, like idols thrown into the furnace of the desert sun. Only after our discourse is emptied out, only then, heart to heart, can we pray for the other to come, the other that we will meet in the stranger and refugee.

Prayers of this sort are common among the mystics and they are synonymous with the experience of wonder, reverence, and awe. When John the Scot Eriugena calls God the "divine desert"—the first to explicitly name God in this way—he was praying in unexpected ways, no longer naming God, but de-nominating, to borrow the language of Marion again.[27] He was developing a theology of absence that is awesome in its sparse and vacuous symbolism: "A more profound interpretation understands it (the desert in Exodus) as the desert of the divine nature, an inexpressible height removed from all things. It is 'deserted' by every creature, because it surpasses all intellect, although it does not 'desert' any intellect."[28] Eriugena's "divine desert" is equivalent to nothingness or emptiness, but of a peculiar sort, an emptiness that is over-full, a nothingness that is everything, a super-saturated presence that appears as absence. It is neither this nor that. Eriugena takes aim at formlessness the way Jewish or Islamic artists would remain faithful to the prohibitions of image and visual representation (considered idolatry).[29]

Whether in Eriugena or others, wonder appears frequently as the footprint of their language of unsaying. Eriugena bequeathed this strategy to many others, including the French Beguine mystic Marguerite of Porete when she would consider the nothingness that is God and the nothingness that dwells in the darkest recesses of the human soul: "They are amazed by what is from the top of their mountain, and they are amazed by the same thing which is in the depth of their valley—by a thinking nothing which is shut away and sealed in the secret closure of the highest purity of such an excellent Soul."[30] To be amazed by thinking nothing: perfectly said and perfectly representative of the desertlike apophasis I am pursuing in this book. For many mystics, amazement is the summit of theology and it takes us to inconceivable heights where language falters and where metaphors like "nothingness," "desert," "emptiness," and "nakedness" point us to the other side. When reaching these summits, wonder or related experiences—admiration, awe, reverence—gain in potency as reason begins to falter and the mystic loses her mind and ego in the arms of the other. No wonder madness has so often been attributed to the mystics: they are out of their mind, distraught and hysterical, and they go to the desert in search of their Beloved like Majnun once did for his darling Layla, with reckless desperation and despair, tearing his garments, smearing his face with dirt, hopeless in love. The result may be madness, but a madness that is a blessing of God.

If nothing else, our brief conversation with the mystics teaches us one fundamental fact about the place of wonder in apophatic discourse: as much as it takes away and deconstructs all concepts and images that have turned idolatrous, it maintains a reverent posture before the bare, denuded metaphors that it loves so much. These metaphors—"nothingness," "emptiness," and so forth—should not be construed as a form of nihilism, in other words. The origins of modern nihilism may lurk in these thoughts, but mystics are too exuberant to succumb to a total annihilation of faith. They are fond of negations and denials, for sure, but resounding affirmations, loves, and pleasures are their salvation, the yes of their "negative theologies."

For this reason, wonder is not reducible to human ignorance in the mystics. Wonder is generated by something affirmative, call it a "presence of an absence" if you will, but it is an absence like no other, something infinitely alluring, something that reveals in and through its withdrawal, that loves in and through its renunciation. In this sense, the experience of wonder in mystical apophasis remains at odds with the cynicism of the modern age. While mystical unknowing is a prefiguration of modern skepticism, it is different insofar as there remains for the mystics a formless beauty like infinity summoning and seducing the soul. For the mystics, infinity can surely be terrifying, but it is also an overflowing goodness, a spring "that gives itself to all the rivers yet is never exhausted by what they take" (Plotinus), the vast sea at high tide spilling onto the shores, the super-saturated excess of love and justice, the wide and immeasurable desert.[31] Wonder is the response of the soul to these kinds of surprising beauty, experiences of the plenitude and surplus of infinity. Or it is the response of the soul to the strangeness of itself, to the foreign mystery dwelling deep within.

Exile and Prophetic Language

While there are numerous moments when mystics and prophets come together like two hands joined in prayer, it is also true that they have their own signatures when writing of wonder or exile, God or the desert.[32] Though wonder is the natural ally of the mystic's purpose—called on to dramatize the unreachable heights of the divine—exile appears so frequently in the prophets' proclamations that it is more emblematic of their identity than the olive branch is emblematic of peace. As a memory that is both wounding and revelatory, exile is a defining theme of these troubled individuals who were almost always the voice of migrants and strangers, the poor and needy, if they weren't the migrants and strangers themselves, estranged members of an estranged people. Though prophets seek wisdom in the signs and symbols of exile, it is also nothing to celebrate, so devastating and ruinous it is, if it was not also the occasion for the prophets' betrothal to God. The prophets carry this memory of love deep in their hearts without ever losing sight of the severe and forbidding nature of exile, every bit as cruel and inhospitable as the desert sun. Indeed, when the prophets turn to the symbolism of the desert, there is an unmistakable tone of suffering and dereliction in their appeals. While the mystics are fond of desert language for its apophatic significance, their theologies often remain confined within an intellectual paradigm about the possibilities and limits of human ideas. With the prophet, on the contrary, the desert is a perfect mirror of the desolation and destitution felt by hungry wanderers and oppressed slaves, by exiles and aliens. Different from mystical exegesis, the language of the prophet is much more tormented, frightening, existential. It captures the coarseness of human history.

Desert imagery in the prophets is, in short, a dark summary of human history. The desert signifies dispossession in history and location, the forced slavery of entire communities, the yoke and cruelty of war, the loss of house and homeland, the hunger and misery of exiles and refugees. The desert is the homeland of the homeless, the region of wanderers and pilgrims. And the desert is, as Juan Rulfo knew so well, our own century, an age that bears a striking resemblance to the town of Comala in Rulfo's surrealistic masterpiece *Pedro Páramo* (indeed, in Spanish *páramo* means a wasteland or barren plain, which makes his novel speech from the void, speech that rises from the barren soil like a scorpion).[33]

To take one example of the desertlike spirituality of the prophets, consider Jeremiah. His speech is like an uncontrollable fire—his metaphor—

because it bears witness to the ashes of history, to burned communities and cities, to the desolation left in the wake of war, captivity, and exile. Like so many prophets, Jeremiah is the anguished chronicler of the heavy hand of history, of the welts and bruises left on the souls of the poor and innocent. He lets loose his words to wreak havoc among the untroubled and complacent consciences of the people. His words are wild and agonizing, full of complaints and protests, sad moans and laments—and full of tears:

> O that my head were a spring of water,
> and my eyes a fountain of tears,
> so that I might weep day and night
> for the slain of my poor people.
> (Jeremiah 9:1)

> A voice is heard in Ramah,
> lamentation and bitter weeping.
> Rachel is weeping for her children;
> she refuses to be comforted for her children,
> because they are no more.
> (Jeremiah 31:15)

Indeed, in Jeremiah and other biblical texts, tears are the most obvious sign of the devastating reach of exile. They are the most visible indication that there is something terribly wrong. The evidence is in their eyes, eyes that suffer blindness for being flooded with tears. When distinguishing the poet from the philosopher, Federico García Lorca captured beautifully the principal meaning of the prophet: "And I tell us that you should open yourselves to hearing an authentic poet, of the kind whose bodily senses were shaped in a world that is not our own and that few people are able to perceive. A poet closer to death than to philosophy, closer to pain than to intelligence, closer to blood than to ink."[34] The prophets are poets of this kind, closer to pain than to intelligence, closer to death than to philosophy. Their proclamations are evocative of imploration and blindness rather than vision, apocalypse instead of enlightenment. If one understands anything about the Bible, it should be how much the prayers of the Bible are bathed in mourning and lamentations, dirges and cries. Derrida picks up on this theme:

> By praying on the verge of tears, the sacred allegory does something. It makes something happen or come, makes something come to the

eyes, makes something well up in them, by producing an event. It is performative, something vision alone would be incapable of if it gave rise only to representational reporting, to perspicacity, to theory or to theater, if it were not already potentially apocalypse, already potent with apocalypse. . . . To have imploration rather than vision in sight, to address prayer, love, joy, or sadness rather than a look or gaze. . . . Contrary to what one believes one knows, the best point of view is a source-point and a watering hole, a waterpoint—which thus comes down to tears.[35]

The biblical prophets do not give us theory or systems, they do not look or gaze—they implore. Their bodies and spirits are embodied apocalypses, they put on the garments and sackcloth of mourning, they become walking dramas of Israel's impending doom. Their words are mournful revelations that announce the death of the old before the new can be envisaged. Jeremiah will literally put on the oxen's yoke to forewarn the Israelites of the Babylonian might. Isaiah will strip his body naked and wander the desert for three years to call attention to the fate of the nations at the hands of the Assyrians (Isaiah 20). Ezekiel is commanded to prepare an exile's bag and to cover his eyes to characterize the impending days of darkness that will fall hard on this nation of wayfarers. In each case, the prophets become one-man shows in a peripatetic theater that has the dispossessions of history as its main act (Ezekiel 12). With feverish histrionics, they cry out, denounce, censure, bewail, bemoan. And above all, they shed tears of blood for the omens of death they notice everywhere.

The prophets are, in fact, obsessed with death, and they succor death as if it was their own beloved who has died, marching arm in arm with him, bemoaning his death, grieving and wailing, singing the blues. Some tremble to name the ghastly specter of death for fear of reprisal or curse, but the prophets are not reserved in this regard. Because they announce the end of all that presumes to be inviolable and unending, death is always a key theme in the prophets, if not their most beloved companion, their most steadfast love, as Octavio Paz once wrote about Mexicans.[36] The funeral they enact is for Israel, of course, or the Temple, or for the dead consciences of the people. Whatever the case, there is no doubt that their pronouncements are peopled by the ghosts of the dead.

And for the prophets, this familiarity with death is impossible to disentangle from their experience of exile. Exile is a break and disruption with death-like features, a wound that can be fatal. As an omen of death, exile takes and strips away all that is dear and life-giving; it peels away our soul, leaving us denuded and bare. It can be catastrophic, this much is clear in the Hebrew Bible:

> I looked on the earth, and lo, it was waste and void;
> and to the heavens and they had no light.
> I looked on the mountains, and lo, they were quaking,
> and all the hills moved to and fro,
> I looked, and lo, there was no one at all,
> and all the birds of the air had fled.
> I looked, and lo, the fruitful land
> was a desert, and all its cities were laid in ruins.
> (Jeremiah 4:23–26)

In fact, most of the prophetic books of the Hebrew Bible prophesy and describe the great catastrophes that befell the kingdoms of Israel and Judah. The prophets are chroniclers of these violent episodes in Israel's history. As speaker's of God's word, they call out and denounce the bloody machinations of world powers: the Assyrians and Babylonians, the Persians, Syrians, and Romans. And closer to home, they see with great clarity and honesty their own nation's sins and injustices. They are harshest and most unforgiving when it comes to Israel's own ethical-political offenses. They jolt the memory of the people when they are likely to forget that that they, too, were once strangers in the land of Egypt (Deuteronomy 10:19). They excoriate the guilty for "crushing the poor into the dust of the earth" (Amos 2:7), for turning away widows and orphans, for not welcoming the strangers of the land. And they are hostile to practices of worship and sacrifice that accompany such acts of injustice and violence. The Hebrew prophet surely wants sacrifices and offerings from the people, but ones that give life to the poor and dying, sacrifices that answer Pablo Neruda's hopes: "the poor hopes of my people: children in school with shoes on, bread and justice being spread as the sun is spread in the summer."[37] They want offerings, in other words, that will be spread evenly, generously, justly. Anything else seems to only invoke their fury.

And there is plenty of sound and fury in their voices. They speak with the same violence and outrage as a tornado, causing all in its path to quake and shiver. Indeed, it is quite natural to associate prophets with the most awesome forces of nature—earthquakes, tornados, blazing fires—because they are possessed by the same earth-shattering power, the same seismic activity.

When they speak, we should beware and prepare for an eruption and upheaval that leaves nothing unaffected.[38] In their desertlike speech, a voice cries out, unsettles and terrifies us, and always forces us to remember the exoduses and dispossessions of human history. The prophet would have no vocation, no calling, then, if exile didn't create the desperate need. Without exile, there would be no tears and no prophet needed to speak on behalf of those who shed so many tears.

The condition of exile is, in short, the definitive feature of the Hebrew prophets and it provided them with an unenviable privilege: a cognitive insight and awareness of human fragility and insecurity, danger and pain. In this sense, exile proved revelatory for the prophets, a disclosure of wisdom gained by combat with the calamities of history. They shunned any other version of religion—no matter how beautiful and seductive—if it did not locate God's face in the naked and tormented face of the poor and oppressed. And this certainly holds true for the understanding of wonder: no version of wonder will pass their scathing judgment if it does not channel the terrible throes of the dispossessions of history. Wonder will always include these raw, sorrowful realities after passing through the hoarse throats of the Jewish prophets. It will always sound different from those without any contact and solidarity with the wretched of the earth.

Wonder and Exile in the New World

Though I have opened with a general discussion of mystics and prophets, I hope to show in what follows the echoes and reverberations of these themes in the figures of the New World. The subjects of this study carry the memory of these voices deep in their hearts and consciences, and when they do not channel them, they at least echo them the way a great jazz musician echoes the sounds and beats of the past while adding their own improvised sound. In this way, the subjects of my study recall the themes and sounds of mystics and prophets, but add their own accent on wonder and exile, an accent that was profoundly shaped by the unprecedented discoveries and conquests of the year 1492.

María Rosa Menocal describes well these new accents and sounds post-1492 when speaking of the mystical significance of the expulsion of the Jews from Spain (the date was changed from July 31 to August 2 by the appeal of Isaac Abravanel). The date of August 2 was preferred because it fell on the ninth of Ab in the Jewish liturgical calendar, the anniversary of the destruction of the Temple. The new date would provide a new occasion for ancient sorrows, a new diaspora in perfect liturgical and kabbalistic continuity with the original diaspora. True to the purpose of ritual, Abravanel and his contemporaries sought to recapture and re-enact an ancient memory—as painful as that memory might be—so that some kind of meaning and order could be assigned to what was otherwise meaningless and chaotic. Menocal's moving prose takes us back to that time and place of August 2, 1492, and recalls for us the tide of tears streaming from Jewish eyes as they wait on the docks of Spain for ships to take them somewhere else, always somewhere else:

> These are the first days of August 1492. If we go down to the docks in the great Spanish port of Cádiz we are overwhelmed. . . . The throngs of people are unbearable, particularly in the damp summer heat, and worst of all are the tears, the wailing, the ritual prayers, all those noises and smells and sights of departures. This is the day, the hour, the place, of a leave-taking more grievous and painful than that of death itself, an exodus inscribed in all the sacred texts, anticipated and repeated. . . . Exile on Diaspora. And, during that summer, all roads led to the sea, to ports such as Cádiz, to the desperately overbooked ships, and they were filled with the sounds of exile, that mingling of the vernacular sorrow of the women and the children with the liturgical chanting of the men.[39]

If all roads led to the sea that summer, the sea also became the passageway to new worlds. In that year, the sea would carry sailors across the deep blue ocean and it would carry exile along with it. Exodus would be remembered, anticipated, and endlessly repeated in this unknown and strange world. And wonder, too: wonder would be endlessly repeated, in some ways honorable, in others, reprehensible. Soon enough, the storied splendors of the New World would attract a vast sea of explorers itching to know the remotest corners of the earth. They would be lured and charmed by the indefinite, half-attained, and unimaginable experience of sublimity that is the phenomenon of wonder, to paraphrase Herman Melville's Ishmael. While this taste of sublimity would lead some to a modest and tolerant understanding of religions and cultures, in other cases, it would help create a new desert and wasteland.

In this regard, the sixteenth and seventeenth centuries would witness the different histories of wonder, the dispossession of knowledge alongside the dispossession of house and home. With a perceptive eye to the histories of both wonder and exile, Michel de Certeau spoke of the defilements of history that appeared on the mystical bodies of the sixteenth and seventeenth centuries: "They were leading lives of exile, hounded from their land by the defilements of history. *Super flumina Babylonis*: the theme of mourning, disconsolate despite the intoxication of new aspirations, was endlessly repeated."[40] Certeau has chronicled well this coexistence of exile with the intoxicating dreams of New Worlds in the early modern period. The conquest of the New World, wars and economic recessions, expulsion of the Jews and Muslims from Spain, outbreaks of famine and plague, the persecution of the "impure" of blood: all these events of the early modern period were visible stains on mystical lives according to Certeau. The theme of exile deepened in intensity in the period and came to disturb all assurances of meaning. The images of a lost paradise and an apocalyptic future—rampant in the age—made it clear that exile had forced its way into every dimension of time, beginnings and ends. There was no sanctuary or haven, past or future, that would be free of exile's despotism. The desert of exile extended its reach into all territories of Europe and soon made its way, as we will see throughout the course of this study, across the great sea into the New World.

Following the mystical and prophetic sensibilities of Certeau, thus, I hope to explore New World poets and writers with a concentration on wonder and exile. If my focus is with poets and writers, it is because I see in them what Kierkegaard saw in Job: "In our time it is thought that genuine expressions of grief, the despairing language of passion, must be assigned to the poets, who then like attorneys in a lower court plead the cause of the suffering before the tribunal of human compassion. . . . Speak up, then, unforgettable Job, repeat everything you said."[41]

In my view, it is mystics, prophets, and poets who best capture the wonders and beauties, the tears and long walks that make up the history of the Americas. It is their language of passion and imagination that enables us to be like José Arcadio Buendía and navigate across unknown seas and visit uncharted territories. And it is their language that is witness to the desert of history, the desert of exiles and migrants, the desert of privation and sorrow.

TWO

Voices of the Dispossessed

Shall I say it again? In order to arrive there,

To arrive where you are, to get from where you are not,

You must go by a way wherein there is no ecstasy.

In order to arrive at what you do not know

You must go by a way which is the way of ignorance.

In order to possess what you do not possess

You must go by the way of dispossession. . . .

And what you do not know is the only thing you know

And what you own is what you do not own

And where you are is where you are not.

—T. S. Eliot, *The Four Quartets*

The travel narrative is a text of observation haunted by its Other, the imaginary.

—Michel de Certeau, "Travel Narratives of the French to Brazil"

The European encounter with the New World remains one of the decisive events of modern world history. The shocking discovery of this continent would soon make only death the final undiscovered country. And neither Europe nor this uncharted world would remain the same. The introduction of this territory into European consciousness would lead to a dramatic expansion and revolution in geographical, cultural, and theological worldviews. For Western observers, this event would come to represent the

quintessential encounter with otherness. Travel to this newly discovered territory was like sailing away into unreality, into unimaginable and uncharted
regions, into a world where truth was mixed with fantasy, and dreams with
reality. And when the chroniclers of this strange new world sat down to
articulate their experiences, facts and fictions were difficult to disentangle.
Indeed, the accounts are a curious blend of the two, which is why so many
writers have seen the colonial-era chronicles as the first attempts at magical
realism. The explorers' accounts give us fantastic and wild portraits of the
New World, as if fantasy and dreams alone had been adequate in preparing
the West for an event of this sort. In direct proportion to the degree and
extent of the mystery, the accounts multiply the number of adjectives and
metaphors to describe the wonder of these lands. As the mystery deepens,
the language of wonder escalates and thickens. In finding ourselves on the
shores of the New World, then, and in meditating on the significance and
import of these historical events, we must notice this language of astonishment and amazement on the tongues of the first Europeans. It will be an
important clue for us in assessing this encounter with radical otherness.

This chapter will consider the language of wonder in the New World
and its relationship with wandering and exile. As suggested earlier, my
concern in this book is with languages of dispossession: wonder as dispossession in the order of knowledge and exile, forced or voluntary, in history
or location. Though they do not look alike, wonder and exile share this
fate of dispossession and displacement, when both mind and body are
threatened by an encounter with unknown and uncertain phenomena,
when familiar and stable truths are suddenly interrupted by an appearance
of something so peculiar and new that it introduces doubt and equivocation, when all confidences are quickly undone. When we speak of wonder, we are trying to name something that happens prior to or beyond
the boundaries of knowledge, and this experience is fraught with the same
baffling, disorienting, and bewildering feelings that accompany an exile in
his new home away from home. In both cases, the homeland of belonging
and truth is badly desired, but forever lost. No wonder, then, that wonder—
like moments of awe or stupefaction—shares with exile the experience
of loss: the loss of words, loss of clear and familiar truths, loss of absolute
certainties. Wonder is closer to absence than presence, dispossession than
possession. Wonder inhabits the gaps and dark corners of knowledge. It
appears in stories of the impossible and among those who dream impossible dreams . . . like mystics. Mystics will always prefer the language of
wonder to any other because it names so well their tireless attempts to

reach the other side of words, somewhere beyond the boundaries of our familiar truths.

As we explore the sympathies between wonder and mystical language in this study, and their affiliation with dispossession and exile, we would do well to follow the lead of Michel de Certeau. In his reading of mystical literature, he found the resemblances between mystics and travelers particularly intriguing, seeing mystics as travelers of the human soul, travelers of the unfathomable and unknown. Regardless of whether they would ever leave the confines of their homeland, Certeau considered mystical language to be stirred by nomadic and restless desires, infinite and insatiable, and filled with an imagination that carried them on journeys to remote lands. In entering territories without a map or chart, mystics were a lot like explorers of new worlds, only now the purpose was an impossible theological one, like seeing the face of God, or naming the unnamable. The language of wonder came to mystics as frequently as travelers because it was the precise word to name this journey into foreign territories, an experience that can be freeing and exhilarating, or else terrifying and dreadful. Capable of these wild extremes, the one who wonders resembles a heavenly body that has suddenly been loosed from its fixed orbit. No longer tied and constrained by the familiar, one is suddenly unfettered and emancipated, now free to imagine the unimaginable, to consider new possibilities, to live differently. How terrifying yet thrilling this can be—and terrifying not only to one's own psyche, but to all the defenders of sameness, to those who draw uncompromising borders and warn against trespassing beyond what we already know and trust.

For this exact reason, wonder is the verbal equivalent of trespassing borders and surpassing limits, and always moving deeper and deeper into the dark. Wonder is a common word in the vocabulary of mystics and wanderers because they are navigating territory that is cloaked in darkness. The travel route of wonder is like entering the cloud of darkness and finding one's way through it with the stick of a blind man, trusting it to lead you with instinct and intuition through unfamiliar regions of knowledge. In this way, the *via negativa* of the mystics—the deconstructive strategy of dispossession and detachment from concepts and worldly desires—prepares one for travel into the unknown, and this journey is always wondrous. The mystical journey takes the route of ignorance and dispossession in order to arrive at what you do not know, at where you are not ("You must go by a way which is the way of ignorance. . . . You must go by the way of dispossession"). And wonder is a key indicator and marker of this journey.

The figures that I will be considering in this chapter—especially Cabeza de Vaca and Bartolomé de Las Casas—were such travelers and wanderers, courageous men who ventured deep into unknown lands and who became voices of the dispossessed in the New World. In some ways, they adopted the via negativa of the mystics—especially the demand for detachment— but their own version of this strategy resembles closer the desert experiences of the biblical prophets. Their via negativa summons the negations and denunciations of the biblical prophets because only this kind of explosive language is relevant to them in a history that knew so many trials and tribulations, so much distress and agony. Only this kind of language—hostile, dissenting, anguished—proved adequate to the negations and catastrophes that they witnessed in their age.

In both cases, moreover, surprising insights and realizations came to them through their long sojourns—particularly tolerance, even affection, for the great variety of cultures that they encountered in the New World. Their passionate advocacy for tolerance and compassion seems to have arisen from the calamities of their lives, as if they were able to suck the marrow out of the dry bones of their travails and learn something in the process. They would achieve a wisdom born of suffering, that rare quality that sees the world through the eyes of other peoples and cultures, especially through the eyes of the downtrodden and brokenhearted. The discovery of the New World was for them a discovery of painful truths and beauties, a discovery that enabled them to see the strangers of the Americas as brothers and sisters to themselves. And, more than that, it allowed them to recognize the strangeness of their own selves. Their discovery of the New World, thus, also included their own agonizing discovery of a new, inscrutable world deep within their own soul, a discovery that revealed to them how alien and wondrous their own being actually was. They would come to notice the shadow of exile as the dark, ghostly creature residing within their own soul and, subsequently, embrace it in the dark-skinned peoples of the New World.

In this sense, the experiences of wonder and exile are fundamental to the discoveries of Cabeza de Vaca and Las Casas. They would not have become voices of the dispossessed if they did not see the foreignness and strangeness in their own histories and cultures. With their capacity to wonder at themselves, the alien nature of other cultures and peoples suddenly appeared to them far less threatening and dangerous.

While the focus on exile in the present study has a particular kinship with wonder, we should not overstate the resemblances and end up overlooking their singularities. If wonder interrupts our drive to comprehend and explain, exile disorients us with greater force and violence, casting us into the tides and maelstroms of history. In assessing the features of exile in the New World we are suddenly faced with realities that a strictly aesthetical approach to wonder is reluctant to acknowledge: the rupture of violence and colonialism in the New World. No consideration of wonder in the New World is worth our attention if the history of exile is left off the pages. There has been too much suffering and too many disasters in the history of the Americas for us to cover our faces from the historical record. As much as some portraits of wonder in the New World would try to elide and disregard exile, it is always there, haunting Latin American narratives like a disturbing, repressed memory buried within the unconscious. The tragic histories of Latin American cultures must be narrated if the patient desires the truth, if he is to face memories both menacing and unsettling, therapeutic and wondrous.

So in this passion for the truth, we must look carefully at the histories of displacement and uprooting in the New World: the slave trade, the genocide and abuse of native peoples, the gross inequalities. European possession of the Americas led to the brutal dislocation and resettlement of the Amerindians to where their labor would be needed, and it led, as Las Casas puts it, to a desert of exile.

Our attention, then, will be drawn by the "desertification" of new lands and the part played by wonder in all of this. This should remind us that wonder is not innocent and certainly not free of impurity. For many New World explorers and conquistadors, wonder was often invoked in the service of control and ownership; when wonder appeared on their lips, it furthered a strategy of possession in which the exotic realities of the New World were to be used and enjoyed for European advantage. The wonders and marvels of the New World became enticing objects to own—or else, signs and proof of their inferiority and barbarism.

In a way, the colonial powers in the New World failed to heed the mystical warnings about idolatry, namely, that the "God beyond God" dwells in silence and darkness, in the cloud of unknowing. Contact with the true God, as Simone Weil once suggested, is given to us by absence.[1] The rush of European powers to "discover" the New World was a race in being present before anyone else (native excluding). By the act of presence—catching sight of the land by one's vision, placing one's foot and body on the land, by a legal record and pronouncement of ownership—Europeans would claim possession. The conquistadors worshipped a god entirely present, one that could be manipulated and controlled, one that would justify and legitimize the possession of the New World. As Las Casas would make clear, this was a god of their own making, an idol that would fill their empty coffers with gold and slaves.

In tracing the different routes of wonder, the title of Emmanuel Levinas's book *Totality and Infinity* is suggestive for this study. In the New World, the theme of wonder is used, for one, as a lure and enticement to possession and totality, as it surely was for Columbus, and as a fragment of infinity for Cabeza de Vaca and Las Casas. When seen through the eyes of the latter, it can be a valuable image of dispossession. This chapter will follow these different routes of wonder and see what it has to teach us about first encounters and the discovery of new things.

Columbus: *Almirans*, the One Who Wonders

When the figure of Columbus turns to the language of wonder—and he does so with great frequency and devotion—it reminds us that we are faced with a medieval man. As much as his tenacious and adventurous spirit suggests something modern, his discoveries and dreams, like his language of wonder, are articulated and named with the only vocabulary that he knows and has inherited from his medieval predecessors. We do not need to look much further than the name he ascribes to the New World (the Indies) for evidence of this. When he comes upon the great river in South America, the Orinoco, he imagines that he is stepping on Indian soil and even approaching the Ganges, where many medieval travelers—Marco Polo, William of Rubruck, Sir John Mandeville—had placed Earthly Paradise.

Columbus, in other words, saw the world with the starry eyes of medieval travelers and was amazed by what he saw and heard in their accounts. Provoked by them, he became a magi of sorts and soon followed the heavenly stars and wonders that enticed his predecessors. And there was plenty to entice him. These travelers, in fact, swam in rivers of wonder and looked to the East as a site where the marvelous was commonplace and the fantastic ordinary. If medieval mystics desired to drown in the sea of God's love, these figures drowned in a vast sea of marvels and imaginary worlds. For classic and medieval travelers, the border between the West and the East might as well have been the border between the living and the dead because the differences between the two were equally vast—and equally frightening. To venture there would mean facing the dangers and anxieties of the unknown, not to mention the dragons, man-eaters, and other terri-fying creatures that made the unknown their home. If one was brave enough to go there, however, the rewards could be immeasurable, like dis-covering the Fountain of Youth, Earthly Paradise, cities of gold. In medi-eval representations, the East resembled the "Orient" of later centuries, "a site of dreams, images, fantasies, myths, obsessions and requirements," to quote Homi Bhabha.[2] Never an empirical reality, the East represented what is totally other: the barbaric and strange, the mysterious and irrational. For the men of this age, as in the time of Columbus, the border between fact and fiction is a curious and ambiguous line, permeable and unclear. Passage between the two occurs with regularity to these explorers of the impossible, which is why their discoveries look like the matter of dreams and fantasies.

It is quite clear that the explorers and travelers to the New World breathed this medieval air, and they certainly craved the stuff of legend and fantasy as much as they dreamed of wealth and glory. When first learning of this discovery, the message to the Old World must have felt like choco-late to a tongue that had only known bland foods, like spices to a palate accustomed to insipid foods. They must have been ravished and thrilled by the news.

Columbus and his men traveled across the great ocean aroused by rumors of this sort, rumors of fabulous truths, cities like Atlantis and Cibao, women like Amazons and mermaids, one-eyed men, cannibals, men with snouts of dogs, people with tails—and as they returned to Europe, no matter what their experience, they were loose with their reports and extravagant with their pens. One might say that they gathered the ocean winds for them-selves and infused their language with it, creating accounts that were tem-pestuous and bloated like hot air balloons. Call it creative license if you will, but one thing is clear: they drew from a deep well of fantasy and gave their readers a wild sea of stories. Like their medieval predecessors, travel accounts of the New World describe experiences with strange and bizarre peoples, with customs entirely new and unfamiliar, and with a curious and wild diversity of religious beliefs. In tales of this kind, they thoroughly astonished and won over their readers the way Othello would win over Desdemona with the stories of his fantastic adventures.[3]

Like Othello, Columbus was a master of wonder's seductions. He knew how to evoke, stimulate, and nurture it. And stimulate it he certainly did, becoming a powerful spinner of tales and maker of myths. His letters stim-ulated delight and wonder. If not for gold and silver, pearls and land, Columbus entices Europeans to the New World for a wild adventure, for a romantic experience of an exotic and strange world. The letters are not satisfied with informing, instead seeking to transform their readers and to evoke in them a sense of the marvelous and wondrous. There is something like intrigue involved in Columbus's letters. They connive more than educate; they tantalize, charm, beguile. Columbus's designs are to cast a spell over Europeans and to convince them that the colonization of these new lands and peoples is a holy and worthy cause. As Stephen Greenblatt mentions in *Marvelous Possessions*, in the absence of gold, Columbus offers the marvelous: "The marvelous stands for the missing gold."[4] The appeal to wonder here becomes an instrument in colonial possession. Wonder is colonized and turned into an exotic object that Columbus and other explorers would exploit in the service of conquest.

Inga Clendinnen explains well the many instances in which wonder and fantasy served colonial purposes, and makes this point in reference to Cortes: "His essential genius lay in the depth of his conviction, and in his capacity to bring others to share it: to coax, bully, and bribe his men, dream-led, dream-fed them. . . . He also lured them to acknowledge their most extreme fantasies; then he persuaded them, by his own enactment of them, that the fantasies were realizable."[5] Or listen to Carlos Fuentes on this same theme: "The two foundations of Buenos Aires clearly dramatizes two impulses of Spanish colonization in the New World. One is based on fantasy, illusion, imagination. The conquistadors were driven not only by the lust for gold . . . but by fantasy and imagination, which at times were an even stronger elixir. As they entered the willful world of the Renaissance, these men still carried with them the fantasies of the Middle Ages."[6]

We might see the play on the names of Columbus as illustrating these two themes. Because of the frequency of Columbus's appeal to the wonder and marvel of the New World, the King of Spain said that Columbus should be known not as *Almirante*, the admiral, but as *Almirans*, the one who wonders. And yet, at the same time, Las Casas once noted that the name he had been born with, Cristóbal Colón, sealed him with the mark of a "colon-izer."[7] Columbus's capacity for wonder coexisted with his dreams of colonization and possession. He is a wonderer and colonizer at once. We might see this duality as the beginning of a history that will endure for centuries in Latin America and claim the lives of millions: the mixture of dreams of paradise with the history of colonization and violence.[8]

How quickly, then, does wonder assume its part in the history of colonization. We should always remain alert to this possibility, especially as we listen to Columbus's wonder-intoxicated language. Columbus never tires of the word *maravilla*. The trees, fish, animal life, the varieties of nature's loveliness, everything is marvelous:

> The fish here are surprisingly unlike ours. There are some the shape of dories and of the finest colors in the world. . . . The colors are so marvelous that everybody wondered and took pleasure in the sight. . . . Flocks of parrots darken the sun and there is a marvelous variety of large and small birds very different from our own; the trees are of many kinds, each with its own fruit, and all have a marvelous scent. . . . Hispaniola is a wonder. . . . This country, Most Serene Highnesses, is so enchantingly beautiful that it surpasses all others in charm and beauty as much as the light of day surpasses the night. Very often I would say to my crew that however hard I tried to give your Highnesses a complete account of these lands my tongue could not convey the whole truth about them nor my hand write it down. I was so astonished at the sight of so much beauty that I can find no words to describe it. . . . But now I am silent, only wishing that some other may see this land and write about it. (C, 65, 70, 83–84)

It is easy to be seduced by Columbus's portrait of Hispaniola. He can be dazzling when speaking of its wonders and idyllic beauty. And he sounds like a mystic in suggesting how little these wonders can be described, how much they require personal experience. He says that the New World brings him to silence, that nothing comparable has ever been seen. The beauty is so intense and surprising that it brings his mind and tongue to a pause. His language falters. "My tongue is broken," as Sappho once remarked.[9] Columbus tells us what it must feel like to be filled with such awe and delight. He gives us signs, but then warns us, like so many mystics, that it is ineffable. In moments like this, Columbus tastes beauty in all its splendor and expresses himself in ways that any mystic would understand. For many Christian mystics—perhaps the lesson learned from paganism—beauty is a sign of grace, a kind of icon in which the One discloses itself. And for those with a trained eye for this beauty, revelation comes to them in these sensual forms with a force that can leave the soul breathless and ecstatic, undone by so much beauty.

Here Columbus is as close as his shadow to this kind of rapture, to the aesthetical intuitions of the mystics. His invocation of the language of inexpressibility is a key feature of his portrait of wonder, and it appears with regularity when he is at pains to articulate his discoveries. Columbus locates wonder in the gaps and silences of language, beyond the boundaries of what can be said in clear and certain terms. And yet, since the naming of islands is fundamental to taking possession, Columbus—in his guise as Cristóbal Colón—wants to name what is unnamable and, thus, betrays his initial intuition about Hispaniola, that it is wonder that cannot be possessed; or else, is it his other identity that he betrays, his beneficent shadow as the Almirans? Regardless, it is clear that Columbus is a knight of possession and conquest: "Generally it was my wish to pass no island without taking possession of it" (C, 60). With this frank admission, we realize that Columbus's approach to the beauty of Hispaniola is nothing like reverence—demanding, it seems to me, respect and awe for the integrity of the other—but, instead, voracity, an insatiable desire to consume and own.

His betrayals have many different facets, but consider one incident that Columbus notes on his fourth voyage (1502–4). He writes of an encounter with magicians on an island he calls Cariay. He expects to find confirmation of the people Pope Pius II wrote of in his *Cosmographia* (a description of the Far East). Columbus writes, "In Cariay and in the adjoining districts there are great and very terrifying magicians who would have done anything to prevent my remaining there an hour. On my arrival they sent me two magnificently attired girls, the elder of whom could not have been more than eleven and the other seven. Both were so shameless that they might have been whores, and had magic powders concealed about them. On their arrival I ordered that they should be given some of our trinkets and sent them back to land immediately" (C, 297). The wonder that Columbus describes here is mixed up with terror and suddenly his tone is noticeably different from when speaking of natural beauty. When speaking of the natives, Columbus begins to tremble and expresses apprehension and foreboding, fear and antipathy. In his perception, these native women are nothing but demons in female form, succubi.

It's almost as if he had landed on the same island that is the setting for Shakespeare's *The Tempest*, a parallel noted by the classic work of José Enrique Rodó, *Ariel* (1900).[10] Remember that this great work of Shakespeare is situated on a mysterious island in the West. Prospero and his daughter find themselves exiled there along with a creature of the earth, Caliban, and his mother, the Algerian witch Sycorax (Caliban is a near anagram of the term cannibal, and in the New World related to the term "Carib"). In this distant and alien world, the characters are at pains to anchor themselves to solid footing. The language of wonder captures the depths of their disorientation in this strange world (the name of Prospero's daughter, Miranda, suggests the wondrous atmosphere of the island and derives from the Latin *mirari*, to wonder, admire, or revere). Strange things happen here, none stranger than the occult powers of Prospero, a great and powerful magician who has nature, even death, at his command: "I have bedimmed the noontide sun, called forth the mutinous winds, and 'twixt the green sea and the azured vault set roaring war . . . graves at my command, have waked their sleepers, oped, and let 'em forth by my so potent art" (*Tempest*, 5.1.41–50). The location of this island somewhere beyond the boundaries of the known world seems to have opened doors to other dimensions of reality and to have invited in the powers of sorcery and wizardry. The uncanny is abundant in this new world.

With Prospero's potent art in mind, we know that the wonders of this island are wild to an extreme, making for a bewildering experience, engendering fear and anxiety. Caliban is the prime instance and embodiment of these fearful wonders. He represents the wonder of the New World, but in a grotesque form: misshapen, bizarre, strange, ugly, unpleasant, and, above all, monstrous. Everything about this island resembles this grotesque creature and it causes some to want nothing more than to flee. Gonzalo's response is a case in point: "All torment, trouble, wonder, and amazement inhabits here. Some heavenly power guide us out of this fearful country" (5.1.104–6).

Like Gonzalo in *The Tempest*, Columbus finds himself in a strange land, and the wonder in his eyes at the sight of these "magicians" is an expression of fear and anxiety. Columbus would not tolerate native magic anymore than Prospero would tolerate an independent and free Caliban. "Magic" is the name of the demonic for Columbus. He attributes "magic" to what he does not understand, to native attire or dress, native ceremonies or rituals. By describing natives in these terms, he transforms the other into a grotesque form, and it becomes a dangerous threat in the process. In the mind of Columbus, there is plenty reason to fear the "magic" of the natives: it is demonic and evil, strange and dreadful. And the best way to handle this threat is to subdue it by violence, to enslave it. Columbus would propose doing to the "Caribs" what Prospero does to Caliban: force him into servitude.

In Columbus's description of "magic" and "whores," furthermore, he links together images of idolatry, sorcery, and sexual deviance in ways that echo throughout the ages. This association between idolatry and sexual danger has an ancient history. For centuries Western perceptions of the East included descriptions of sexual license and carnality (if not earlier, beginning with biblical perceptions of the Canaanites and Philistines). What is surprising, at least in this instance, is that Columbus lets them be, does not abduct them. In most other cases, Columbus would make up the absence of gold by abducting natives for slaves. In one instance, a lieutenant of Columbus, Michele de Cuneo, tells of a native woman that was given to him by Columbus: "While I was in the boat, I captured a very beautiful Carib woman, whom the said Lord Admiral gave to me. When I had taken her to my cabin she was naked—as was their custom. I was filled with a desire to take my pleasure with her and attempted to satisfy my desire. She was unwilling. . . . But . . . I then took a piece of rope and whipped her soundly. . . . Eventually we came to such terms, I assure you, that you would have thought she had been brought up in a school for whores" (C, 139).

Whores and objects to be used and given away: these two passages are representative of how Columbus perceived native peoples in general. When Columbus expresses fear, it is most commonly negotiated away by his acts of conquest and possession. The experience of wonder at this point in Columbus is loaded with fear and ignorance, and, like an animal that is afraid and threatened, becomes hostile and violent in response. If Aristotle sought to remove wonder by philosophizing, Columbus responds to wonder by a desire to colonize it. There is a combustible mixture of fear and ignorance throughout all of this, and if we have learned anything from the Conquest, we should know that the result is often explosive violence.

What makes the case of Columbus particularly interesting, if not sacrilegious, is his assurance that God is behind it all, that God is, in fact, the wind beneath his sails, sustaining and succoring him, even speaking directly to him when the tsunamis of his life threaten to unmake him. When failure and disaster seem to gain the upper hand, he fights off disillusionment with the resilient and stubborn conviction that he is acting under the mandate of God and Spain in support of the Reconquista of Andalusia and of the crusade to reconquer the Holy Land. He quickly turns to the divine for such consolations, as in this case when he speaks of Mary's presence in his life: "When I was much afflicted and on the point of abandoning everything and escaping, Our Lady miraculously consoled me and said to me, 'take courage, and do not faint nor fear, for I will provide in all things'" (C, 293). And in another instance, on the verge of despair, he falls asleep and hears "a compassionate voice saying, 'O fool, slow to believe and serve thy God, the God of all! What more did he do for Moses or David his servant than he has done for thee? . . . He gave thee the Indies'" (C, 122).

The religious experiences of Columbus are a strange rendition of mystical themes. Traditional mystical discourse of detachment and abnegation are altogether absent. Instead, mysticism here is a tool of conquest and a confirmation of possession—"He gave thee the Indies!" Instead of demolishing and dispossessing the idols of thought and desire, Columbus's mystical revelations seem to act as the servants of covetousness and appetite. Of course, his cupidity is never more obvious than in his devotion to gold, but when Columbus's dearest idol could not be found, he would devise an alternative plan, one that would substitute Indian bodies for missing gold. In 1494, he captured more than a thousand natives and sent some five hundred of them to be sold in the slave markets of Seville. In his letter on his first journey, he assures the Sovereigns that he will procure as much gold and spices as they desire—something which at this point he could not deliver—and also as many slaves as possible: "I will also bring them as much aloes as they ask and as many slaves, who will be taken from the idolaters" (C, 122). While the Sovereigns initially approved the sale of Columbus's slaves, they soon withdrew their consent pending a study by a commission of theologians and legal experts on the ethical and legal implications.

Columbus's version of mysticism, thus, resembles fantasy more than Christian mysticism. His confessions of faith echo mystical themes and desires, but they are often profane and idolatrous perversions of mysticism. Columbus substitutes fantasy for mysticism the way he had substituted native bodies for gold and hoped that no one would be the wiser for it. Instead of mysticism, the fantasies of Columbus capture with precision the meaning and aim of idolatry, the ignoble consecration of profane images and desires. In fantasy, as in idolatry, the human gaze settles in "arrested, fixated forms of representation" and, thus, proscribes ahead of time the discovery of something different (Bhabha).[11] Columbus perfectly embodies this kind of look, ego-centered, narcissistic, self-important. He would not discover the Americas any more than he would discover God for one obvious reason: his perception of both was frozen and fixed, already determined by what he expected and anticipated to find. He would never capture the truth of native lives and cultures because his vision was blocked by a cataract that produced tunnel vision. He would see only what the mirror reflected back to him, his own image and the projection of his own desires, wants, and beliefs.

It is also true, however, that the desires of Columbus cannot always be reduced to base motives. There are sublime and transcendent emotions swimming in his soul that fuel his relentless drive for exploring the unknown.

Even when he doesn't explicitly name these desires, it seems clear that he wants to play the part of the biblical patriarchs and become the new Adam or Abraham of his age (to give names to creation when it is still fresh and young like Adam; to migrate from the known to the unknown in search of promised lands like Abraham). In this regard, his journeys are not only into undiscovered regions of the world but back in time, to the place and time of human origins when Adam and Eve wandered the earth. Recall that in his third voyage, Columbus claims to have come upon the end of the East, where Paradise can be found: "For I believe that the earthly Paradise lies here, which no one can enter except by God's leave. . . . It lies at the summit of what I have described as the stalk of a pear, and that by gradually approaching it one begins, while still at a great distance, to climb towards it" (C, 221). Columbus craves contact with the place of human origins, the womb of the earth, the sacred place where God dwells. His mind is filled with an erotic and religious longing for something that always escaped him, "for the kingdom or the paradise or the Jerusalem that he could not reach."[12] Like a troubadour who can never possess his beloved except in his dreams and fantasies, the desires of Columbus are always unrequited and unfulfilled. In this sense, his capacity for wonder is a manifestation of what he does *not* possess, of the undefined and elusive goal for which he is passionately searching. And, for Greenblatt, insofar as this dimension of wonder in Columbus carries with it the sense of absence and lack, it continues the medieval sense "that wonder and temporal possession are mutually exclusive."[13]

We know well, however, how Columbus eventually betrays this intuition and conflates wonder and temporal possession. He could not be a troubadour, or even less a Christian mystic, if only because he does not respect the distance and inaccessibility of the other. If Columbus fails the mystical heritage, it is in his devotion to divine immanence without transcendence, to aesthetics without ethics, and, ultimately, to his love for idols. Wonder and temporal possession go hand in hand for Columbus because he knows only a god that he can name, control, possess, and make his own. In place of YHWH, the golden calf has assumed its throne in the life of Columbus, and it is in his honor, not for God, nor for the natives of the New World, that he would devote himself. In this desire for a tangible, material deity, entirely present and determinate, Columbus would seemingly take no notice of a fundamental dimension of mystical thought, namely, divine absence and, thereby, the need for dispossession and emptiness in the life of one seeking to mirror this divine emptiness. Columbus couldn't appreciate the meaning of divine emptiness or nothingness among Pseudo-Dionysius, John the Scot Eriugena, or Eckhart because he was so eager for fullness, for what would fill the emptiness of his heart and pockets.

If we are to attribute any mystical or Adamic qualities to Columbus, therefore, we know that these also include the great catastrophic sin of Adam as well. Columbus brought original sin from the Old World like a plague that would infect everything and everyone. True to his biblical ancestor, Columbus's descendants would suffer long and hard for his inability to resist taking and eating the fruits of paradise, fruits that included human bodies alongside apples and such. The heritage of this serpentine American patriarch will always include this original and decisive sin that stained the American soul and cast a pall over this beautiful, troubled continent. In Billie Holiday's haunting rendition of "strange fruit hanging from the poplar trees," I recognize the history of Columbus's effect, the history of exile and slavery he left in his wake:

> Southern trees bear strange fruit,
> Blood on the leaves and blood at the root,
> Black bodies swinging in the southern breeze,
> Strange fruit hanging from the poplar trees.[14]

Billie Holiday sounds out an elegy on behalf of all the strange fruit of the Americas that has been violently plucked from its branches, never allowed to ripen. These American trees stained with blood share the malediction and curse brought on by Adam's primal deed and that of Columbus. The result has been a long history of people hanging from trees, crucified peoples.

Long before Billie Holiday's lament for crucified peoples, however, other American voices cried out in favor of the dispossessed.[15] The second route of wonder that I want to map in this chapter shows us how wonder can be a force that explodes ethnocentric, European assumptions of superiority and that can reveal to us a glimpse not only of diversity and pluralism, but of infinity, the iconic face of the other. I am suggesting that an articulation of the wondrous and marvelous, as readily as they can become assimilated and exoticized by the colonial enterprise, can also be thought of as fragments of infinity, as metaphors of the unknown and unknowable, as gestures of silence that leave us stunned, uncertain, tolerant. In the figures we will now be analyzing, wonder is chastened by a sense of exile. These remarkable figures recognize the marvelous and alien nature of native cultures as also residing deep within the depths of their own soul. As Stephen Greenblatt wrote, "The movement is from radical alterity—you have nothing in common with the other—to a self-recognition that is also a mode of self-estrangement: you are the other and the other is you."[16] We are the aliens and exiles.

Voices of the Dispossessed: Cabeza de Vaca and Bartolomé de Las Casas

In *Marvelous Possessions*, Sir John Mandeville appears as Stephen Greenblatt's great hero, a "knight of dispossession" he calls him. Although I want to focus on figures of the New World, beginning with Mandeville and Greenblatt's approach on "wonder" will help us better understand the contributions of Cabeza de Vaca and Las Casas.

Up to this point in my study, I have been suggesting that the evocation of wonder in the Middle Ages and Renaissance was a common strategy by which something new and unfamiliar, alien and foreign, or even terrible and hateful was assessed. We have already explored the way that wonder can operate in the service of possession and colonialism, but too little has been said thus far about the liberating impulse of wonder. The enriching possibility of wonder lies, for Greenblatt, in its indeterminacy. It is a metaphor of the absence rather than fullness of knowledge, the partiality and deficiency of human reason more than its wholeness.

It is not enough to call to mind the intellectual indeterminacy of wonder, however. There is also something sensual about wonder, something that strikes at the core of the human person, that thumps the chest and attacks the heart. No wonder, then, that Aquinas's famous teacher Albert the Great described wonder with affective metaphors. It is "a constriction and suspension of the heart caused by amazement at the sensible appearance of something so portentous, great, and unusual that the heart suffers a systole."[17] The systole here is the affective response to something that appears incomprehensible to the mind. Wonder is the body and soul's gasp at the unexpected and surprising, the extraordinary and strange. It is an electric current and feeling that suffuses the body with an untamed mixture of curiosity, desire, and fear. For Greenblatt, then, wonder incites human desire as much as it reminds us of human ignorance.[18]

While different approaches to wonder are evident throughout the Middle Ages—from philosophy's search to remove ignorance to the enhancement or intensification of wonder in art or mysticism—wonder is especially abundant in travel narratives, and Mandeville's text, *The Travels of Sir John Mandeville*, is a great example of wide-eyed wonder. Around every corner of his journey he encounters people, places, and things startlingly new and different, and he never ceases to be amazed by it all. In entering foreign territory, wonder comes as naturally to him as fear comes to a child suddenly lost and alone. While there are manifestations of this primal fear in Mandeville's travels, the stronger impulse is actually courage—there is a lot of nerve and audacity in Mandeville's willingness to take leave of his home and wander through unknown lands. And he is clearly changed as a result: Mandeville's journey from the West to the Holy Land and then into regions further east resulted in this remarkable knight's suspension of all he had known prior to the journey and, subsequently, in a new vision—more catholic, more liberal, magnanimous. Mandeville is a border crosser, an illegal alien, trespassing across walled cities and across the boundaries of European preconceptions and prejudices, and it took heavy doses of courage for him to scale walls of this sort.

Mandeville's experiences in the East (Turkey, India, China), for instance, instill in him a remarkable sympathy and appreciation for human diversity (I leave aside the question of whether Mandeville ever actually traveled to these regions in person or whether they are the journeys of a remarkably imaginative reader). Not only does he withhold condemnation and judgment of different cultures and religions, he speaks admiringly of Orthodox Christians, Muslims, and Hindu Brahmins. In a memorable passage about Brahmins—who "always go about naked"—Mandeville writes:

> Even if they are not Christians, nevertheless by natural instinct or law they live a commendable life, are folk of great virtue. . . . And even if these people do not have the articles of our faith, nevertheless, I believe that because of their good faith that they have by nature, and their good intent, God loves them well and is well pleased by their manner of life, as He was with Job, who was a pagan, yet nevertheless his deeds were as acceptable to God as those of His loyal servants. And even if there are many different religions and different beliefs in the world, still I believe God will always love those who love Him in truth and serve Him meekly and truly. . . . For we know not whom God loves nor whom He hates. (*SJM*, 178–80)

We learn a lot about Mandeville from this passage. He reveals to us a man who is charitable and benevolent toward all of God's creatures and who contends on their behalf, speaking of their goodness and natural faith, their ability to love God however different and idiosyncratic their religions may appear to the Christian mind. But he also tells us about his theology, how little we know the mind of God, how little we can presume about anything about God's ways. Although there are many precedents for this Christian approval of pagan traditions—medieval theology's practice of baptizing the Greek philosophers—Mandeville is a path breaker both for his emphasis on travel and for his almost anthropological interest in non-Christian religions. He is not, after all, speaking of Greek philosophy as in most Christian theology, but of the various religions and beliefs of the world. Quite unlike a sequestered theologian—say, Thomas Aquinas—Mandeville's narrative is the tale of a man who achieves wisdom through all he experienced about the other, through the people he came to know, the friendships created, the relationships developed. If the hero of the narrative realizes that God loves everyone "even if they are not Christian," it comes at the end of a long journey and through experiences that are closer to the writing of history than to philosophy, closer to Herodotus than to Thomas Aquinas (in fact, a lot like the traveler of Thomas More's *Utopia*).[19]

The protagonist of the narrative, in short, finds his classroom in the wide world of human experience. Like a peripatetic philosopher or naked Brahmin wandering the world, he is not confined to a cell or university. His pedagogy is tied up with his wandering outside the walls of universities, cities, cultures, civilizations. He is a champion of what the medieval Latin tradition referred to as *sapentia*, an experiential wisdom distinct from a scientific, theoretical approach to knowledge (*scientia*). Mandeville is a medieval pilgrim driven by curiosity and wonder at the strange and peculiar creations that God has put on the earth. His path is remarkably inventive and original.

To take another example, Mandeville tells a fantastic story about the first approach of Alexander the Great into the lands of the East. As Alexander approaches the land of the Brahmins, one daring sage confronts Alexander and challenges his conquering impulse: "Wherefore then do you gather the riches of this world? . . . Out of this world you will take nothing with you, but naked as you came hither shall you pass hence, and your flesh shall turn back into the earth from which it was made. And yet, not having any regard to this, you are so presumptuous and proud that, just as if you were God, you would make all the world subject to yourself; yet you do not know how long your life will be, nor the hour of your going" (*SJM*, 179–80).

The lesson is a clear censure of all dreams of invincible wealth and power. Alexander's conquering drive is a subtle subterfuge hiding his essential nakedness and mortality, says the Brahmin. If Alexander has come to the East to conquer, wearing his pride and presumption like a coat of arms, Mandeville has come for the wisdom of the East. He has come for understanding, to enlarge and expand the horizons of his being and, even more, his culture's own self-understanding. His exploration of foreign lands teaches him, as Greenblatt remarks, that no one is ever quite at home. His travel narrative is a sketch of homelessness, a disruption of any secure sense of belonging. It is a journal of permanent displacement and alienation, of wandering without possessing. The end of Mandeville's wandering amounts to an uprooting in his origins.[20]

All of that is to say that Mandeville has a large, capacious soul, and only by the route of dispossession does he make room for the largesse that he demonstrates in his writings. By dispossessing himself of his ego's darkest impulses, he suddenly notices manifestations of this drive in his culture at large and does not hide his disapproval and displeasure. European and Christian triumphalism now appears to him just as shameful and disgraceful as any other deadly sin. As Mandeville crosses borders in his wandering, he is interrupting and dislocating his entire culture's haughty and vain feeling of centeredness (ethnocentrism, Eurocentrism, Christocentrism, etc.). As unsettling and disquieting as this experience can be, Mandeville finds virtue in this cultural derailment the way he finds wisdom in his nomadic ways. He finds value in dispersion.

As much of this ethic of dispersion demonstrates his intellectual magnanimity, it surely also includes an ethics of barrenness and poverty. He tells us numerous stories in the book, but many of them return to the theme of renunciation and abnegation. In his travels to the Middle East he tells us that he lived and served the great Sultan for a long time and even fought on his behalf in wars against the Bedouin. Consequently, the Sultan sought to reward him for his loyalty: "And he would have arranged a rich marriage for me with a great prince's daughter, and given me many great lordships if I had forsaken my faith and embraced theirs; but I did not want to" (*SJM*, 59). "I did not want to": this concise comment typifies his renunciation. He turns away from the lure of wealth and power as Jesus had when facing similar temptations in the desert. His ethic is desertlike, sparse and meager, a Quaker-esque spirituality.

The wisdom Mandeville gains from his encounters with other cultures returns him to his homeland a changed man. He now sees his Western church and culture as an outsider might and the portrait is unflattering. He appeals to the wisdom of the East in hopes that it might help Christianity recover what has been lost, a spirit of humility and simplicity and an appreciation for the rich diversity of God's creatures. While Columbus carried with him the tales of Mandeville's journeys to the East, he provides us with a good case of the prophetic warning "they have eyes but they do not see." Because whatever Columbus saw in these tales, he did not tend to the narratives of dispossession—and they might have been redemptive to his soul.

At the very least, Columbus might have walked away with a richer understanding of wonder, one that is a "disclaimer of dogmatic certainty, a self-estrangement in the face of the strangeness, diversity, and opacity of the world."[21] Wonder might have been rescued from Columbus's profane version, his execrable conflation of wonder and dogmatic certainty. And it would have also been far more faithful to other more ancient, venerable wanderers, like Herodotus. For Herodotus and Mandeville both, dogmatic certainty is denied by wonder if only because there is so much of the world to see and so much variety and difference under the sun. Dogmatic certainty is surrendered the moment these travelers enter foreign lands and confront the bewildering uncertainties of various cultures, the dizzying variety of truths, the plurality of conceptions of the good, the different faces of beauty. Their narratives are thick with wonder because they are at pains to explain phenomena that are like nothing encountered before, like nothing imagined or dreamed. Short of remaining speechless and stupefied— short of remaining silent, that is—they indulge in the language of wonder as a way of remaining silent while speaking, as a way of communicating what is incommunicable.

In reference to the travels of Herodotus, Greenblatt highlights the epistemological significance of his nomadic method: "Herodotus had raised to an epistemological principle and a crucial rhetorical device the refusal to be bound within the walls of a city. Knowledge depends upon travel, upon a refusal to respect boundaries, upon a restless drive toward the margins. . . . Scythian nomadism is an anamorphic representation of . . . the historian's apparently aimless wandering."[22] If Herodotus's historical method follows the example of Scythian nomadism, Mandeville follows in the footsteps of the desert nomads of the Bible, including the descendants of Ishmael, Muslim Saracens (the word Saracen derives from the Greek generic term *Sarakenoi*, for "nomadic peoples," and was eventually attributed to Arabs in the seventh century as Islam conquered *al-Andalus*).

Herodotus and Mandeville might have never approached these insights if not for their refusal to remain put. These prophets without a home found wisdom in wandering the earth.

In the age of the Conquest of the New World, there were numerous prophets of Mandeville's breed. They would come to record with their feet as much as the pen the catastrophes of the age. Cabeza de Vaca was one of the most fascinating of them.

Cabeza de Vaca

With Cabeza de Vaca we get another kind of wanderer, even more striking than Sir John Mandeville since Cabeza de Vaca plays a key role in the exploration of the New World, and the account of his adventures and captivity (covering the 1527–36 period) is the first narrative of the land and cultures of North American territory. Cabeza de Vaca's experience in the New World is the stuff of which fiction is made. The events and circumstances of Cabeza de Vaca's life seem to have rolled off the pages of some great novel—and a fantastic one at that.[23] For nine long years, Cabeza de Vaca fights to stay alive after being shipwrecked off the coast of Florida with three hundred other Spaniards sent to conquer more New World territory. Only four of them survive.

After being separated from the leader of the expedition, Pánfilo de Narváez (a seasoned colonizer who had achieved wealth and fame in the conquest of Cuba and Jamaica), Cabeza de Vaca eventually wanders from Florida to the territories of Texas, Arizona, New Mexico, and finally into northern Mexico. He survives against all odds after being enslaved, enduring cold winters, fighting various sicknesses, and, most of all, battling against the relentless and cruel effects of hunger and thirst. His extraordinary ability to survive would have made him a star of the recent genre of "reality television." How he survives is, perhaps, what is most curious and fascinating about his story: he becomes a trader among North American Indian tribes as well as a renowned healer. In that dramatic process, he somehow empties himself of his former identity as conquistador to become, in his nakedness, part Indian, the first mestizo of the Americas.

Like so many of the chroniclers of the New World, Cabeza de Vaca wrestles with naming the unknown. He is another Adam searching for nomenclature for places without names. Everything is strange and new to him, and he reels, body and mind, to assign it meaning, to orient himself in an environment that is profoundly disorienting. In the first pages of the account, he warns (and entices) the reader to prepare for an account of so many new things that many will choose not to believe (CV, 4). His subject matter will be the surprising and unbelievable, the fantastic richness and diversity of human beings. If nothing else, he tells us, his travel account will satisfy the curiosity that human beings have for one another. When he describes a particular manner of Indian cooking, for instance, it serves as a general metaphor of the great diversity and strangeness of human cultures: "Their way of cooking them [beans and squash] is so new and strange that I want to describe it here in order to show how different and queer the devices and industries of human beings are" (CV, 85).

Something so ordinary—the preparing of vegetables—becomes for Cabeza de Vaca an example of how extraordinary and marvelous human behavior is to someone with the eyes of a foreigner. What is banal and commonplace to natives is fantastic and idiosyncratic to Cabeza de Vaca, like reality in the eyes of a child, or ice in the eyes of a Buendía. Perhaps most remarkable, however, Cabeza de Vaca knows that he is seen this way by other peoples, that he and his strange brood of European explorers are just as unusual as the most eccentric of barbarians. And he certainly knows that all the foreknowledge he has brought with him is inadequate in this New World, null and void, empty like the desert. As Cabeza de Vaca travels through these mysterious territories with his small, dwindling band of Spaniards, he is navigating through vast, labyrinthine deserts, and he confesses to us that his knowledge about these lands and cultures is equally desertlike, barren, desolate, and devoid of familiar truths and certainties: "Neither did we know what to expect from the land we were entering, having no knowledge of what it was, what it might contain, and by what kind of people it was inhabited" (CV, 11). Fear is a natural response to this, but he survives by his ability, in Rolena Adorno's words, to negotiate this fear.[24]

His most remarkable achievement in this regard is his uncanny ability to alter and transform his identity as a Spanish conquistador and to somehow reinvent himself as an Indian trader and shaman. He is now brother to New World Calibans. In this guise, at times naked and starving, Cabeza de Vaca proves himself valuable to various Indian groups by bringing them hides and red ocher (with which they would smear their faces and hair) as well as flint and canes for arrows, and possibly tobacco and peyote. The service that he provides various native communities gives him brief tastes of freedom during a time when he was otherwise enslaved by various groups (the Malhado Indians, as well as the Quevenes and Marianes Indians).

But now comes the strangest part of the story. Cabeza de Vaca somehow becomes what the Indians of these regions most needed and most revered, a shaman and healer, now resembling Prospero in the ways of magic—and, of course, the figure of Jesus. As physician of the body and soul, Cabeza de Vaca begins to minister to a wide variety of native groups, performing acts of healing for individuals desperate for a touch of the miraculous. By making the sign of the cross, breathing on them, and praying in earnest to God, he is able to heal. His reputation as a wonder-worker soon blossoms and spreads among native groups, so that when he is able to escape from his captivity under the Marianes, he flees to a group called the Avavares and is treated with respect, even reverence, "because they had heard of us and of how we cured people and of the marvels our Lord worked through us" (CV, 55). And he travels to other communities to attend to the sick and dying. In the most dramatic case, Cabeza de Vaca is summoned to heal a very sick man only to arrive and find that he is already dead. He follows the pattern that he has established, making the sign of the cross, breathing on him, and praying to the Lord. Later that night, the Indians rush to him, "saying that the dead man whom I attended to in their presence had resuscitated, risen from his bed, walked about, eaten and talked to them. . . . This caused great surprise and wonder, all over the land nothing else was spoken of" (CV, 60).

Cabeza de Vaca now has an uncanny power at his command. He himself has become a wonder-worker with awesome powers like Shakespeare's Prospero ("graves at my command"). When Cabeza de Vaca is rescued and returns to the Old World, evidence of his healing power ends. Beyond the borders of the New World, Cabeza de Vaca's shamanistic power is canceled and invalidated. It's as if it could happen only there, in the margins of the world, where normal laws of reason are suspended, a world teeming with the extraordinary and marvelous.

Whatever one thinks of these wondrous stories of healing, the most marvelous and extraordinary fact of these events is the metamorphosis that occurs to Cabeza de Vaca. He is the one that undergoes a magical and wondrous change. He is a soldier after all. All of a sudden, naked as the day he came from his mother's womb, he is a New World wanderer, an Indian trader and shaman. He sheds his previous identity as a snake changes his skin: "We went in that land naked, and not being accustomed to it, we shed our skin twice a year, like snakes" (CV, 63).

Like this shedding of skin, the numerous references to nakedness in Cabeza de Vaca's account is a major hermeneutical key to his writing. His account opens up with a sense of the strangeness of the land and, above all, the strange, naked being that he has become in the New World: "No service is left to me but to bring an account to Your Majesty of the nine years I wandered through many very strange lands, lost and naked" (CV, 3). This sentence is key. Cabeza de Vaca multiplies the references to his nakedness, never wanting the reader to forget his lowly and debased condition. His nakedness is a picture of the most extreme and complete dispossession possible. It is a symbol of the misery and disaster that had befallen this group of proud and noble citizens of the Spanish Empire. And it is a symbol of the fragility and impermanence of imperial dreams, which in the fate of these explorers had turned to dust. Or, perhaps, Hamlet gives us yet another interpretation equally valid: Cabeza de Vaca's dispossession is his confrontation with death, with the final undiscovered country; his dispossession, thus, is the shuffling off of his mortal coil (*Hamlet*, 3.1.67). Ecclesiastes says the same thing: "You are dust and unto dust you shall return" (12:7).

Even before their enslavement by Indian groups in Texas, to continue our story, Cabeza de Vaca and his group had journeyed inland from Florida seduced by rumors about gold and abundant food supplies in the land of Apalachee. What they found there instead were hostile Indians as well as very limited and scarce amounts of food—surely, no gold. At times, the desperation of the Spanish was so intense that some resorted to cannibalism: "And the last one to die was Sotomayor, and Esquivel made jerky of him, and eating of him, he maintained himself until the first of March."[25] Almost as desperate, when Cabeza de Vaca and his group made it in their makeshift rafts to an island off the coast of Texas (which they named "Malhado," bad fortune), they are a company of emaciated and lifeless bodies. Their boat gets stuck in the sand, which requires them to take off their clothes: "Because the shore was very rough, the sea took the others and thrust them, half dead, back onto the beach on the same island. . . . The rest of us, as naked as we had been born, had lost everything. . . . It was November, and bitterly cold. We were in such a state that our bones could easily be counted and we looked like death itself" (CV, 33).

The winter setting only aggravates his naked condition. Exposed to the inclement and merciless winter, his skin (and life) is all the more vulnerable. He is as naked as a deciduous tree in the winter. The winter has done to him what it does to these trees, left him bare and unprotected, completely undressed. In this condition, with his life ebbing away, a group of Indians comes upon them and saves them from certain death: "Upon seeing the disaster we had suffered, our misery and misfortune, the Indians sat down with us and began to weep out of compassion for our misfortune. For more than a half an hour they wept so loudly and so sincerely that it could be heard far away" (CV, 32).

This act of compassion saves Cabeza de Vaca's life in more ways than one, spiritually as much as physically. His old life and person dies and something else is born in its place like a renascent tree in the spring. Through this display of Indian kindness and affection, Cabeza de Vaca gradually comes to recognize what escaped him as a Spanish soldier, the shared humanity of native and Spaniard alike. In this naked, totally vulnerable condition, Cabeza de Vaca was stripped bare of his Spanish code of honor, of any titles and past achievements, and, above all, of his feeling of European cultural superiority. Only in this wasteland experience of Cabeza de Vaca, in this abject and wretched setting, does he recognize his solidarity with native peoples: "I spent six years in this country, alone with them and as naked as they were" (CV, 43).

Clothes were surely an important mark of status and class throughout European history, and for the Spanish they would have represented certain levels of civilization. To be naked, then, represented a fall of sorts, a diminishment and debasement of civilization that brought one to the level of the uncivilized and barbaric. Nakedness, in the words of Paul Schneider, "was a symbolic turning point, after which the Spaniards could no longer differentiate themselves from those whom they had come to conqueror."[26] Or take Ilan Stavans's thoughtful assessment of the issue: "[The word] *naked . . .* signifies bewilderment, even embarrassment on the part of the voyager, and is also used to indicate an uncontaminated, natural disposition toward the environment by the natives."[27]

The metaphor of nakedness appears in many New World chronicles, but one of the most intriguing cases is the account of another shipwrecked Spaniard, Gonzalo Guerrero, who "went native" after being shipwrecked off the coast of the Yucatan in 1511. Though the historical record on Gonzalo is scarce and contradictory, the narratives told about him (by Andrés de Cereceda, Francisco López de Gómara, Bernal Díaz del Castillo, and others) emphasize his renunciation of European civilization and his embrace of native ways. Like Cabeza de Vaca, this renunciation leaves him indistinguishable from the natives. In the words of Cereceda, "This Gonzalo has gone about naked, his body tattooed and in the garb of an Indian."[28] And for Bernal Díaz, in taking on this new denuded identity and in marrying an Indian woman, Gonzalo, "the Warrior," is the father of the mestizo.[29]

Whether Gonzalo was a flesh and blood person is unclear, but we do know how many chroniclers perceived and interpreted his intimate relationship with native peoples. For some, he is an apostate and traitor, for others he represents the beginning of American miscegenation. As the legends about Gonzalo were developing (Gómara published his version in 1552), there must have been a renewed interest in the reports of Cabeza de Vaca (published in 1542 and then republished in 1555, with the title of *Naufragios*). How fascinating these tales of wandering, lost, naked Spaniards must have appeared to Europeans. Especially to those disturbed by the reports of violence and abuse in the New World, the cases of these men were refreshingly different. Instead of triumphal narratives of war and plunder, these legends gave us examples like Cabeza de Vaca, men who adopted nakedness and dispossession above the will to power. They gave us individuals far less certain and self-assured, but infinitely more capable of tenderness and compassion than their conquistador counterparts. William Pilkington thinks it was the suffering and debasement that Cabeza de Vaca endured that made him the extraordinary person he was: "The knowledge of human suffering and its psychological, if not physical, alleviation seemed to expand and alter his vision of life; it chastened him, taught him humility, and encouraged his spiritual growth—growth which paralleled . . . his geographic progress."[30]

His life, then, comes to mirror his geographic wandering, and his spirituality adopts the look of desert ecologies—barren, arid, empty, unadorned. Even his skin color must have changed hues to resemble the brownness of desert dwellers, of people burned by the sun and darkened by suffering. He must have begun to look a lot like so many migrants and refugees of our own age, wandering through the deserts of the modern U.S.-Mexico border in search of water and promised lands, like the biblical Hagar and her son, Ishmael—themselves exiles—frantically searching for springs of life.

If there wasn't enough drama and suspense in the narrative thus far, when Cabeza de Vaca and his three companions (a North African slave, Estevanico; Andres Dorantes; and Alonso de Castillo Maldonado) finally are reunited with their countrymen, it is with a group of Spaniards hunting for slaves. Though we would expect a moment of elation at this point—like a child being reunited with his mother—Cabeza de Vaca is suddenly tentative and he is not at all clear where he belongs, whether he is one of the hunters or the hunted. He has a hard time recognizing himself in the rapacious acts of his countrymen and tells us in no uncertain terms how much sorrow it caused him to witness the devastation the slave raids were having on the

Indian communities (led by Nuño de Guzmán and Diego de Alcaraz). He comes across villages once full of life and now deserted, the people in exile and hiding in the mountains. He saw with his own naked eye villages that were depopulated and set on fire by these slavers, a "scorched earth" campaign:

> We traveled through much land and we found all of it deserted, because the inhabitants of it went fleeing through the sierras without daring to keep houses or work the land for fear of the Christians. It was a thing that gave us great sorrow, seeing the land very fertile and very beautiful and very full of waterways and rivers, and seeing the places deserted and burned and the people so emaciated and sick, all of them having fled and in hiding. And since they did not sow, with so much hunger they maintained themselves on the bark of trees and roots. We had a share of this hunger along the road, because only poorly could they provide for us, being so displaced from their natural homeland that it seemed that they wished to die. . . . They brought us blankets, which they had been concealing from the Christians, and gave them to us, and told us how the Christians had come into the country before and had destroyed and burned the villages, taking with them half the men and all the women and children. (CV, 90)

"We had a share of this hunger along the road": Cabeza de Vaca's comment here again represents the new direction his life had taken. His own experience of desperation and hunger was the condition that made possible this expression of sorrow that he feels for the fate of these communities. This passage is filled with pathos and it is an exact, vivid, poignant, and moving description of native dislocation and destitution. In the face of the threat of "the Christians," Cabeza de Vaca swears to the Indians that he will not allow them to kill any of them or abduct them as slaves. Eventually, when Cabeza de Vaca and his companions reach the Spaniards a standoff ensues between Cabeza de Vaca and the leaders. One of the slavers, Diego de Alcaraz, was insistent that Cabeza de Vaca use his influence with the Indians to get them to come down from the mountains, out of hiding. Cabeza de Vaca relents and proceeds to call for the Indians, expecting peaceful cooperation. It soon becomes clear, however, that the Spanish have no intentions of letting the Indians be: "Thereupon we had many and bitter quarrels with the Christians, for they wanted to make slaves of our Indians, and we grew so angry at it that at our departure we forgot to take along many bows, pouches, and arrows, as well as the five emeralds, so they were left and lost to us" (CV, 95).

Cabeza de Vaca tells us, at this point, that Alcaraz had also attempted to discredit Cabeza de Vaca and his companions by saying to the Indians that they were disloyal renegades and people of little heart. The Indian response to Alcaraz demonstrates how far Cabeza de Vaca had gone in becoming American: "The Indians paid little attention to this talk. They talked among themselves, saying that the Christians lied, for we had come from sunrise, while they had come from where the sun sets; that we cured the sick, while they had killed those who were healthy; that we went naked and barefoot, whereas they wore clothes and went on horseback and carried lances. Also, we asked for nothing, but gave away all we were presented with, while they seemed to have no other aim than to steal what they could, and never gave anything to anybody" (CV, 96).[31] In his role as a wandering beggar, Cabeza de Vaca has become one with the natives in dress and disposition. His complete dispossession—as I've been saying, his nakedness—is a visible indication of his faithfulness to native peoples. His body wears the signs of a wanderer on the earth, a desert pilgrim. His nakedness is an icon of his newfound American identity. This is particularly evident in the episode where the Spanish slave raiders first catch sight of Cabeza de Vaca. Their response to him is one of pure wonder: "The next morning I came upon four Christians on horseback who, seeing me in such strange attire and in the company of Indians, were greatly surprised. They stared at me for quite a while, speechless. Their surprise was so great that they could not find words to ask me anything" (CV, 93).

To these Spaniards, Cabeza de Vaca had become the greatest wonder of all, surpassing anything they imagined about the New World. In his exile in the Americas, Cabeza de Vaca had succeeded in becoming a strange and wondrous being, not only a voice of the dispossessed but one of them. I repeat, he has become brown like them, a savage and impure mixture of European and American cultures, brown as Richard Rodriguez sees it: "I write of a color that is not a singular color, not a strict recipe, not an expected result, but a color produced by careless desire, even by accident; by two or several. I write of blood that is blended. I write of brown as complete freedom of substance and narrative. I extol impurity."[32]

Cabeza de Vaca is brown like this, an impure product of an accident—a shipwreck to be precise—that was both his ruin and his salvation. And in response to this sudden brownness, the "Christians" respond with stupefaction and incomprehensibility. His person causes them to marvel because he himself has become something strange and fantastic, as wild as anything they would encounter in this New World. In speaking of the New World Baroque, Octavio Paz describes well the fascination that this new creature would cause: "In the seventeenth century the aesthetics of the strange expressed with rapture the strangeness of the criollo. . . . The criollo breathed naturally in a world of strangeness because he was, and knew himself to be, a strange being" (OP, 58–59). Cabeza de Vaca is this kind of strange creation, a criollo or mestizo avant la lettre.

Cabeza de Vaca's real and direct knowledge of native peoples is nothing like the romantic and prejudicial versions of Columbus. He knew the Indians to be people of great compassion and tenderness as well as cruelty and violence. They were, in short, very much like him. And yet, through his wandering and living among them, he learned that there is a great diversity of human beings and that he himself is as strange and wondrous to his fellow Indians as they are to him. It is Cabeza de Vaca's experience of abject failure and disaster that allowed him to see himself on the same human plane as the Indians: as a vulnerable, mortal, and wondrous being. The great Dominican friar Las Casas, a reader of Cabeza de Vaca, would be undeniably impressed with this message and would himself come to a similar conclusion about the Indians and about himself.

Bartolomé de Las Casas

When Columbus first returns to Seville from the New World, he carries with him a group of Indians in chains. As a young man in Seville, Las Casas was said to have been there for the epic event. This young man would later build a theological defense of the Indians around this principle of "being there," of witnessing firsthand the events and circumstances of the Conquest of the Indies. Las Casas would eventually take his place in a long line of historians and prophets—the two blend into each other for Las Casas— who were chroniclers of the victims and oppressed of history. Las Casas arrives at this point, however, with more than his own personal experience of the New World. It took a revelation of a classical biblical nature to jolt him from his slumber. And it was the biblical prophets that brought him the message that would be crucial to his life: that God is on the side of the poor and dispossessed.

It is unquestionable that autobiography and personal testimony are cornerstones of Las Casas's intellectual life. Any consideration of dispossession in Las Casas should begin with his own story, at the moment when he renounces his life as a slaveholder and *encomendero* after witnessing a massacre of Taíno Indians in Cuba (1514).

Las Casas went to the Antilles as early as 1502 (at eighteen years of age), where he helped manage his father's *encomienda* on the island of Hispaniola (granted to Las Casas's father for traveling with Columbus on his second voyage in 1493). Later, for taking part in the conquest of Cuba under Diego Velásquez and Pánfilo de Narváez, Las Casas had been granted a large *encomienda*. Privileges like this come at a heavy price, gained at the expense of innumerable individuals and communities. This fact would not be lost on all Europeans in the New World. Already at this early stage in the Conquest there were friars and priests in Cuba and Hispaniola who were protesting the bloodshed and atrocities. Several Dominicans, in particular, would heavily influence Las Casas. In one case, a Dominican friar—possibly Pedro de Cordoba, the leader of the Dominican community in Hispaniola—refused Las Casas absolution for being an encomendero and possessing Indians. Las Casas once remarked that his attitude toward this Dominican at the time was one of respect, "but as to giving up his Indians, he was not healed of his opinion."[33]

Pedro de Cordoba was the superior of a group of Dominicans from the Convent of St. Stephen in Salamanca intent on reforming the Order and recovering the original spirit of contemplation and poverty.[34] The Dominicans are mendicants, after all, a word from the Latin verb suggesting "to beg." When faithful to St. Dominic, they would wander like rolling stones forever on the move, seeking stillness in and through movement, contemplation through action. This itinerant lifestyle was a parable of exile and perpetual displacement on this earth. The betrayal of this nomadic virtue—for these Dominicans, the impulse to settle down and take possession—represented the victory of the "City of Man" over the "City of God." For the reform-minded Dominicans of the age of Conquest, this victory was almost total and absolute in the New World, so much, in fact, that the "City of Man" had achieved totalitarian authority. Those homesick pilgrims that belonged to the "City of God" were, by contrast, few and far between, like revolutionaries on the verge of defeat, disunited and routed. The Dominicans, however, would try to rally them.

Las Casas would never forget one mendicant preacher in particular, the Dominican friar Antonio Montesinos. Las Casas sat calmly in the church pews as Montesinos mounted the pulpit and began his tirade. In opening his mouth, a dam broke and a flood of accusations and denunciations accosted the congregation like volcanic lava burning up everything in its path. The biblical text for the sermon was the passage relating the ministry of John the Baptist, the voice crying out in the desert. Montesinos went on to describe himself as a "voice of Christ in the desert of this island":

> You are all in mortal sin! You live in it and you die in it! Why? Because of the cruelty and tyranny you use with these innocent people. Tell me, with what right, with what justice, do you hold these Indians in such cruel and horrible servitude? On what authority have you waged such detestable wars on these people? . . . Are they not human beings? Have they no rational souls? Are you not obligated to love them as you love yourselves? Do you not understand this? Do you not grasp this? How is it that you sleep so soundly, so lethargically? (LC, *HI*, 141)

Montesinos's thunderous words rained on the audience with fury. On that day, Montesinos channeled the best of the Hebrew prophets.

Needless to say, Montesinos caused an uproar. His congregation wanted sweet and sentimental sermons, not this fury that thickened like the dark clouds of a hurricane. Montesinos's superior in Hispaniola, Pedro de Cordoba, supported his sermon, and himself turns to the king to tell him what is happening in the New World. The colonists are "depopulating" rather than populating the lands. The Indians have the appearance of "painted corpses" rather than living human beings. The cruelties and servitude in the New World are worse than those committed by the Pharaoh and the Egyptians.[35]

When Las Casas recalls the preaching of the Dominicans, however, he places himself in the company of those who slept soundly and lethargically. It is not until later, under the spell of a passage from Scripture, Sirach 34, that Las Casas's life is changed, which seems to me to highlight how much his life was influenced not only by historical events and atrocities (like the massacre of Taíno Indians in Cuba that he witnessed) but by texts, including the Bible and the accounts of the New World that he was reading (e.g., Cabeza de Vaca). Las Casas's encounter with the biblical text is nothing short of a shock of recognition, a bomb within the contentment and comfort of his previous life. He reads the lines of Sirach—"The Most High approves not the gifts of the godless, nor for their many sacrifices does he forgive their sins. . . . The bread of charity is life itself for the needy, he who withholds it is a person of blood"—and he is jolted from his slumber. He

tells us that at this point, "He agreed to condemn openly the distribu-
tions or encomiendas as unjust and tyrannical, and then to release his own
Indians."[36]

Now gathering within him the voices of the biblical prophets, Las Casas
excoriates the guilty for "crushing the poor into the dust of the earth"
(Amos), for withholding the bread of love to the afflicted, for turning away
and mistreating the stranger. As any prophet would, Las Casas first targets
the problem of idolatry and its most glaring manifestation in the New
World: the religious consecration of the Conquest, in particular the "dona-
tion" of the Indies to Spain by the papal bull of Alexander VI. For Las Casas,
the Indies belongs to no one but God, a theology as simple as it is radical.
Rolena Adorno shows, for instance, how this thought shaped the thinking of the great Inca Guaman Poma de Ayala. Using Las Casas's work *The
Twelve Doubts* as his source, Guaman Poma makes this claim: "You must
consider that all the world is God's and thus Castile belongs to the Spaniards and the Indies belongs to the Indians, and Guinea, to the blacks . . .
each one of these is legitimate proprietor."[37] For Las Casas and Guaman
Poma, this principle meant that the natives have the right of sovereignty over
their own lands and that the rights granted by the papal bull concerned
only the right to evangelize, not to conquer and subdue foreign peoples.

Theologically, then, this thought would strip bare and nullify any claims
of possession by church or state. Claims to private ownership in the New
World was another manifestation of the idolatrous impulse, with the Indies
now playing the part of the Golden Calf. In practical terms, though, Las
Casas argues that the papal bull is null and void by failing to observe its
primary objective: the peaceful spread of the Gospel. Since the bull was
designed for this purpose—and included recognition of the legitimacy of
native rulers as well as the free consent of the Indians—it ceases to be valid
when these conditions are flaunted. On papal authority, Las Casas has this
to say: "The pope has no jurisdiction over temporal things, or concerning
the area of the temporal, or over secular and worldly states, except for the
sake of the spiritual."[38]

Lacking in temporal and worldly authority, the pope's authority is confined to the spiritual realm, and even this authority is jeopardized by the
sins and transgressions of Spain. The savage actions of Spain, argues Las
Casas, have in effect abrogated the papal bull and, of greater concern to this
theologian, put Spain on a path to damnation, not salvation. Las Casas, in
fact, prophesies the death of Spain if it continues in this regard. Las Casas
invokes death as threat and curse, yet again echoing the prophets of old.

As the biblical prophets announce the end of the holy city, Jerusalem, or holy Temple, Las Casas's imprecations speak of the death of Spain for its part in the destruction of the Indies. The omens of death in the New World spell only one thing in his mind: disaster.

So, the prophetic word is an epitaph for Las Casas, an inscription in memory of the dead. In fact, this sort of epitaph bears a surprising resemblance to the inscription on Walter Benjamin's monument in Portbou, Spain, on the French-Spanish border (Benjamin died here while fleeing the Nazis in 1940). Las Casas could have written the inscription: "It is more arduous to honor the memory of the nameless than that of the renowned. Historical construction is devoted to the memory of the nameless."[39] For both of these great intellectuals, the written word is always devoted to the memory of the nameless. They used the word to conjure memories that had a dangerous, subversive edge, memories that cut like a knife and defeated the oblivion that threatened to bury the nameless from being remembered among the living.

The logic that joins Las Casas with Benjamin is particularly plausible and convincing if we consider that Las Casas explicitly allied himself with the Hebrew face of Christianity, with its emphasis on history and ethics. With the same open-eyed attention of the prophets, Las Casas would look for traces of God in the strife and tumult of the events of the day and listen for God's word through the sounds of fury and war. Thus, when it came to the question of history writing, Las Casas would look for a guide in a Jewish writer, Josephus. For Las Casas, Josephus's greatness as a historian can be explained by his unique vantage point as a Jew who records the events of his community as it came under the dominion of the great beast of his age, the Roman Empire. Josephus, in this reading of Las Casas, was witness to the devastation caused by Roman imperial dreams just as Las Casas was to the nightmarish realities that emerged from Spain's imperial dreams. Anthony Pagden has written of this relationship between Las Casas and Josephus: "Las Casas's own motives, however, were like those of Josephus, the historian of another race—the Jews—who had been destroyed by a rapacious imperial power and to whom his own theoretical remarks are heavily indebted."[40]

These two distant brothers come together, then, when addressing and confronting the horrors of their respective epochs. Death had undone so many in their ages and they turned to the prophets—Las Casas more than Josephus—to articulate and release their outrage. The prophetic word haunts Las Casas, never releasing him from its grip, the way exile would prove so inexorable and unrelenting for native peoples. And exile, of course, is the minion of death. Exile takes and strips away all that is dear and life-giving; it peels away our soul and leaves us denuded and bare. Las Casas seeks lessons in these morbid thoughts, however. The ghosts of the dead will inform his theology, and this fact will produce a kind of theology that has an elegiac quality, resembling a dirge or requiem more than the logical disputations of a philosopher. It will be a theology comprising the broken shards of native histories and cultures.

Thus, amid the storm of suffering in the New World, Las Casas's theology is first battered and broken before it is reborn as something different, something more fragile and modest than what he had before—a theology of dispossession. Decisions that he makes in his personal life—like becoming a Dominican in 1522—reflect this ongoing effort at dispossession, with his life changing form and content under the spell of the written pages of sacred texts, a case where life imitates art. For several years Las Casas withdraws from the public arena only to return with greater intensity as defender of the Indians. In my reading, part of this reemergence is the formulation of a new theology, a restless theology of exile.

It seems to me that Las Casas returns with a greater awareness on the incompleteness and nomadic nature of any theological formulation. His theology will increasingly capture his own restlessness and his newfound life as an itinerant, mendicant preacher. Insofar as the Indian communities are scattered, exiled, and oppressed, no authentic follower of Christ is permitted rest. His new theological vision will be governed by the following sources: "The love of Jesus Christ," for one, "which knows no measure nor seeks any rest while on this pilgrimage"; and "the distress and endless misery which, in these lands these unfortunate infidel peoples here have suffered for so long a time now, without a day of rest, respite, or relief, but with more agony still."[41] Any theology of his time, he tells us, must mirror and represent these two images: the pilgrim of Christ wandering without rest and without security, and the restless wandering of the displaced, oppressed Indians in the Americas.

Several years later when Las Casas is Bishop of Chiapas, in 1544, the experience of exile would visit him personally, as he is driven away from Chiapas to escape irate colonists, angry at Las Casas's use of excommunication for slaveholders and encomenderos.[42] Drawing on papal writings, Las Casas in *Sublimis Deus* (1537) and *Pastorale Officium* (1537) excoriates and condemns the abuses of the colonists. A passage from *Sublimis Deus* reads as follows: "The aforementioned Indians . . . although they be outside the faith of Christ, neither are nor ought to be deprived of their freedom or dominion over their goods. Indeed, they may freely and licitly use, possess, and enjoy freedom and such dominion and must not be reduced to slavery."[43] *Pastorale Officium* went further and provided cause for the excommunication of slaveholders, but later, under pressure from Charles V, the bull is revoked. Needless to say, this action does not weaken his determination. Las Casas will continue to draw on these documents in his fiery preaching against the colonists. His experience of exile would be a predictable consequence of this prophetic vocation. We might see this experience of Las Casas's exile as a tragic foreshadowing of the fate that many great intellectuals would endure in the history of Latin America for being voices of dissent. Las Casas is the beginning.

Or else, as I've been suggesting in this chapter, the biblical prophets are the beginning. And for this Christian, of course, the suffering God is the beginning, the alpha and the omega of his prophetic theology. From this theological perspective—where Christ crucified is discovered among the poor and oppressed of history—Las Casas associates the Indians with the crucified God of Christianity. The ethnocentrism and Christian triumphalism of his time is upset by a theology that regards the face of the other as the site of God's revelation. Take this powerful text as a case in point: "I leave, in the Indies, Jesus Christ, our God, scourged and afflicted, buffeted and crucified not once but millions of times, on the part of all the Spaniards who ruin and destroy these people."[44]

This remarkable passage from the pen of Las Casas sets the tone for much of his theology of the cross. Las Casas doesn't simply argue that the Indians are human like us and deserving of dignity and respect. He's more daring: we encounter God in the face of the other; their lives are sacraments of Christ, and their bodies part of the mystical body of Christ. The enslavement and murder of the Indians is nothing short of blasphemy akin to the crucifixion of God, or the profanation of the Eucharist.

Las Casas, in other words, redirects the charges of blasphemy and idolatry against the Christians. Anticipating a philosopher like Kierkegaard, he would complain that there is no Christian to be found in Christendom and its empire, no authentic faith in the adoration of a warring, conquering God, no real passion for the God of the cross, this humiliated, ignominious, and lowly figure, Jesus of Nazareth. Who are the idolaters, then? Spanish behavior in the New World exceeds in iniquity and barbarity any transgressions of the natives, including human sacrifices. The colonists commit sins more egregious by "substituting things for people," adoring wealth and glory before love of neighbor and love of God (LC, *HI*, 106). Las Casas anticipates what Montaigne would say on the subject generations later: "I think there is more barbarity in eating a man alive than in eating his dead; and in tearing by tortures and the rack a body still full of feeling, in roasting a man bit by bit, in having him bitten and mangled by dogs and swine . . . than in roasting and eating him after he is dead."[45] This passage captures Las Casas's sentiments exactly, expressing the same outrage at European hypocrisy in decrying the barbarism of other cultures without facing the barbarian within. Before Montaigne would articulate these thoughts, Las Casas had already called attention, like a psychoanalyst of history, to the darkest drives and inclinations in the human soul. In this case, Las Casas channels Augustine to reveal a European soul that resembles a madhouse of the grotesque, hideous and malevolent in its disorder. Such a condition is like a soul come off its hinges, unmoored and adrift. "Such a type is like someone out of his mind and gone crazy. His mind is not his own, it is enveloped in clouds, dimmed by fog. . . . Such a type is hardhearted, merciless, does not have faith, does not love peace, lacks love, feels no pity, owns no father, no mother, trusts no one, relative or friend, has no compassion" (LC, *HI*, 104). As he put it in the prologue to *A Short Account of the Destruction of the Indies,* such men have ceased to be human in any meaningful sense of the word.

In forcing his readers to face the grotesque and monstrous possibilities within their own souls, Las Casas changes the conversation on the theme of wonder. The language of wonder takes on a darker, more dreadful form, closer to what is awful and ghastly in the experience of wonder than to what is delightful. Wonder has blacker tones in Las Casas, as if Goya's macabre scenes—images of hideous violence, demonic possessions, witches, evil sprites, fiends, and so forth—had influenced his judgment on the events of his age. Malevolent forces run wild and with impunity; wickedness and shamefulness has subdued goodness; chaos has swallowed up order and harmony; the world is, in short, experiencing the groans and pangs of the end times. For Las Casas, then, wonder is marked by apocalyptic omens, by baleful auguries inscribed on the forehead of wonder, as it were. If Columbus called on wonder as an expression of ineffable beauty and sublimity, Las Casas evokes wonder to signify a wrenching dismay in what is happening in the Indies. Las Casas's sense of wonder is a kind of mute reaction before the horror of it all. The profundity and gravity of suffering has him stupefied and perplexed. The opening to *A Short Account* illustrates this well:

Everything that has happened since the marvelous discovery of the
Americas . . . has been so extraordinary that the whole story remains
quite incredible to anyone who has not experienced it firsthand. It
seems, indeed, to overshadow all the deeds of famous men of the past,
no matter how heroic, and to silence all talk of other wonders of the
world. Prominent amid the aspects of this story which have caught
the imagination are the massacres of innocent peoples, the atrocities
committed against them and, among other horrific excesses, the ways
in which towns, provinces, and whole kingdoms have been entirely
cleared of their native inhabitants. (LC, *DI*, 3)

The wonder of the New World, he writes, is so extraordinary and unique
that it "silences all talk of other wonders of the world." For Las Casas, any
consideration of wonder is quickly interrupted by the devastating fact of
human suffering; the pleasure of wonder gives way to what is frightening
and awful in the experience. He will not, therefore, linger long with an
aesthetics of wonder. There will be no account of the ecstasies and rapture
of beauty, or any kind of indulgence in poetry, art, or music. Las Casas is
like a disenchanted intellectual amid the Holocaust, glancing with scorn
and contempt at celebrations of beauty and romantic love when death is
ravaging the innocent. His sense of wonder is chastened and conditioned
by the historical reality of exile, of whole kingdoms made into deserts. If
the seeds of wonder have been sowed throughout the New World with fantastic expectations and hopes for a magnificent harvest, Las Casas sees only
a harvest choked by weeds and overrun by flowers of evil.

If Las Casas resorts to the theme of inexpressibility, therefore, it is often
to indicate the severity of suffering: "And no account, no matter how
lengthy, how long it took to write, nor how conscientiously it was compiled,
could possibly do justice to the full horror of the atrocities committed" (LC,
DI, 43). So, Las Casas attempts to register something that cannot be spoken
of, something that exceeds the mind's capacity to possess and grasp, but it
is neither beauty nor a mysticism of nature. It is the reality of "horrific excesses," of tragedies that paralyze the mind by manifestations of a cruel madness. For Las Casas, the age of Conquest is an age of disaster and tragedy,
so when he references the marvelous and fantastic tales of chivalry, it is to
underscore this point: "All that I have seen and all your reverences have
heard, will seem perhaps like the fables and lying tales of Amadis of Gaul,
for all that has been done in these Indies is by natural, divine and human
law, null, inane and invalid, and as if it had been done by the Devil."[46]

The characterization of wonder in Las Casas, then, forces us to ponder realities scarcely thinkable, realities that cause the soul to recoil for being so unnerving and appalling. Arthur Cohen's reflections on the terrifying events of the Holocaust parallel moments in Las Casas: "Thinking and the death camps are incommensurable. The procedures of thought and the ways of knowing are confounded. . . . The death camps are a reality which, by their very nature, obliterate thought and the humane program of thinking. . . . The death camps are unthinkable but not unfelt."[47] Las Casas's writings are something like Cohen's conundrum—this vicious dilemma of thinking and writing about something that confounds and obliterates all procedures of thought. If Las Casas's theology bleeds with so much passion and emotional intensity, it is because he wants the reader to feel the unthinkable and to be moved to tears by the dreadful story he has to tell. His language is tortuous and outrageous because only this kind of language—morally outraged, furious, explosive—can communicate the fullest extent of the horror.

Las Casas turns to apocalyptic images to suggest all this, what is "unthinkable but not unfelt." Las Casas is the voice of a prophet wandering in the desert, speaking on behalf of whole communities in exile. In his *Apologia*, he speaks of what he witnessed in Cuba: "The extent of the natives' destruction is unbelievable, and they wander about, hiding in woods and forests, scattered, unarmed, naked, and bereft of all human aid, are quartered by the Spaniards, stripped of their fortunes, reduced to wretchedness and landlessness. They stumble about aghast and terrified by incredible fear at the sight of the monstrous crimes perpetrated against them by those tyrants."[48]

This passage mirrors the depopulation and devastation of what Cabeza de Vaca witnessed in native territories. Las Casas describes numerous incidents of terror against native peoples, wanting to give the reader a portrait of lands and cultures destroyed. The New World has become a wasteland, a desert of exile and death. Again, speaking of Cuba: "They did terrifying massacres there. That way they wiped out the population of the whole island. We see few left today. It is an awful pity to see it, a wasteland, a man-made desolation" (LC, *HI*, 147). And of Mexico: "Afterwards there was a succession of others, cruel monsters who laid waste to the region, the provinces of Naco and Honduras, by massacres and fearful cruelties, by making slaves of people and selling them to the ships that brought wine and clothing. . . . And these provinces were an earthly paradise to behold, they were heavily populated. . . . We travel them today and as we do we see them so thinned out, so ravaged that they would move anyone to pity" (LC, *HI*, 231). Las Casas does not tire of recounting the burning and looting, the scorched-earth campaigns, the slavery and abuse of the Indians of the Americas. It would be too cumbersome to mention all of his passages on these matters. Suffice it to say that his *History of the Indies* is laden with a profusion of tragedies. He piles up example on example the way a Baroque artist will bring together a profligate variety of exotic forms and colors (the subject of our next chapter). Excessive and extravagant displays of suffering are as necessary to Las Casas as aesthetical surplus is to Baroque art. Las Casas describes the Conquest with the memory of the defeated and conquered always before him, haunting his mind and spirit, demanding that he write and speak on their behalf. The dead are never quite dead for Las Casas because their specters remain with him, and his prophecy is speech on their behalf as much as it is speech on behalf of God.

Another historian of his age, Pedro Cieza de León, gives us a perfect image of the age: "There remains no other testimony of the country having once been peopled than the great cemeteries of the dead, and the ruins of the places where they lived."[49] There could hardly be a better summation of the age of the Conquest, nor of Las Casas's theology. Cemeteries and ruins: Las Casas builds his theology on these images. His theological imagination is saturated with such images, none more important than the symbol of the cross. In his mind, the New World has become a labyrinth of crosses, a desertlike crown of thorns. Where others bend their knees to the triumphal god, Las Casas adores the crucified god as he is revealed in the innumerable agonies and ruins of history. Las Casas wrote his theology from the cemeteries of the dead and in the ruin of native civilizations. And he preached from the belly of the beast, within the vast wasteland that was the New World.

The target of his preaching—with a voice that was a howling gust of wind—was always the covetousness of European nations. His voice was to be a typhoon that exposed the vulgar, savage motives hiding behind European appeals to Christian doctrine. Barbarism was plainly evident to Las Casas in the "cruel, inhuman, wild and merciless acts."[50] If Las Casas identifies barbarism with this kind of mad, merciless behavior, he also wants to deepen our understanding of it, all for the sake of an enlightened tolerance. His thoughts on this topic presage a future age of pluralism, soon coming with the modern age: "A man will be called barbarian in comparison with another man because he is strange in his ways of speaking and because he pronounces the other's language badly. . . . But from this point of view there is no man or race which.is not barbarian in relation to another man or another race."[51] Montaigne's version is this: "Every man calls barbarism whatever is not his own practice."[52] In both cases, the implication holds true that each culture is strange and incomprehensible to the other and that "barbarism" is the pejorative designation for otherness. It is the prejudicial nomenclature for an experience a lot like wonder—that is, radical alterity—but with ethnocentrism firmly in place. If we would follow Las Casas and Montaigne in discovering the barbarian and foreigner within, we would expand our capacity for wonder.

In his reflections on barbarism, moreover, Las Casas follows a code that he has established early on, the principle of empathy in cultural understanding, to see things "as if he were Indian." In an argument with the Scottish theologian John Major, Las Casas employs this principle of empathy to evoke recognition of the common humanity of European and native alike: "If the Hungarians or Bohemians . . . were to despoil him of his dignity and his realm, were he a king, in the first moment of contact with him, sowing uproar everywhere and terrorizing his provinces with the tumult of war . . . by any chance would John Major graciously and joyfully accept this 'good cause'? . . . I in no way think that John Major himself would tolerate a situation so impious and brutal if he were an Indian."[53] The biblical text of Matthew 25—"When you did it to the least of my brothers and sisters," Jesus says, "you did it for me"—must have preoccupied his mind when Las Casas spoke of empathy. It provides a perfect model for this kind of identification with the other in need and for the divine summons of infinite compassion and solidarity. But then again, it is not only Jewish texts saturating his mind and spirit. The great master of theology of his Order, Thomas, would bequeath to Las Casas certain Greek thoughts (even though Las Casas's beloved is clearly Jerusalem before Athens).

With the Greek inclinations of the Dominicans, Las Casas finds one principle particularly significant and relevant: the tradition of the natural knowledge of God. Las Casas, in fact, assumes the theological claim that every human being—created in the image of God—has an intuitive knowledge of God (and he cites not only Aquinas but also several Church Fathers in this regard): "And in all truth, the universal concept of God is oriented toward the true God and does not rest until it reaches him" (LC, *A*, 296). Las Casas assumes that this universal concept of God is, well, universal and present throughout the great and strange diversity of human cultures and lives. There is no people, he avers, so barbarous as to be devoid of knowledge of God. He even insists that the natives of the New World already possessed a "refined, quite accurate knowledge of the true God" prior to the arrival of Christianity (LC, *A*, 307).

On this point, Las Casas found further confirmation in the observations of Cabeza de Vaca. In reading him, Las Casas's attention must have been most acute and sharp when Cabeza de Vaca recounted the destruction and decimation of the Indian community at the hands of slavers in the area of North America (quoted above), but there was more to it that intrigued Las Casas. As Rolena Adorno explains in her work *The Polemics of Possession in Spanish American Narrative*, Las Casas cited and utilized Cabeza de Vaca on at least these following issues: first, regarding Cabeza de Vaca's claim that the Indians "worshipped a man in the sky," and, thus, had a natural knowledge of God; second, that they had "found neither sacrifices nor idolatry" among the Indians; and third, that the natives had a moral aptitude and disposition to receive the Christian God.[54] Las Casas saw in Cabeza de Vaca someone like himself, one who favored the Indians, and, concomitant to this ethical choice, someone who testified on behalf of a natural knowledge of God among the Indians of North America.

Even if one conceded to Las Casas this argument about the natural knowledge of God, however, the more difficult problem for him was to explain the potential perversion—a demonic perversion—that can occur in the natural state of humankind. The problem of human sacrifice was a case of this sort. Las Casas, nonetheless, argued that the practice of human sacrifice was an instance of the natural knowledge of God, albeit of a primitive kind. Las Casas suggested that human beings worship God according to their natural abilities and instincts, and that the practice of human sacrifice stemmed from the desire to offer to God what is most precious to oneself, human life. Las Casas's arguments accumulate in degree, so that by the time he finishes with the matter of human sacrifice he contends that the natives are not only justified, but, in fact, obligated in order to defend their religion and communities (of course, in the minds of many, the practice of human sacrifice warranted and justified colonization): "Until the true God is preached to them with better and more convincing arguments and especially with the examples of Christian behavior they are surely obliged to defend the worship of their gods and their religion and to sally forth with their armed forces against anyone who would attempt to deprive them of such worship or religion. . . . They are obliged to struggle against the latter, slay them, or take them captive, and exercise all rights that qualify as corollary of just war."[55] It seems to me, and here I wind the chapter to a conclusion, that Las Casas's ability to place himself within the cosmos of the other and see things from their perspective—the Christians, not the Indians, are the idolaters; the Indians wage just war, not the Spanish; native religion is a legitimate and credible understanding of God—originates from his recognition of the proper moment of silence in theological speech, in a theological modesty.

Following in the footsteps of Aquinas, Las Casas draws on one further strategy in his defense of the lives and religions of native peoples, namely, the incomprehensibility of God. Las Casas surely knew that the master of theology in his Order, Thomas, had clearly stated in his *Summa Theologica* that human beings can know very little about God: it is not given for us to know *what* God is, only what God is *not* (Aquinas is clearly influenced by Pseudo-Dionysius on this point). And if this claim isn't enough, toward the end of his life Aquinas is reported to have stated that everything he had written was nothing compared to what God had revealed to him directly, as if Aquinas himself placed a large asterisk next to his great *Summa*, warning the reader to consider all that is written as a grain of straw, as a modest experiment or broken fragments, hints followed by guesses.

In proof of this insight, Las Casas will invoke the spirit of Thomas at a key moment in the debate with the Aristotelian theologian Sepulveda over the issue of human sacrifice and the theological status of the Indian: "We are ignorant of more about God than we know." With this concise claim, Las Casas builds his defense of the Indians. As to whether God will punish the Indians for offering human sacrifices, he retorts, "I know not that judgment of God; it is inscrutable." As one might guess, Sepulveda's response is grounded in an appeal to the certainty of faith. Las Casas's incertitude is, according to Sepulveda, contrary to Catholic faith: "He says near the beginning of the eleventh reply that *he knows not what God judges* of the idolaters who sacrifice innocent human beings. But to doubt the judgment of God is a thing manifestly contrary to Catholic faith and the precepts of the Decalogue . . . since 'knowing' here is done with the certitude of faith according to the common understanding of the doctors" (LC, *A*, 212). It seems to me that Las Casas recovers a sense of wonder at this point. Wonder returns to signify something positive and enriching, something at odds with presumptuous and possessive claims to knowledge of God. Wonder here is an icon of infinity, and what seems to me most marvelous in Las Casas is that he views Indians as icons, not as idols. The infinity of God is etched on the bodies and faces of the natives, and Las Casas receives them with the same degree of humility and adoration as he shows before the Eucharist. In seeking to understand his brothers and sisters of the New World, Las Casas stands before the greatest wonder, the ultimate marvel, the uncanny and surprising mystery of God.

The experience of wonder is now given theological significance and places us before the presence of an alluring and intimate mystery. The incomprehensibility that Las Casas alludes to at this moment echoes mystical language and produces a wide-eyed and open-minded theology. It is a distant enemy of what Sepulveda advocates, a closed theological system built on absolute certainty and totality. Las Casas gives us a freer model, more restless and expanding, more dynamic and nomadic, than what we see in Sepulveda's dogmatic system. Here Las Casas finds his company not only with his fellow Dominican Aquinas, but with wanderers like Sir John Mandeville ("We know not whom God loves nor whom He hates") and Cabeza de Vaca.

All of these wanderers share the wisdom that King Lear arrived at late, only after he is deposed and exiled. Reduced to the condition of a beggar, the once proud and powerful king now is nothing less than a naked man vulnerable to the "winds and persecutions of the sky" (*King Lear*, 3.2.14–15). When coming across a bedlam beggar, Poor Tom (the disguised and fugitive Edgar), Lear has this to say, as he starts to peel off his clothes: "Thou art the thing itself; unaccommodated man is no more but such a poor, bare, forked animal as thou are" (3.4.107–8). Lear learns humility, then, only after being humiliated, and wisdom only after being denuded of his pomp and glory, when he is on his knees instead of the throne. And, above all, he learns compassion, as Edgar remarks:

A most poor man, made tame to fortune's blows,
Who by the art of known and feeling sorrows,
Am pregnant to good pity.
(*King Lear*, 4.6.221–23)

Lear peels off his clothes as Hamlet shuffles off his mortal coil, as Cabeza de Vaca changes his skin, as Las Casas is reborn as a mendicant preacher and prophet. The capacity for wonder and compassion in all of them— from Las Casas to Shakespeare—was related to a sense of human vulnerability and fragility, an awareness of exile and dispossession. All of them saw themselves as pilgrims and beggars on this earth, drifters with no place to lay their heads. And in this abject condition they became explorers of the frontiers of human possibility, pioneers of hard-won truths. The success of their lives and writings was possible only through the failures and disasters of the age in which they lived, one savage in its violence and profound in its capacity for wonder.

THREE

THE HIDDEN GOD OF THE BAROQUE

Baroque Wonders, Baroque Tragedies

Wipe away, with death, the day of my birth;

may it be forgotten forever, and never

come back in the sweep of time. And if it ever

returns, eclipse the sun and blacken the earth.

Let all light fade and disappear. Let wild

omens reveal everything must die.

Let monsters be born. Let blood rain from the sky.

Let every mother not recognize her child.

Let all the stunned and terrified people, with tears

streaking down their faces, pale and worn,

believe their world is doomed and overthrown.

You, frightened people, accept these wonders and fears,

for this was the wretched day on which was born

the most miserable life that ever was known.

—Luís de Camões, "Curse"

If this poem by the great Portuguese poet begins as a personal lament, it suddenly becomes something broader in scope, a lament for an entire epoch. The anguish of this poet is let loose on his age to become a dark prophecy of things to come. The poet summons wonders and fears like a biblical prophet of doom or an apocalyptic seer. As both prophecy and curse, the poet chants these gloomy lines as he notices misery and darkness gathering strength to overthrow all traces of light. Camões's lines have a sad and ominous beauty to them and they augur a new, post-Renaissance age, the age of the Baroque. The allure of wonder continues in the age of the Baroque—an age that is both a disruption and expansion of the Renaissance—but it also undergoes significant transformations. Wonder metamorphoses, changing forms to become more ominous, more frightening, monster-like. Wonder is now loaded with the sentiments of dread, anxiety, and anguish, and the burden of it is so severe that wonder is gravely wounded.[1]

The narrative that I want to follow in this chapter concerns the changes that the experience of wonder undergoes in the Baroque as it relates to the tragic sensibilities of the age, including its anguished theology that felt distant from God, exiled from God in fact. Indeed, the sentiment of exile intensified in the Baroque and disrupted everything it touched. Neither wonder nor conceptions of God would be the same. In both the European and the New World Baroque, the language of wonder would be increasingly marked by the sign of the cross, and the hidden God was a key symbol of this, as was the tone of fear and trembling, the preoccupation with monsters, and the pervasive feelings of loss and death in the age.

In exploring this claim, we will see how crucial the Baroque has been in the histories and cultures of Latin America. Though the Baroque clearly had European origins, it was soon changed as a result of its new home in the Americas, like a man in exile who soon learns to adapt to his new environment. The Baroque's ability to acclimatize and negotiate with its new location left an indelible mark on the New World, and this influence extended to everything, including the themes of wonder and exile. To appreciate the distinct qualities of the American Baroque, however, we need to familiarize ourselves with the Baroque in the Old World. In fact, it strikes me as profoundly shortsighted to ignore the European context. As I suggested in the introduction, we cannot divorce the study of the New World from the history of Spain and Europe, which is why in this chapter we will examine the Spaniard Calderón vis-à-vis the great Peruvian scholar Juan Espinosa de Medrano (and in the next chapter, Cervantes in light of Sor Juana Inés de la Cruz). To be sure, the Baroque that is born on the shores of the New World is a unique and original creature (especially in light of the Conquest and the cultures of Amerindians), but it also has the same genes as its parental figure. To understand one, we need to know the other. So, as we make our way tracing the history of wonder and exile, we will cross the ocean, to and fro, numerous times, all in the hope of understanding the dark age of the Baroque and the image of the hidden God that flourished in these difficult times.

The Renaissance and Baroque

The age of the Baroque awakens as the Renaissance sun is setting and night is fast approaching, as the earth is blackening and monsters are being born. A pall of dark clouds has settled over the age and eclipsed the sun, and it begins to rain without end as it does in the mythical town of Macondo. Indeed, when the plague of rain comes to Macondo in *One Hundred Years of Solitude*, it heralds a new period in the novel when the town begins to succumb to decline and decay. As it was in Macondo, so it is in the Baroque: everything is soaked in sadness and gloom, everything is out of joint, and everything displays the beastly marks of apocalypse. Wonder takes on tragic tones, in short, and is tied to the fears and anxieties of the period, to the loss of certainties and confidences, to the widespread experience of crisis and conflict in this age.

If wonder takes on monstrous forms in the Baroque, it is because the aesthetics of the period have suddenly undergone a sea change. The Baroque shifts away from classic and Renaissance ideals of beauty—imitation of nature's perfections, dreams of human nobility and dignity, harmony between the cosmos, man, and God—to prefer the disharmonious over harmony; oddity and strangeness over sameness; ruins and fragments in lieu of completeness; the ugly and grotesque in lieu of classic beauty; the mad and absurd instead of the reasonable; terrified and tortured subjects instead of serene and tranquil ones. The Baroque collects and gathers these strange fragments in a desperate effort to shore itself up against its ruin.[2] Indeed, ruin and disaster are felt so deeply by the Baroque artist that madness is always a danger, like a savage beast lying in wait, ready to pounce and devour. If the Baroque artist succeeded in fighting off the madness and terror, it was because he learned to face it by wrestling with the beasts of evil instead of evading and ignoring—thus the tragic wounds of the age, thus its tragic sense of life.

Despite crucial differences, however, the Baroque developed its tragic vision in continuity with themes from the Renaissance, in continuity, especially, with the "darker side of the Renaissance," to quote Walter Mignolo once again.[3] Think of Michelangelo's *The Last Judgment*, for instance. After the noble beauty of the Sistine Chapel (1512), the gloom and terror of this painting comes as a shock and an explosive interruption of his earlier work. As is well-known, the atmosphere of the world had grown more grave and ominous in Michelangelo's later years. After the sack of Rome in 1527, the experience of dread haunts this once great capital of the Western world. Michelangelo will paint the scenes of *The Last Judgment* with a tragic brush. It is known that in preliminary drawings for this painting he had sketched an image of Mary with her arms wide open, as if appealing to her son to remember his mercy and compassion. By the time he begins work on the painting (1536) he has changed the position and pose of Mary. Now her arms are closed and she turns away from Christ, her face suggesting fear. The time for merciful intercession is over. Nothing now can stay God's judgment. David Tracy says this about the change in Michelangelo's world:

> With Raphael already dead, with the city of Rome ferociously sacked, with the northern Reformation and southern Counter-Reformation crushing the Renaissance Christian humanist hopes of his youth, Michelangelo was forced to abandon the noble dreams of his own youth—the tenderness of the *Pieta*, the classic dignity of *David*, even the tensive triumph of the Sistine Chapel. Michelangelo turned, for his final vision, to his extraordinary *Final Judgment*: a judgment where Christ was all judgment, no mercy—judgment upon Christianity itself; a judgment where even the beloved figure of Mary seems to move away from her traditional iconography of tenderness and compassion to fear for humankind.[4]

The poems that Michelangelo put to paper also reflect this anguish of an artist so close to sin and far from God, a particular Baroque anxiety. In a meditation on the cross of Christ, Michelangelo writes:

> Oh flesh, O blood, O wood, O ultimate pain,
> in you may all my sin be justified,
> sin I was born to as my father's seed.
> Sole good, may now your supreme pity deign
> to succour my predicted evil state,
> so near to death and yet so far from God.[5]

It is clear, then, that Michelangelo gradually abandoned the noble humanism of his youth as the walls of Rome came crumbling down. Like

Camões, Michelangelo prophesied the sadder mood of the Baroque. Louis Dupré makes this same point about another great Renaissance figure, Tasso:

> Tasso, whose work still belonged to the Renaissance, forefelt this sadder mood. More than glorifying its heroes, his great epic laments the transitoriness and futility of even the greatest human accomplishments. In the end, only forgetfulness—*tacita e nera*—awaits the heroic deeds of the past. . . . Tasso's brooding awareness of the instability of all things marks a clear departure from the optimistic confidence of the Renaissance. The worm of corruption inhabits all human enterprises. . . . Tasso even felt abandoned by God, and the uncertainty of ultimate salvation tortured him even while it inspired his sublime poetry. Few artists expressed the somber mood of the Baroque epoch more poignantly than those who stood at its beginning—Tasso and Michelangelo.[6]

Dupré's reading of the Baroque age explains well the continuities and breaks with the Renaissance. The hints and intimations of a tragic spirit in the Renaissance become dominant motifs, fully blown and come of age in the Baroque. The Baroque would embellish and exaggerate the sensibilities that it inherited from the Renaissance. The shallow wounds felt by its forbearer became deadly and gaping abscesses in the Baroque artist, the gray atmosphere became black. Everything was marked by an emptiness that came to resemble an aggressive and fast-spreading disease. Even the idea of God would be susceptible to its spread and would soon show symptoms of a chronic absence or hiddenness threatening to expand to epidemic proportions.[7]

The Hidden God and Christian Tragedy

> What can be seen on earth indicates neither the total absence, nor the manifest presence of divinity, but the presence of a hidden God. Everything bears this stamp.
>
> —Blaise Pascal, *Pensées*

It should come as no surprise to anyone familiar with intellectual life in the twentieth century that when the question of God is concerned, the prevailing sentiment seems to be one of absence. The calamities of the century make belief in God to be something like a risk and gamble taken against all odds, with little degree of certitude and assurance. And yet, to millions of people on the planet—more in developing countries than among rich and powerful nations—God is somehow there, like a hope that survives the severest of tests. Among many intellectuals, however, the absence of God has become a dogma widely accepted.

On this problem concerning God, the Baroque is an intermediary or link between these conflicting positions. It is an age thoroughly absorbed in God and, yet, mourning the signs of God's absence. In dirgelike tones, the poetry of the period bemoans the loss of a premodern wholeness, and nothing makes this anguish more evident than its affection for ruins and fragments. Walter Benjamin, in fact, spoke of the "cult of ruins" in the Baroque, and argued that the modern taste for ruins, allegory, surrealistic shock effects, and historical catastrophe all came from the Baroque: "In this state of disruption, the present age reflects certain aspects of the spiritual constitution of the Baroque" (*T*, 55).

To this list of Baroque sensibilities, I would add this conundrum of the hidden God, this simultaneous affirmation of divine presence and absence. Benjamin, again, knew that this theological paradox was fundamental to the Baroque. In his study of the German Baroque, he would claim a role for theology that would make many of his contemporaries uneasy: "If, in the concluding part of this study, we do not hesitate to use such concepts, this is not a transition to a different subject. For a critical understanding of the *Trauerspiel*, in its extreme, allegorical form, is possible only from the higher domain of theology; so long as the approach is an aesthetic one, paradox must have the last word" (*T*, 216).

In the twentieth century, a host of intellectuals would share some of Benjamin's preoccupations in this regard, searching for a God that resembled neither the God of theists nor that of atheists. Intellectuals like Simone Weil, Lucien Goldmann, and David Tracy have all been searching for alternatives to simplistic dichotomies of this sort. Many of them have been drawn by the thought of a hidden God, if not for orthodox reasons, for a way of addressing the continuing allure of the *mysterium fascinans*, on the one hand, and its terrifying and ominous twin, the *mysterium tremendum*. The modern age is so close to this hidden God if only because it is conflicted and fragmented in a similar way. Neither satisfied with premodern confessions of presence nor content with the modern dogma of absence, many twentieth-century intellectuals want something totally other, call it a "presence of absence" or call it the hidden God. Regardless, I take this trend to mean that we are all looking for divine traces even in the rubble and ruins of our times. Many of these intellectuals, to put it another way, will be looking for something meaningful in absence, a gesture almost Buddhist-like in its search for truth in emptiness, for fullness in nothingness. And make no mistake about it, this version of nothingness has little in common with nihilism. Instead of the despair of nihilism, we are offered another possibility, a version of nothingness that is alluring and beautiful for its stark and bare nature. To find this denuded beauty, however, requires a courage that will not flinch in the face of disaster and suffering. Toward this purpose, tragedy is invaluable.

The Baroque, it seems to me, is the first age to attempt an integration of tragedy with Christian thought, for centuries viewed as irreconcilable spirits, as elements that could not be mixed, oil and water. This chapter will sketch some of the evidence for this claim that the Baroque embraced a host of contradictions and aporias, including this seeming opposition between Christianity and tragedy, and, in the process, gave birth to a blacker, more brooding and menacing version of wonder than what came before, to a portrait of wonder wounded by exile.

To test this claim, we should begin with a consideration of the Latin meaning of hiddenness, *in abscondito* or *absconditus*. The term suggests a movement of truth as it retreats into invisibility, as it withdraws from view and absents itself.[8] In English, therefore, to abscond means to depart or escape under the cloak of secrecy, a stealthy and furtive action like the movement of a criminal who prefers the night to the day so that he can disappear without being known or captured. In the Baroque, truth behaves in this way: deceptively, discretely, surreptitiously.

And yet, in this age in crisis, *absconditus* does not signify only an intellectual movement as suggested above; it is not simply synonymous with incomprehensibility. In the post-Reformation and Baroque ages, *absconditus* has a Hebrew accent, a shibboleth that reveals its kinship with emotions of anguish and affliction.

In this regard, the Reformation scholar Heiko Oberman makes an important observation about the history of *absconditus*. Oberman tells us that by the sixteenth century, the understanding of *abscondere* and *absconditus* had taken a different form than what is found in Greek mystical apophaticism (e.g., Pseudo-Dionysius). It is much more anxiety-ridden for the Latins of the early modern period, particularly Luther. "By 1514, it is already clear," Oberman writes, "that 'darkness'—*tenebrae, umbra,* or *caligo*—shares in the double meaning of *abscondere* and *absconditus*," and that this fellowship of terms is now encumbered with trials and tribulations, hardships and ordeals.[9] *Abscondere* and *absconditus*, in other words, are yoked to the theme of darkness and increasingly come to represent the distress of someone groping in the dark, dazed and confused. "Darkness" now casts a far wider shadow, one that reaches beyond classic notions of incomprehensibility—as in Gregory of Nyssa, Pseudo-Dionysius, or Eriugena—and suggests something more frightening, like long, sleepless nights (John of the Cross) or feelings of God's displeasure or withdrawal (Luther). Fearful premonitions abound in the age. Everything in the sixteenth and seventeenth centuries seemed to point to the gloomy state of the world, a world that seemed to have reached its natural end like an overripe apple fallen to the earth, rotten and decomposed. No wonder, then, that Luther emphasized that unrest and struggle is the norm for the *viator* on earth, for the pilgrim inhabitants of this valley of tears in the end days. In the early modern period, *absconditus* increasingly captures the motto of an age haunted by traces of divine absence. *Absconditus* becomes the feature of existential crisis and spiritual *anfechtung*.

If anything, this perception of crisis in the age of Reformation intensifies in the Baroque age. In a famous study of Pascal and Racine (*The Hidden God*, 1955), Lucien Goldmann demonstrates the line of continuity on this theme of the hidden God between the Reformation and the Baroque, and refers to this tradition as the Christian face of tragic thought in the seventeenth century: "This is one of the fundamental points of tragic thought. 'Vere tu es Deus absconditus,' quotes Pascal. The hidden God."[10] In Goldmann's reading of Pascal, the hidden God is seen as an allegory of exile in the early modern period, of human separation and alienation from God.[11]

As Pascal understood, therefore, to speak of divine hiddenness in the Christian tradition means meditating on the revelation that occurs through the lowly, broken, and crucified figure of Jesus of Nazareth. In writing about Luther's theology of the cross, David Tracy has this to say about "hiddenness": "God's revelation is principally through hiddenness—i.e., God discloses God's self to sinful humans *sub contrariis*: life through death; wisdom through folly; strength through abject weakness. A hidden God is not merely humble but humiliated: *deus incarnatus, deus absconditus in passionibus*."[12] God is, thus, hidden beneath the cloak of suffering. So startling and revolutionary is this hidden God that all one's expectations and preconceptions are upset and reversed: you will find God where you least expect it, where poverty and suffering holds dominion, where the marginal and destitute struggle for their daily bread, where the refuse and waste of history gathers, the way Job encounters God on the dung heap that had become his life. God is disclosed, in short, through all the distorted and defeated, shattered and fragmented forms of history.

Baroque artists and theologians adopted some elements of this tradition—at the very least, the centrality of the cross and the principle of failure. Even amid celebration and festival, death had a pride of place in the Baroque and no one would escape from its cold grasp, neither Jesus, nor Mary, nor the saints of the Church. Baroque iconography would represent them all in tortured and distressed forms. Though inherited from the Reformation, the Baroque would leave its own mark on the theology of the cross, by extending and enhancing it, by making it appear grotesque and disjointed. Instead of triumphal images of the resurrected Christ—ones that correspond to economic success and well-being—the Baroque of Spain and the New World embraced theological images of failure.

Because of the proximity of the Baroque to the image of Christ crucified, then, it seemed to share the protest that was uttered by Jesus on the cross: "My God, my God, why have you forsaken me?" (Mark 15:34). This disquieting protest from the mouth of Jesus echoes throughout the ages, but it seemed to get louder in the early modern period and eventually came to characterize the Baroque's agonizing struggle with God. David Tracy contends that experiences of this kind—innocent suffering above all—correspond to a more terrifying and tragic moment of divine hiddenness than the one just noted (e.g., a classic theology of the cross where God is revealed through Jesus Christ). This second interpretation is forced on us by the undeniable presence of evil in human history and by the roaring sound of God's silence amid so many cries, so many griefs and tribulations: "At the very least, this literally awe-ful and ambivalent sense of God's hiddenness is so overwhelming that God is sometimes experienced as purely frightening, not tender: sometimes as an impersonal 'It' of sheer power and energy signified by such metaphors as abyss, chasm, chaos, even horror; sometimes even as a violent personal reality."[13]

On this second face of the hidden God, the affinities with Greek tragedy are especially obvious. Beyond the tender, loving image of Jesus, this impersonal and frightening image recalls the God who would leave Jesus to his cruel fate on the cross, the God who is portrayed in the Bible in violent terms, the God who is absent in the face of historical eruptions of catastrophe. In either case, to suggest that God is somehow hidden echoes the Greek conception of fate, that cold and brutal force that is unintelligible and intractable to rational thought, that obeys no idea of justice and has the power to crush and destroy the greatest or lowliest of human beings.[14]

As I explore the interpretations of the hidden God in this chapter, we should keep in mind the variations of this theme discussed thus far. In the Baroque age, to summarize, *absconditus* may include the intellectual awareness of divine incomprehensibility—a mystical and cryptic approach to the hidden God that emphasizes exile from truth, we might say—but the most conspicuous sense of "hiddenness" was felt down deep to the bone, and, thus, is a symbol of the tragic soul culture of the Baroque age. Given the social and political crises of the age, including large-scale exiles and displacements, the hidden God theme was an emblem that embodied all the grief and sadness of an age that felt infinitely close and, yet, at the same time, distant and estranged from God. It would seem, in short, that the Baroque had a lot in common with Prospero's sentiments at the end of *The Tempest*: "Every third thought shall be my grave" (5.1.315). With one eye to the grave, the other one turned, or so I am arguing, to the thought of a hidden God. It was this tragic soul culture that produced the geniuses of the period, figures like Calderón, Cervantes, and Sor Juana, and eventually the twentieth-century "magical realists." The Baroque set the state, then, for a Christian form of tragedy that would blossom in oppressive circumstances.

Rescuing the Tragic Spirit of the Baroque

In the Baroque, thus, this vision of a hidden God produced a tragic theology that was especially alert to the ruins and catastrophes of history. For this reason alone, many modern and postmodern intellectuals have taken up efforts to excavate and rescue the Baroque from disrepute. Walter Benjamin, as I just suggested, left nothing in doubt about the value of the Baroque for twentieth-century intellectual life. In his brilliant apologia for the Baroque, he emphasized the value of the "baroque explanation of history" as one shaped by the image of the Passion, by the cross of history (*T*, 166).

With this eye for the crucifixions of history, Benjamin describes the Baroque as an age that recognized wisdom in defeated and subjugated forms. The Baroque was collector of history's waste products. It wandered through the alleyways of history picking up the scraps that others left behind, seeking something precious in what had been discarded, something sacred in the relics that were lost to memory. In Benjamin, Baroque allegory, in particular, had a talent for this salvage activity. Allegory sought to preserve all the discarded fragments of the past, everything about history that was failed, forgotten, and marginalized. "In allegory," Benjamin writes, "the observer is confronted with . . . everything about history that has been untimely, sorrowful, unsuccessful" (*T*, 166). Or elsewhere: "Allegories are, in the realm of thoughts, what ruins are in the realm of things. This explains the Baroque cult of the ruin" (*T*, 178). With a magnanimous and extravagant memory, Baroque allegory sought to preserve the ruins and repressed fragments from cultures far and wide: Greek and Roman myths, the hermetic traditions of Egypt, the Kabbalah of Judaism, Indian gymnosophists, Chaldean astrologers, Persian Magi, Aztec gods. Like a lover suddenly pained by an irredeemable loss, the Baroque is desperate in its affections, indiscriminate and dissolute, giving itself to a wide variety of lovers. With Don Juan, the Baroque turned everywhere to satisfy its insatiable desire, to fill the gaping emptiness of its heart. Its indulgent and wild behavior is a reflection of the void it feels within and without. Carlos Fuentes describes this nicely in the following passage: "Defeat, misery, insecurity, and historical excess can only be recounted in a language that preserves immediate evidence, an instrument capable of including everything because in a world where nothing is known for certain everything must be preserved. . . . The Baroque, language of abundance, is also the language of insufficiency."[15]

The Baroque prefers the language of abundance because it is so anxious and insecure about all human achievements. It embellishes and indulges like a man suddenly told he has months to live. Death may be rushing toward him, but he chooses to exit the human drama with flair, panache, grandeur—carpe diem. So, if the Baroque artist must fail, if he lives in a world where nothing is certain, in a world that has grown old (*senectus mundi*), he lives his remaining days with intensity and vitality, in an embrace of the bounty of human life. Through music and dance, poetry and painting, drama and ritual, fiesta and procession, mysticism and eroticism, the Baroque would celebrate the art of living through the art of dying.

The secret desire of the Baroque is, thus, plenitude, but no matter how badly it is desired, the Baroque comes away empty like a failed mystic. In this sense, allegory, to return to Benjamin, tries to save everything, but it always fails, "it goes away empty-handed" (*T*, 232–33).

For those familiar with mystical discourse, these Baroque strategies recall ancient practices of naming and un-naming God. In his studies of mystical languages of the sixteenth and seventeenth centuries, Michel de Certeau describes these practices beautifully. The text before him is the work of Diego de Jesus, a Discalced Carmelite. The following by Diego is a meditation on the language of "excess" in the Bible and in the theology of Pseudo-Dionysius: "The variation that mystic theology employs also declares, marvelously, the divine perfection and its ineffability, speaking one moment regularly, that is, with the terms it finds ordered and perfect, the next moment, not content with those words, throwing itself into a holy excess, as if of madness and dissoluteness."[16]

To signify divine ineffability, Diego remarks, the Scriptures resort to language seemingly offensive and mad. Diego insists that metaphorically lavish, even dissolute language, is badly needed when the task is strictly impossible (naming the un-nameable). In this case, references to a God "enraged," "cursing," or "drunk and hung over" are even more desirable than more pious ones (e.g., God is truth), because we are less likely to literalize the former metaphors and, thus, we avoid the potential idolatry always lurking in theological discourse. Following Diego and Pseudo-Dionysius on these points, then, Certeau describes the use of barbarisms and vulgarity to remind us of the one fundamental point of mystical language: "It is never anything but the unstable metaphor for what is inaccessible."[17]

And so we learn something valuable in looking at mystical discourse relevant for our study of the Baroque: that it is in the bountiful profusions of theological affirmations of God (cataphatic language) that we enter the dark silence of the apophatic realm, where we recognize, wondrously, the insufficiency of all human language. The language of abundance is also the language of insufficiency. Roberto González Echevarría has a nice description of this same point: "the crowded page saturated with signs," he writes of the Baroque, "counterpoints of silence."[18]

Like mystical speech, then, Baroque allegory signifies silence. Baroque artists loved allegory because it was a perfect representation of what they thought about the world, the human condition, or God: that they are indecipherable. If allegory is, as Christine Buci-Glucksmann has written, from the Greek *allos* ("other") and *agoreuein* ("to speak"), then it is speech of the other, a strategy that hides and conceals truth behind the literal and plain sense.[19] Allegory behaves a lot like magic in this regard, with a sleight of hand that preserves secrecy and mystery with the use of disguises and masks (hieroglyphs and theater motifs being among the age's favorites). To those initiated in allegory's arcane wisdom—the magician or mystic—allegory is as deep and unfathomable as the sea, never fully plumbed by human efforts of reason and knowledge. Indeed, as Walter Benjamin suggests about the German Baroque, reason is left dizzy and dismayed by the extravagance and bombast of Baroque allegory (*T*, 201). In saturating the mind's eye with excessive language, reason is reduced to silence, shocked and awed by so much splendor, so much infinity (*T*, 56, 201). Mystery is present in the Baroque in great abundance like the angels in its architecture, like the saints in its processions and ceremonies, the colors of its churches.

In putting mystery on display, allegory was the favorite form of the Baroque, one that forced the human mind to recognize its boundaries and limitations. Though speaking of the place of allegory in late antiquity, Peter Brown makes this point with his accustomed eloquence: "By Augustine's time, the idea of allegory had come to sum up a serious attitude to the limitations of the human mind. . . . The religious philosopher explored a spiritual world that was of its very nature 'ever more marvelous, ever more inaccessible.' The worst enemies of such inquiry, of course, were superficiality, the dead-weight of common-sense, habitual stereotypes that made a man cease to be surprised and excited, and thus veiled the most vertiginous complexities with a patina of the obvious."[20]

Augustine's description of allegory's purpose—manifestation of a spiritual world "ever more marvelous, ever more inaccessible"—captures Baroque purposes as well. As speech of the other, allegory entertained the mind with stories and characters, myths and ideas that surprised so much that one would feel vertigo and yet, somehow, enlivened and exhilarated by the complexities of life under the sun. It made for good theater by speaking to unconscious instincts, emotions, and dreams in addition to the faculty of reason and logic. And it discovered that this kind of drama would be at its finest when it sought out deviations from the norm, exceptions to the general rule, the oddities and rarities of culture and religion. In this way, it adored the marvelous if only to unsettle the most common, predictable, and banal standards of knowledge (the "patina of the obvious" in Peter Brown's words).

Baltasar Gracián once described poetic wit in these terms, as the enemy of habitual stereotypes and moderate principles: "Wit attempts excesses and achieves marvels" (quoted in OP, 54). Or Francisco de Quevedo would write that his verses were like a flood, not calm and gentle, but a deluge. Octavio Paz is at his best when describing this feature of the Baroque poet:

> The baroque poet hoped to astonish and astound; Apollinaire proposed exactly the same thing when he extolled surprise as one of the basic elements of poetry. . . . That is why it sought out and collected all extremes, especially hybrids and monsters. Conceit and cleverness are the sirens and hippogriffs of language, the verbal equivalents of nature's fantasies. In such love for the strange we find both the secret

of baroque art's affinity with criollo sensibility and the source of its fruitfulness. To the baroque sensibility the American world was marvelous, not only for the vastness of its geography, the fantasy of its fauna, the delirium of its flora, but for the bizarre customs and institutions of its ancient civilizations. (OP, 53, 58)

In its love of the strange, then, the Baroque fell for the Americas, love at first sight. The Baroque imagination came to life with the sudden and shocking introduction of the American continent—it became the Baroque artist's muse, its sun and moon, its Beatrice. In the Americas, it found a profusion of new marvelous realities to delight and satisfy its love of the uncanny: the flora and fauna of the Americas, its myths and rituals, its cultures and peoples. The Baroque artist of the New World may have shared Augustine's reverence for the greatest wonder of all—God—but it added other preoccupations that swelled and burst the boundaries of theological thinking to now include a fantastic variety of wonders from the American world. The Baroque artist would come to play a key role in defining and identifying the new creatures of this continent (mestizos, criollos, etc.), like a midwife giving birth to new, previously unknown monsters. By putting on display these monsters and freaks of nature, these wild hybrids and savage spiritualities, it would set the tone for the cultural and literary future of the continent. Magical realism would take its name centuries in the future, but the artistic infatuation for the astounding and monstrous was born in these early days of Latin America, long before the last remaining Buendías, Amaranta Úrsula, would give birth, as prophesied, to a monstrous child with the tail of a pig.

Baroque Times in Spain and the New World

The more deeply that exile is suffered, the stranger and more grotesque wonder becomes: this is the hypothesis that I've been exploring in this chapter, and I want to continue looking at this Baroque metamorphosis with further attention to Spain and the New World.

The Spanish historian José Antonio Maravall has shown with thoroughness and depth how pervasive exile and social crisis was in the age, beginning with the expulsion of the Jews and the Reconquista of the Moors in 1492. This key date in the history of the West would establish a pattern of intolerance and exclusion that would prevail in Spain and its colonies throughout the Baroque age. While the Moors are not officially exiled from Spain until 1609 (when Miguel de Cervantes was writing part 2 of *Don Quixote*), by 1492 the writing is already on the wall. The creation of legal institutions like the Holy Brotherhood and the Inquisition is a sign of an emerging empire seeking to define and unify itself. Empire building would require efforts toward national integration and centralization, and the Catholic kings of Spain would not shrink before the task. They created legal networks—patterned on Roman bureaucratic models—of discipline and punishment that would monitor not only human behavior, but also the beliefs and desires of its citizens. The long arm of the law grew yet longer. For this age and others, empire building would promote and sanc-tify conformity and solidarity with the newly formed nation. Such a task would require, as it always seems to, the creation of others that deviate from and threaten these communal bonds.

In extending their reach into every nook and cranny of its lands, the laws of Spain would spawn and produce a wide-ranging host of illegal aliens and depraved, sinister criminals—and countless exiles. The legalistic network of Spain's empire would produce as much as it would punish transgressors of the law. The development of new forms of literature beyond the epic poem—the picaresque and the novel—reflects this new atmosphere of legal-ism and surveillance. The novelty of these genres can be traced to the in-troduction of new voices and new experiences previously invisible to the Middle Ages and Renaissance. The picaresque (e.g., *Lazarillo de Tormes* or *Guzmán de Alfarache*) would give its readers a glimpse into a deviant under-world of prisoners and prostitutes, thugs and pimps, galley slaves and fugi-tives, the way the culture of hip-hop would for late twentieth-century North America. The picaresque and the novel became the voices of the other.

The picaresque and the *relaciónes* of New World explorers were, in fact, framed as legal depositions and give preference to realistic and contingent accounts of human conduct in lieu of systematic, philosophical methods. This recording of the specificity and uniqueness of human behavior—especially in its deviant, monstrous forms—signals a profound change from Renaissance thought and a step toward the modern age. Roberto González Echevarría describes this change very well: "From the perspective of liter-ature . . . what is most relevant is that in presenting the life of the *hampa*, or underworld, the authors of picaresque novels were laying bare the most frightful manifestations of the human, all too human in general, bereft of the embellishments of morality and customs. If the Renaissance was interested in the study of man, the picaresque constituted a deeper probe than the analyses of princes, courtiers, ironic self-analysts, and Platonic lovers (Machiavelli, Castiglione, Ficino, Montaigne). . . . For literature the most compelling aspect of picaresque life was the individuating detail, the originality of the deviant, his bizarre behavior."[21]

The Baroque age provided the context for the coming of this new underworld to the stage. In this regard, the Baroque was more vulgar than was its Renaissance cousin, more inclusive of deviant behavior, deviant thoughts, deviant cultures. The first inkling of the modern novel—to be discussed in chapter 4—is the product of the *eloquentia vulgaria* of the Baroque age. With its learned vulgarity, the new genre of the novel is something like the creative explosion of black music in North America: the novel disrupts the Renaissance the way jazz disrupts classical music with its improvisational madness, the way the blues scandalizes folk music, the way hip-hop reinvents, poeticizes, and vulgarizes rock and roll. The noble and dignified project of philosophy is disrupted and mocked. The Wu-Tang Clan puts it this way: "I bomb atomically, Socrates's philosophies and hypotheses can't define how I be dropping these mockeries."[22] The Baroque dropped mockeries on Renaissance decorum by introducing disreputable characters into the sedate and exclusive world of princes, courtiers, and educated elites. It gave us dark truths and black beauties.

The attraction for misfits and thugs in the Baroque was born, then, in social circumstances that were shady, unclean, out of joint. The social context of the Baroque provides us with unmistakable clues about the age's distress and confusion—it certainly was not only epistemological in nature. With a historian's eye for detail, Maravall has described the Baroque age as a period in extreme crisis: incessant wars, persecutions, acts of expulsion, continent-wide economic recessions, ballooning rates of poverty, plagues, famines. The popularity of images of death, the unpredictability of fortune, metaphors of decay and impermanence: all of these were symptoms of an age in ruins. Maravall estimates that as high as a quarter of Spain's population lost their lives to the seventeenth-century plagues, and the estimates are higher with the losses of war. In a letter of 1638, a Jesuit writes that the effects of war and plagues have produced a situation in which "the needs and hunger are so unprecedented that they go so far as to consume their neighbors," adding a bitter realism to the proverb that "man is a wolf to man."[23]

While Maravall argues that the Baroque was a deeply conservative age—meant to reinforce and shore up Spain's empire and monarchy—he also notes the explosions of rebellion and resistance in the age. Given the state of poverty and depression, it is not surprising that there were outbursts of violence throughout Spanish territories.[24] In some cases, organized rebellion was the response, but the most widespread and common form of protest was banditry and vagabondage. An increase in the depth of social misery was equaled by an increase in the numbers of bandits and beggars, wanderers and drifters:

> This extreme form of antisocial protest and deviant conduct grew at an alarming rate in the seventeenth-century crisis. . . . If the adverse economic conditions at the end of the sixteenth century, which were accentuated in the following century, brought to all of Europe an alarming increase in misery, vagabondage and banditry, . . . such consequences were well marked in the Spain of Philip III and Philip IV, giving rise to what has been called the banditry of the baroque. . . . Those masses of the needy, deviant and full of animosity, emerged from the wars, epidemics, oppression by the powerful, and from the unemployment made obligatory by the economic crisis.[25]

Given this atmosphere—joined with the heightened legal surveillance and centralized bureaucracy—it is natural that the numbers of prisoners in Spain grew exponentially (not unlike the escalating rates of incarceration in North American ghettos in the 1980s when "gangster rap" was emerging). In describing Seville, Agustín de Rojas expressed astonishment at the "infinity of prisoners there for strange crimes"; in Madrid, Barrionuevo states that there are so many prisoners that the jails can't possibly hold them all.[26] The punishment of "strange crimes" would have included sexual misconduct, as famously dramatized by the galley slaves that Don Quixote frees. And let us remember that Cervantes himself spent time in Spanish prisons on more than one occasion. This familiarity with the dregs and rejects of Spain's empire must have served him well when he sat down to narrate the fugitive existence of Don Quixote.

In the face of this social turmoil, Baroque motifs of a "world upside-down" or "out of joint" were telling images of the times. It was the tragic conflicts of the age—according to Louis Dupré—that gave the age its depth and complexity.[27] The harsh realities of the age would convert even the most enchanted and uncompromising dreamers (e.g., Don Quixote) into melancholic and disillusioned souls.

And, of course, the realities of the age drove Don Quixote insane, a motif that caught on like wildfire in the Baroque because "madness" seemed to capture the turmoil and uncertainty of the age. In such unsettling, disturbed circumstances, who could maintain his or her sanity? For Maravall, the topos of madness at the time reflected the abnormality of the events taking place. To Quevedo, the world is suffering from a delirium "that today appears to be raving mad." Lope de Vega wondered "what madman will surpass this madman." And Barrionuevo describes the people of the time walking "through the streets as if madmen and spellbound," coming to the conclusion that "we are all madmen, each and every one of us."[28] The metaphor of madness would capture for Baroque man and woman the irregularities of a reality intractable to reason. Reason bangs its head against the wall of reality, unable to produce order out of the chaos, unable to render it intelligible, comprehensible. For this reason, the Baroque artist was painfully aware of reason's limits and ever mindful of the deceptions and broken mirrors that veil as much as reveal the truth. The madness motif, then, wanders down the same road as other Baroque themes—for example, the world as labyrinth—and is another image of being alienated from one another, from God, from ourselves.

The widely popular theme of *peregrinatio* is another instance of this.[29] If the theme of pilgrimage is as old as the biblical age—developed with brilliance by Augustine—it takes on a new significance in this age. For one, the wanderings of the Baroque pilgrim produced a different person than his medieval or Renaissance ancestor (e.g., Sir John Mandeville). The pilgrimage of Baroque men and women is permeated by new anxieties and heartaches, fraught with dangers and fears. Gracián says this with a clear Baroque accent: "Various and great are the monstrosities which one rediscovers every day in the dangerous pilgrimage of human life. The greatest among them is the appearance of deception at the world's entrance and of disillusionment [*desengaño*] at the exit."[30]

Gracián's pilgrim will have to face a confused and uncertain world, a world gone mad.[31] The experience of wonder takes on tragic, pessimistic tones here, suggestive of bewilderment, danger, and crisis. And Baroque pilgrims never cease wandering, never adopt fixity. If they lay their heads anywhere, it is in temporary and provisional abodes like inns (the setting for many of Don Quixote's adventures). Baroque pilgrims take shelter at inns the way Jews reside in a sukkah during the celebration of Sukkoth, always mindful of human exile and dispossession. To commemorate wandering in the desert of exile, Jews are to build and dwell in a temporary, porous, and dilapidated hut. The roof must be open to the heavens, signifying vulnerability and impermanence of all humans dwelling on this earth. This condition of beggary unites the Baroque inn with the Jewish sukkah, but with one very significant and profound difference: the disreputable and shady nature of the inn. In the Baroque age, the inn is the meeting place of outcasts and disgraced types: prostitutes and bandits, pretend pilgrims and deceivers, the mad and abnormal. You would meet at the inn not only *errant* knights and wanderers, but particularly *deviant* ones. You would meet monsters.

The passion for movement in Baroque architecture is a good emblem for the movement of wanderers like Gracián's pilgrim and Cervantes's Don Quixote. The restless mobility of this architecture is like the endless wandering and unease of these figures inscribed on stone. Whether on church walls, monuments, or statues, Baroque architecture captured movement through the mysterious corridors of time and into the greater mystery of death. Indeed, the unease of this architecture is another manifestation of the aching and erosive nature of time, of how ephemeral and impermanent everything is under the sun. "Time finishes off and estranges everything," wrote Quevedo. Góngora would add a similar sentiment: "You, time, are what stays behind and I am the one on the way out."[32] We are always on the way out in Baroque thinking, always situated in an estranged condition looking toward death.

In truth, though, these complaints about time masked a more profound argument with God, it seems to me. The Baroque artist sees all around him allegories of decomposition, an expanding rigor mortis, and he cannot help but wonder where God is in all this. He is wrestling with the hidden God, trying to uncover fragments of God amid ruins. He is looking for signs of life in a culture of death.

It would seem that the pilgrim of the age tries to imitate Theseus's journey through the labyrinth to kill the beastly Minotaur (half-man, half-bull), but unlike the classic hero, Baroque man gets lost in the corridors. He fails. Like the great bullfighters of Spain (Theseus is the first great matador), Baroque men and women are fighting with a monstrous enemy (death perhaps) and the outcome is a tragic realization that the bullfighter cannot win, that man is no greater than the beasts of the land and that they both must die, man and bull alike.

Many of these Baroque images—the labyrinth, madness, pilgrimage, death—are, thus, further illustrations of the spirit of exile that obsessed the Spanish soul in the Baroque period.[33] Calderón de la Barca's obsession in this regard produced great art, magnificent in its grief and beautiful in its anguish. In focusing on Calderón and, subsequently, Juan Espinosa de Medrano, I hope that we can get a better idea of the transmutations of wonder and exile in the Baroque, particularly of the grotesque and misshapen forms that wonder adopts in this age on both sides of the Atlantic.

Calderón's Christian Tragedy

If there is an embryonic shadow of magical realism in the Baroque, as I am claiming, it is especially evident in the strange wonders and ghostly forms that it loved so dearly—again, the monsters. If the Baroque artist thought of her times as disjointed and misshapen—at times, deranged—then we can almost expect something like a monster to be the mental image and effigy of the age. In times like this, disfigured, grotesque, and muddled forms will be preferred over dignified, composed ones (as with the figure of Caliban in Shakespeare, seen in the last chapter). Take the case of Pedro Calderón de la Barca. Calderón's great tragedies are littered with references to monsters: at least three of his plays have the word "monster" in the title and his greatest work, *Life Is a Dream*, describes the two main characters, Segismundo and Rosaura, as having monstrous features (Segismundo is called a "mongrel mix of man and beast," and Rosaura, a "monstrous and unnatural freak"; 2.6.1547; 3.10.2725). More than any other Baroque poet, Calderón gave his audiences a host of monsters and marvels, prodigies and chimeras, and he used these images not only to unsettle and shock his audiences, but as parables of his times, images of an age that is haunted by the specters of death and disease, conflict and catastrophe.

Roberto González Echevarría takes us to the heart of the matter in clarifying the artistic affection in Calderón for this idiosyncratic being. To the Baroque artist, a monster is a mixed-up, contradictory, and hybrid entity, something as yet unclassifiable, but suggestive of chaos and confusion. We know we are approaching something monstrous when our first impression is confused and uncertain, an encounter with the unknown. Rosaura is described as a "monstrous hybrid" because it is uncertain whether she is female or male—her androgynous appearance signals her monstrosity. Segismundo's monstrosity, on the other hand, is a symbol of his beastly features (1.6.675). Segismundo sees himself as Pascal described the human condition: "What sort of freak then is man! How novel, how monstrous, how chaotic, how paradoxical, how prodigious! Judge of all things, feeble earthworm, repository of truth, sink of doubt and error, glory and refuse of the universe!"[34] Pascal took the words right out of Calderón's mouth. They shared this confused and ambivalent anthropology.

Calderón gives us further clues about the Baroque fascination with monsters in his play about the New World, *Dawn in Copacabana*. Here Calderón has an Incan priestess, Guacolda, stare in bewilderment at the first sight of a Spanish galleon reaching her shores. She is at pains to comprehend what comes into her line of sight.

> If I say it is a large fish, it is true that I would ignore
> the wings with which it flies, and if I say it is a sailing bird,
> that is swimming, I would also inevitably contradict myself:
> so that of four aspects, it is a monster of such strangeness,
> as high as a reef, as swift as a cloud,
> the prodigal offspring of the wind and the sea,
> made up of different species,
> a swimming fish and a flying bird.[35]

The language of strangeness and monstrosity here captures beautifully the encounter with the unknown, with an otherness comprising different species, incommensurable to all previous knowledge. The poet resorts to paradox and contradiction as the mind struggles to resolve the mystery (a flying fish or swimming bird?). Echevarría explains, then, that there are at least two elements at work in the designation of monster: "On the one hand, a logical and discursive impossibility, as it is a matter of contradictory attributes; on the other hand, an impossible, ambiguous vision, which is difficult to interpret because of its warring appearances. We are confronted here with an epistemological and expressive impasse, a kind of aporia."[36]

The monster brings reason to an impasse, a border that cannot be crossed, face to face with the impossible. As we've seen earlier in my study, the experience of wonder suggests a similar occurrence—an experience of unknowing—but the monstrous form of Baroque wonder now signals something new, the preoccupation with ambiguous and warring appearances. Guacolda's language is heavy with contradictions and hybrid images because she cannot definitively determine whether what she sees is real, whether it is a dreamlike appearance or something more substantial. Calderón dramatizes Guacolda's encounter with this unknown entity as the dilemma of his age, how to classify and define the unclassifiable, how to distinguish between reality and illusion. Her vision and mind are mixed-up and puzzled by the sight of this strange ship—this "prodigal offspring of the wind and sea"— and in the turmoil and perplexity of Guacolda's vision, Calderón describes one of the important symptoms of the age, the erosion of epistemological certainties. Guacolda's muddled and mystified vision epitomizes the theme of the age. Every human encounter with reality is fraught with the same mixture of Guacolda's confusion and bewilderment: reality is inscrutable, contradictory, strange, and monstrous. And reality can be—as an encounter with monsters proves—frightening.

Luther certainly knew how the unknown could cause a man to shake and tremble. He set the tone for the early modern period when he began to doubt, seriously and obsessively, the certainty of his salvation. In the Baroque, the shadow of ambiguity and uncertainty has only lengthened. There is growing doubt in the validity of appearances, now seen as inextricably caught up with deceptions and lies, illusions and dreams. If Luther is comforted by the hope of faith alone, the Baroque artist is left without either confidence, in a condition of anxiety and uncertainty. It is a humbling portrait of the human condition:

> Attend these words for your soul's sake:
> Be humble, man, and less extreme,
> For all you see might be a dream,
> Though you may think you're wide awake.
> (*LD*, 2.6.1528–32)

> What's life? A frenzied, blurry haze.
> What's life? Not anything it seems.
> A shadow. Fiction filling reams.
> (*LD*, 2.19.2182–84)

It is not surprising that an age so obsessed with appearances would turn so passionately to the theater and stage to understand the human predicament. If the world is an illusion, then perhaps the dramatic arts are the best clue to what the human being is, a reflection in a mirror, an insubstantial shadow, a player on the stage, a fiction. The fact that representations of life on the stage are put together with great care and pageantry but then suddenly disassembled is enough to remind us of the impermanence and transience of all things—any actor would know this.

Calderón gave us these kinds of truths, fleeting and short-lived, ones that rain on us and then evaporate in the heat of the desert sun. Tragic beauty was what he was after and, in this, he both continued and disrupted the Renaissance. Renaissance humanism, according to Paul Kristeller's classic account, paints a picture of "man" as the great miracle of nature, superior to all other creatures, divine in origin and destiny.[37] The response from the Baroque, on the contrary, would echo the words of Qoheleth on the vanity of knowledge, the impermanence of life, and the beastly features of humankind: "Man has no preeminence over the beasts of the land, for they all have one breath. As one dies, so dies the other" (Ecclesiastes 3:19). This passage alone is a bomb in the camp of Renaissance humanism. In Ecclesiastes, man is no greater than a beast of burden. We are all dust, as Hamlet was to lament in 1601: "What a piece of work is a man, how noble in reason, infinite in faculties . . . in action how like an angel, in apprehension how like a god; the beauty of the world, the paragon of animals; and yet to me what is this quintessence of dust" (*Hamlet*, 2.2.285–300).

The confidence that Renaissance man placed in the dignity of humanity and the nobility of reason has now deteriorated and decomposed. For the Renaissance, man may be the paragon of animals, but the Baroque calls man a wolf, *homo lupus* (a line from Plautus that had wide appeal in the Baroque long before Freud recalled it). The Baroque artist gathers and finds himself among the broken glass and decomposed debris of early modern life. Wholeness is for Renaissance man; Baroque man is scattered in pieces, torn by conflict, cast out.

In this regard, the Baroque gave us what Benjamin saw in Paul Klee's grotesque images (angels, masked figures, demons, puppets, madmen, beast-men, plant-faces): "a creature sprung from the child and the cannibal: not a new man, a monster, a new angel."[38] In Benjamin's reading, Klee gave us a portrait of humanism that exposed the ghostly demarcations and frightening contours of the human person, a humanism that explored the undiscovered Indies in the recesses of the human soul. "Man" is not the noble, innocent, and handsome figure that appears in the European mirror of knowledge. He is a beast-man instead, a wild mix of madness and sanity, angel and demon, humanist and cannibal. For Benjamin, no true "humanism" can do without the nonhuman: the unreason in reason, the madness in logic, the barbarism in culture, the primitive and ugly in classic aesthetics, chaos in harmony; the nefarious in virtue; the interruptive force of suffering in all systems of thought. Benjamin had learned from the Baroque that the monster could be a prophet.

With these beastly figures in mind, let's look at Calderón's *Life Is a Dream*. Doomed by his father—if not by the heavens—Segismundo finds himself imprisoned in a dungeon and can recall nothing else but this life in darkness and shackles. His cradle, he tells us, is equivalent to his grave; the womb of his mother has been his sepulcher. Out of fear that his child

would grow to become a murderous and bloody tyrant—an astrologi-
cal portent—the King of Poland, Basil, has his son, Segismundo, confined
to the bowels of the earth in a makeshift prison in the mountains. From
the time of his birth, ominous prophesies—earthquakes, eclipses, rivers
of blood, clouds raining stones—announce the child's black future (signs
reminiscent of the bloody moon and black sun, "black as sackcloth," in
Revelation 6:12–15). And if this isn't clear enough that this child's future
was doomed, while still pregnant with Segismundo, his mother is visited
by terrifying dreams of a "monstrous form not quite human, but resembling one, which disemboweled her from within. Once covered with her
body's blood, the brute would then kill her, then emerge half mortal man,
half viper slough" (*LD*, 1.6.670–75). Half-man, half-snake, Segismundo is
identified as being hideous, gruesome, dreadful.

Echoes of Revelation are evident in this birth scene, especially in the
image of the pregnant woman "clothed with the sun, the moon under her
feet and on her head a crown of twelve stars. She was pregnant and was
crying out in birth pangs, in the agony of giving birth" (12:1–2). As proof
of one's expulsion from Eden, the agony of childbirth would be shared by
every daughter of Eve, but there is something uniquely terrifying in the
apocalyptic visions of the Book of Revelation and *Life Is a Dream*: childbirth must survive the looming threats of beasts and monsters. In apocalyptic literature, one enters the world with cries and tears for being so suddenly
expelled from the womb and cast into a web of danger and misfortune.
The monsters that pervade the pages of apocalypticism suggest how dangerous the times are, how much evil governs the world, how sin, disease,
violence, and death are loosed upon the earth. This is the Baroque world
of *Life Is a Dream*.

In looking back to apocalyptic literature, Calderón also looks forward to
magical realism in his concern with monstrous traits—I have already mentioned the prophesy that spells doom for the family history of the Buendías,
the birth of a half-man, half-pig. Long before this prophesy is realized,
however, we are given many indications of monstrous traits that already
affect the characters in *One Hundred Years of Solitude*. Colonel Aureliano
Buendía, above all, turns monstrous as he fights war after war, thirty-two
in all, none successful. Though he had noble reasons for becoming a revolutionary—after witnessing four soldiers kill an innocent woman—he soon
loses his soul in the morass and quagmire of endless civil wars. Soon enough,
we cannot tell him apart from his enemies, so dehumanized has he become.
"Lost in the solitude of his immense power," he is "rotting alive," the narrator

tells us (*OHYS*, 159–60). Indeed, the extent of this rot is never more obvious than when he has a former enemy, General Moncada, executed after establishing a friendship with him. General Moncada sees what is happening to the Colonel, how power is corrupting his soul and turning him into a monster. Once about justice, the Colonel now is all about power, wanting nothing else but to wield and possess it, as if this taste for power could defeat the curse of his solitude. On the contrary, his actions do nothing but exacerbate his solitude, making it impossible for him to love.

In a yet more egregious case, the Colonel is tempted to kill his own comrade, Gerineldo Márquez, for simply disagreeing about the terms of a peace agreement, and this brings his mother, Úrsula, to a boiling point as she swears to kill him if he carries out the threat: "It is exactly what I would have done if you'd been born with a pig's tail" (*OHYS*, 163). This comment reminds us that his mother, not unlike Segismundo's mother, had ominous premonitions during her pregnancy with Aureliano and, in fact, feared that he would be born with a pig's tail. In the case of Úrsula, she saw this happening the moment she noticed the child weeping in her womb. His tears signaled to her an individual that would succumb to the basest of human emotions—fear, solipsism, anger, sadness, nostalgia—without knowing the most sublime of emotions, love. And now we know what this monstrosity means to the narrator: synonymous with the lust for power and violence, it translates to an incapacity for love.

Like Aureliano, Segismundo was well on his way to acting the monster he was supposed to be. When he is first released from prison, he acts with mad impunity and arrogance and, at one point, hurls a servant over a balcony to his death. And he threatens everyone—aristocrat or commoner—with a similar fate should they oppose him. He is becoming the kind of tyrant Shakespeare depicts in the characters Richard III or Macbeth, both of whom are described as monstrous in their iniquity—with his deformed body, Richard III is called a dog, hellhound, wolf, toad, spider; and Macduff has this to say about Macbeth:

> We'll have thee, as our rarer monsters are,
> Painted upon a pole and underwrit,
> "Here may you see the tyrant."
> (*Macbeth*, 5.8.25–27)

It is not until Segismundo is returned to his dungeon by the king that he begins to learn humility. And this lesson is equivalent to a tragic truth:

that truths and lies, dreams and realities, are inextricably entangled and that human life, even in its most powerful and majestic persona, "dissipates entirely like the blossoms on an almond tree" (*LD*, 3.3.2330–31). Segismundo learns to restrain his hubris, then, only because death has become his companion, and he knows he cannot spurn this inexorable power, fiercer than any human king. The specter of death is omnipresent in Calderón's world:

> The wind grows still, the sun turns to a blot;
> Each rock will be a headstone to revere,
> Each flower the marker on a fresh grave's spot,
> Each edifice a lofty house of death,
> Each soldier but a skeleton with breath.
> (*LD*, 3.6.2471–75)

And so Segismundo learns early enough to save himself from a monstrous fate by adopting a Socratic axiom on the way of wisdom: meditation on death. Like the half-human, half-animal Socrates—recall that Socrates was known as Silenus, the chief of the Satyrs, the half-human, half-goat worshippers of Dionysus, portrayed as short, bald, and unattractive on the outside but full of a concealed wisdom within—Segismundo cultivates wisdom by wrestling and defeating his serpentine demons, by asserting his free will against a dire forecast and, in short, by taming his beastly inclinations: "I'll start with my most dogged foe and quell myself" (3.14.3257–58). In the process, he adopts a learned ignorance about the "wondrous pageant play" that is human life (3.14.3230). Only now is Segismundo capable of love.

The rather hopeful or redemptive ending to *Life Is a Dream* does not detract from its character as a tragedy. Besides the fact that more than half of Greek tragedies end with redemption (Aeschylus's *The Oresteia* is a good example), Calderón gives us a world—a great theater of a world—in which woes and horrors "stalk humans cravenly in packs" (*LD*, 2.13.1840).[39] In the case of Segismundo, fate is exactly like this, a pack of wolves that stalked and even raised him ("raised like a savage beast"). Compassion is aroused in the reader for Segismundo—despite his own brazen and fool-hearted deeds—because we know that he has been unjustly and cruelly imprisoned since the time of his infancy and we feel for him. In the narration of Segismundo's life, Calderón, a Catholic priest, renders innocent suffering with a compassionate and sensitive brush. He avoids reducing suffering to an effect of sin. He is a postmodern priest of sorts, something like the priest that appears in *One Hundred Years of Solitude* as Aureliano Babilonia asks him whether he believes the strange events of the history of Macondo. The priest looks at him "with a look of pity" and answers, "Ay, my son, he sighed. It would be enough for me to be sure you and I exist at this moment" (*OHYS*, 376). Ontological assurances have dissipated for Calderón and Márquez both. The world is an enigma, and suffering the greatest enigma of all.

With acute sensitivity to the cruel enigma of suffering, then, Calderón lets his protest resound throughout the play as he considers the suffering of the innocent and the hiddenness of God in the face of such injustice, a tragic motif if there has ever been one. Segismundo's complaints are those of all innocent sufferers. Here is his Job-like lament:

> Oh abject wretch! To bear such misery!
> I've struggled, heavens, night and morn
> To comprehend what horrid crime was perpetrated at the time
> When I, offending you, was born.
> At last I grasp why cosmic scorn
> Should be my portion after birth:
> Your justice may enlist no dearth
> Of reasons to be harsh with me
> As being born, I've come to see,
> Is mankind's greatest sin on earth.
> But still I venture, stars, to learn,
> If only for some peace of mind,
> Discounting my dark birth, what kind
> Of crime could warrant in return
> A punishment as fierce and stern
> As this I live, a living hell?
> (*LD*, 1.2.102–18)

Calderón's poetry here is a lacerating cry and protest, a tragic articulation and confession. It is neither diluted nor softened by the redemptive ending—the cry goes on.

With this portrait of the terrors of the earthly condition, we can be assured that the sense of hope in Calderón is nothing like optimism. And still, the hope is there, manifested in the artistic depiction of suffering and the transformation of the brute experience of suffering into something with purpose and meaning, even if silence is the final word. This redemptive moment in the Baroque age is yet another thing that Benjamin got right: "The bleak confusion of Golgotha, which can be recognized as the schema underlying the allegorical figures in hundreds of the engravings and descriptions of the period, is not just a symbol of the desolation of human existence . . . but an allegory of resurrection. Ultimately, in the death-signs of the baroque the direction of allegorical reflection is reversed; on the second part of its wide arc it returns, to redeem" (*T*, 232).

Calderón wants his audience to "look to the eternal" to envision—as a hope against all hope—the possible impossibility of redemption. Like the slave spirituals in North America, hope is stolen in Calderón from moments of anguish, and the resolution to "keep keeping on" rises from the ashes of destitution and depression. Or if a closer parallel with Calderón is desired, recall the similar counsel of Prospero at the end of Shakespeare's *The Tempest* concerning the mad hopes and dreams that are the substance of prayer:

> Now I want Spirits to enforce, art to enchant;
> And my ending is despair
> Unless I be relieved by prayer,
> Which pierces so that it assaults
> Mercy itself and frees all faults.
> (5.1.13–18)

The Baroque age was undoubtedly tempted by despair, but in figures like Calderón and Shakespeare linguistic festivity—playfulness, prayerfulness, laughter—held off the beasts of hopelessness and fatalism.[40]

As we turn to the New World Baroque, we should keep in mind the condition of Segismundo's imprisonment and banishment from the throne. It remains a revealing metaphor for an age that saw itself in such traumatic and alienated terms. If the Baroque artist in Europe "felt thrown out of, beside himself, alienated," according to Maravall, this feeling would only deepen in the New World.[41] For Octavio Paz, the criollo and mestizo, "victims of ambiguity," were "thrown out" like Segismundo, and they belonged nowhere, neither in Spain nor in the New World: "If the criollo, born of Spanish blood, was the victim of ambiguity, the mestizo, born of mixed blood, was doubly so: he was neither criollo nor Indian. . . . The mestizo was literally a man without resource or recourse. A true pariah, he was destined to the most dubious livelihoods: from beggary to banditry, from vagrancy to soldiering. . . . They were New Spain's true novelty" (OP, 32–33).

Monsters in the New World Baroque:
Juan Espinosa de Medrano

The allure that many New World artists feel for the Baroque can be explained in many ways, but one explanation can be traced to the obsession with exile. As in Europe, the sense of alienation haunts the New World Baroque, but in their case this sentiment has an unmistakable beginning: born from the ashes and ruins of the Conquest. If the term "horror vacui"—horror of emptiness or absence—describes the Baroque obsession with leaving no space unfilled and the desire to occupy blank spaces, the New World had its own version of this horror. While European intellectuals were feeling the effects of modern scientific discoveries—a world now alone, exiled from God—the American Baroque was desperately searching for resources and strategies to fill in the blank spaces left by conquerors and gold diggers. A concern with absence is common to both, but the New World embraced an art of exuberance to manage the gaping abysses and abscesses created by European empires. Carlos Fuentes describes this beautifully: "Above all, it [the Baroque] gave us, the new population of the Americas, the mestizos, a manner in which to express our self-doubt, our ambiguity. . . . And nothing expressed this uncertainty better than the art of paradox, the art of abundance based on want and necessity, the art of proliferation based on insecurity, rapidly filling in the vacuums of our personal and social history after the Conquest with anything that is found at hand."[42]

Although the Americas surely had other origins outside of European paradigms, "Latin America" emerged out of the vacuum left in the wake of colonialism. Exile is at the origin. Naturally, then, these first creatures of the New World—criollos, mestizos, and the wild variety of other hybrid creatures—would have to find their identity through the rubble and squalor left behind, picking up the pieces to forge new cultural possibilities unknown to Europeans and natives alike. Conscious of being unusual and singular—illegitimate and inferior in the eyes of many—these strange new beings would create art that would agree with their dissonant and irregular identities, an art, in other words, that was a gathering of divergent and cacophonous fragments. As discordant as it might seem, this art came to capture the New World's savage variety and beauty, like a concert that brings together African and Indian rhythms with sounds from classical music (what Alejo Carpentier calls a *Concierto barroco*).[43] This sort of music is idiosyncratic and marvelous, a perfect mirror of what the first explorers thought about the New World.

Indeed, seen through the eyes of the first explorers, the cultures of the New World bred the strangest and queerest of creatures. Mutants and hybrid monsters peopled the land in extravagant variety. Fernández de Oviedo insisted that the tales of Theseus and his minotaur would "turn silent, for, if truth be told, those metaphors, when reduced to their real history, are but jokes and child's play if they are likened and compared to what in these our Indies has been seen."[44] López de Gómara discovered a creature half-fish, half-man; Pinzón spoke of a Brazilian creature, part simian, part fox, with legs like a human; Columbus tells us of two islands, Cibán and Anán, where the people are born with the tails of animals.[45] With monsters of this sort roaming the world, Calderón's beasts seem ordinary by contrast. The monstrous is never more monstrous, the fabulous never more fabulous, than what appears in this land called the Indies (a perfect misnomer for a land that is synonymous with fantasy).

Artists born and nurtured in these Indies are fabulous for these reasons. For breathing this fantastic air, they would evolve accordingly and adopt the peculiar traits of American cultures. The great Peruvian poet Juan de Espinosa Medrano, known as "Lunarejo" because of the birthmark and blemish on his face ("mark of the moon"), is a good case in point. Like a hieroglyph of sorts, the visible defect on his face ("defect" is another possible meaning for the term "lunar") is loaded with significance. For one, the blemish makes Espinosa Medrano something of a monster, not unlike the characters that appear on the pages of Calderón's plays. Lunarejo wears his physical deformity like the grotesque characters of Baroque theater (I'm borrowing again from González Echevarría on this).

And yet, unlike Calderón's monsters, Lunarejo is a new creature of a new world, sprung from the remote Indies. For this reason, he offers us fresh eyes on the condition of these strange and monstrous creatures. He gives us, in the words of Echevarría, a monstrous and exorbitant criollo poetics, one that is exorbitant for emerging outside the "orb" of the cultural center in Europe.[46] From the perspective of an outsider, he creates a new vision of Baroque poetics, different from the models of the Old World. In my view, he addresses perfectly the creative possibilities of exile as described by Leszek Kolakowski. "Any experience of exile," Kolakowski writes, "can be seen either as a misfortune or as a challenge; it can become no more than a reason for despondency and sorrow or a source of a painful encouragement."[47] In the case of Lunarejo (and the Baroque as a whole), the sense of exile certainly included the sentiments of despondency and sorrow, but the dominant sentiment is something like painful inspiration, a creativity that arose out of the risks, dangers, misfortunes, and insecurities of displaced and misshapen identities.

Lunarejo's exorbitance is, thus, the source of his creativity, but it comes at high costs, especially if we consider the history of European prejudice and colonialism in the New World. This characterization of monstrosity is surely not innocent nomenclature. The attribution of sensual and animal traits to New World creatures by the European gaze would have disturbing implications. Lunarejo knows as much. He is conscious of the fact that Europe regards him and his American siblings as brutes; or else, like chthonic creatures, monstrous for dwelling under the earth and comprising both spirit and mud, intellectual and sensual traits. Lunarejo's genius, in fact, has these wildly divergent traits, but instead of being a defect, he demonstrates its explosive and revelatory potential. With his wit and cunning, he transforms European insults of New World creatures into an apologetics for those dwelling in dark and remote locations. His reflections on these conditions, then, are something like notes from the underground.

So, in the case of Lunarejo, the mark of the moon on his face is only a visible symbol of a deeper blemish felt by all New World Calibans—the blemish of inferiority. He feels alienated and estranged because of European disdain for *Indianos*: "In Spain, *Indianos* are reputed to be barbarians, and it would contribute to such falsehood not to sweep away even the slightest traces that could corroborate their suspicion."[48] Lunarejo wants to cleanse the spots and traces of this stigma, but he usually chooses indirect methods as his strategy, the way some African American slaves would outwit their masters by language games (irony, satire, parody). When Lunarejo writes the prologue to his *Apologético*, for example, he reveals in a uniquely combative way his resentment for being thought of as a barbarian, as a satire of this insult: "Should the Duke, my Sire and Benefactor, not be displeased by the humble offering of this paper, he should take me to be encouraged to greater tasks. . . . I dare not be disillusioned, but treasure any consideration. But what can there be of value in the Indies? What can there be to please Europeans, who have doubts on this point? They take us for satyrs, perfumed by Tritons, with the souls of brutes. Vainly do our human masks attempt to prove them wrong. . . . The parrot is worth as much as he can talk."[49]

Taken for satyrs and parrots: a sense of resentment and anxiety is impossible to miss in these lines. He knew well the sense of marginalization and illegitimacy that was deep-seated among criollos and mestizos (a point fundamental for Octavio Paz; see OP, 59). Lunarejo is, indeed, quarreling and wrestling with these feelings as he is quarreling and wrestling with European presumption, if not blatant prejudice. Indeed, if we recall that many non-European peoples would be defined as parrots—thus, capable only of mindless imitation—we should recognize Lunarejo's complaint as a battle with European arrogance and bigotry. Lunarejo is challenging a sentiment expressed with unabashed clarity by David Hume when he described Africans as parrots without original thoughts and feelings.[50] Later in the nineteenth century, this metaphor would lead to a related metaphor, that of the mockingbird.[51]

Regardless of which metaphor one considers, the European prejudice is already known in the age of Lunarejo, and he felt it like a harpoon striking the heart and soul. He knows that there is value in the Indies, but it takes a lot for him to fight with his doubts and anxieties. "It is clear that Espinosa Medrano's self-definition," Echevarría writes, "issues from his resentment, born of feelings of alienation and estrangement provoked by the disdain of Europeans. His self-definition, even his naming of himself and his group, is always based on how Europeans name Americans. *Lunarejo's* is a reflexive sense of being strange."[52] According to Alicia Colombi-Monguio, moreover, this self-doubt was a condition widespread in the sixteenth century, especially in the Indies: "The anxiety to appear learned hounded the sixteenth-century writer in a Europe in which he could harbor no doubt about his belonging to a tradition and to an intellectual homeland. How could this feeling not be increased when one lived in the Indies, feeling exiled from the native land and from the cultural centers in the West?"[53]

As a satyr in the far-off Indies (or as he says, a quill from the Indian orb),[54] there is no doubt that Lunarejo felt exiled from European cultural centers. His resentment of this fact is plainly evident in this sentence: "We criollos live very far away, and if they don't fly on the wings of greed, Spanish things travel here quite lazily."[55] He may not sound off against Spanish greed with the booming voice of Las Casas, but Lunarejo is hardly naive. It is clear to him that Spain comes to the distant ends of the earth in search of wealth and power, and with sails impelled by the windy conceits of Spanish pride. In confronting these facts, he is seeking to deflate some of this overweening confidence and, perhaps, gather some of it for himself and his native siblings. Lunarejo belongs to a strange and exotic world and he is at pains to make sure this fact becomes, in his gifted hands, an advantage rather than insult. The question is, in other words, what he would do with this unrelenting and pervasive sense of exile and illegitimacy.

As we can see with Lunarejo, the feeling of alienation can indeed produce bitterness and resentment, but it also can be the source of new discoveries, and the best New World poets recognized these creative possibilities and opportunities in their disadvantages. And they recognized that the masks they constructed in their exotic world corresponded to a reality they themselves would create. Reality was malleable in Baroque hands, and Lunarejo knew he had the power to re-create himself. He knew that his own being was a piece of art. Echevarría makes this point: "The creole lives in a world of art in which he is the artifact par excellence. That is his oddity. He is a trope incarnate."[56]

Thus, when Lunarejo entertains the question "What value is there in the Indies?" he is answering the question by producing and fashioning a value for himself and his American compatriots. What could a man with the soul of a brute and the plumes of a parrot offer Europe and its learned elites? Beneath these self-deprecating questions lies a combative and intelligent critique of European presumption. The mask of the satyr taken up by Lunarejo (and by criollos and mestizos in the New World) is used as a duplicitous strategy of criticism. He is a signifying monkey of sorts who uses the "satyrical" mask attributed to him by Europe to satirize European value judgments. He is a mockingbird that knows how to mimic and mock and, in the process, when least expected, gives us a new song by combining and shuffling around previous sounds, images, models, topics.[57]

In Lunarejo's description of poetry (through his defense of Góngora), he gives us a good example of this process that merges the technique of imitation with the spirit of ingenuity and originality. He suggests that the nature of poetry stems from the word "verse," and that a great poet is someone who is capable of "reversing terms, inverting style, and intermingling [*entreverar*] words."[58] Baroque poetry may begin with *imitatio* but it develops and proceeds by a shuffling and reconstitution of various fragments to create something new and unexpected. It is *imitatio* taken to extremes and exaggerated so that it suddenly appears unfamiliar and strange. Poetry is strange for Lunarejo because it reverses and inverses ordinary experiences or descriptions; it draws together words and ideas seemingly at odds with one another; it intermingles and unites terms that are not naturally seen together and, thus, creates something unnatural and monstrous. In the process, it evokes surprise and wonderment in the reader.

We might see the mark of the moon on Lunarejo's face with these elements in mind. For the Baroque artist, the moon is a heavenly symbol with mirrorlike qualities. As the moon receives light from the sun, the mirror receives the image that enters its space. Mirror symbolism is omnipresent in the Baroque age and would signify the inexorable reality of change and flux, the theatricality of existence, the vanity and narcissism of the world, and beauty's impermanence. Lois Parkinson Zamora's fine study of the New World Baroque describes nicely the significance of mirror symbolism in this age: "During the Baroque period, the mirror acquires a negative charge. . . . In painting, the mirror is often a moralizing emblem, an emblem of *vanitas*—wrong-headed worldliness, undue investment in one's own youth and beauty. . . . Over time, the iconography of *vanitas* blurred into *memento mori*; the beauty reflected in the mirror depends upon youth, and youth will fade. Skulls begin to provide regular company to the mirror, reminding the viewer of the speciousness of pleasure and the falsity of appearance."[59]

All of these themes are present in Lunarejo (memento mori, the speciousness of pleasure, falsity of appearance, etc.), so, in a way, he sees himself through the mirror that Europe held up to him (especially in its classics from Horace to Petrarch and Góngora). His face bears the mark of the light of the sun (Europe), though the greatness of his poetry—and that of other New World poets—is his ability, like a moon/mirror himself, to receive the images of Europe and transform them into something else, something stranger and more fantastic. He looked at Europe, we might say, through the kind of mirror found at carnivals, one that deforms, disfigures, and twists the visible object. The resulting image is disorienting, aberrant, and unnatural, but still beautiful in its wildness and unfamiliarity.

Thus, Lunarejo takes up the task inherited from the early explorers on how to name the New World, and he does so in his own unique Peruvian way, with a penchant for hybrid language (talking parrots, American satyrs). As most great Baroque poets understood, he too knew that he was inventing himself as an actor on a stage, playing a part assigned him by Europe but transformed by the resources of his own native culture. So, if the moon causes the werewolf to emerge, it was also the provocation and inspiration that produced the monstrous criollo poetics of Lunarejo.

Mariano Picón-Salas famously described this project that produced a poet like Lunarejo as the *Barroco de Indias*, the first Latin American artistic movement.[60] In this regard, it's clear that the New World saw in the Baroque something that resonated with its own imagination and spirit. It is not an exaggeration to say that the New World's conversion to the Baroque was something like a shock of recognition. Robert Harbison's explanation of why the Baroque would flourish in the Americas is telling: "Perhaps this offers a clue to why the Baroque was so successful in Latin America. . . . Even before it attempts to accommodate exotic cultural material, it seems that the Baroque thrives on contradictions and flowers in those perverse enterprises which try to insert contrary motives into a prescribed format, prefiguring European genres as the medium for rambunctious native imagination. . . . The formal principles on which the Baroque is built more easily lend themselves to stimulating intimations of primeval chaos than the establishment of classic order."[61]

As a product of the primeval chaos in the Indies, the Baroque would flourish in the New World and the result was a transformation in the nature of the Baroque and the New World at once. If the growing consciousness of infinity in the European Renaissance and Baroque had the effect of decentering the stubborn hold of the Ptolemaic cosmos, the New World Baroque would gradually begin to decenter Europe's place as the cultural center of the world. The polycentrism of the New World Baroque would unsettle and disturb the Renaissance vision of the *studia humanitatis* centered in Egypt, Greece, and Rome. In the Indies, this never amounted to a denunciation of classic learning, but was more like a form of mimicry, an imitation that was parody at the same time, a willful and conscious distortion—even perversion—of the classic tradition.

In discussing the great Indian architect Jose Kondori—responsible for the extraordinary churches of Potosí—Carlos Fuentes gives us a case of this disfigured poetry and movement in stone facades: "Among the angels and the vines of the facade of San Lorenzo, an Indian princess appears, and all the symbols of the defeated Incan culture are given a new lease on life. The Indian half-moon disturbs the traditional serenity of the Corinthian vine. American jungle leaves and Mediterranean clover intertwine. The sirens of Ulysses play the Peruvian guitar. And the flora, the fauna, the music, and even the sun of the ancient Indian world are forcefully asserted."[62]

Crazy hybrids comprised defeated cultures and Mediterranean antiquity: all of this amounts to an untamed novelty. What is strange in the New World Baroque is not exactly the unknown, therefore, but the "known displaced and blown out of proportion."[63] If Gracián had described a literary conceit as "a very clever sophism to set forth the sentiments of the soul with the wildest exaggeration," the New World Baroque was exactly this, a wild exaggeration of its parent figure.[64] The soil of the New World—the abundance and diversity of fruits and spices, animals and natural minerals, the wonders of the ancient cultures—would stimulate the imagination of those who walked its lands. Because of the Manila galleon, which carried to Mexico merchandise from the Far East, Mexico became a center where one could find a wild variety of cultures and products. In Bernardo de Balbuena, the Americas had a poet who celebrated this colorful exoticism. Picón-Salas describes Balbuena's contribution in this way: "Words have scents like Oriental spices and sparkle like a mythical treasure. The passage 'pearl, silver, gold, coral, incense, and cinnamon,' appears repeatedly in Balbuena's diction. His eye . . . is so all-embracing that it is not selective but transmits, with equal delight, everything that it views—natural phenomenon, fruits, buildings, theological systems, animals, utensils, or heraldry. . . . As the seventeenth century dawns Mexico lies on the exact meridian where the most exotic regions overlap and it is also the point from which they radiate."[65]

Baroque theology breathes this same atmosphere. The heterogeneous voices in the New World Baroque have a religious corollary in the hybrid forms of religion in the Americas, where Quetzalcoatl could become St. Thomas, or Tonantzin could assume the form of Guadalupe. In this light, the Jesuit theologian Athanasius Kircher was widely read in the New World—by Carlos de Sigüenza y Góngora and Sor Juana, for instance—because he represented in philosophical and theological terms what Baroque poetry was: an immoderate and mad syncretism. Jesuit syncretism in the New World would try to incorporate the native gods and legends into Christian theology as Jesuit missionaries did in the Far East (e.g., Francis Xavier and Matteo Ricci). A long tradition of "baptizing" the pagans in Catholicism legitimized this effort, and, according to Paz, this Jesuit syncretism would prove key to the development of an independent American consciousness among the criollos that soon led to the wars of independence (see OP, 34–43).

In calling to mind the Baroque's role in Latin American wars of independence, Paz corrects the impression that the New World Baroque was always conservative and reactionary, a force in the colonizing of the New World. The Baroque had these elements, but like Proteus it could suddenly become something else mutable and versatile, rebellious and revolutionary, perhaps even "postcolonial."[66]

And it is certainly this protean and rebellious quality that many contemporaries want to remember and rediscover in the Baroque. Though the Baroque played its own part in the colonization of the New World (and, thus, has plenty of blood on its hands), in some cases the Baroque proved itself more congenial to New World Calibans than the Enlightenment model, and it rose to prominence in the Americas when it created family pacts with Indian and mestizo artists, when it demonstrated that it could speak the same distressed language of colonized peoples, when it demonstrated that it could change as a result of New World encounters.[67] As Gonzalo Celorio remarks, these changes produced an eccentricity that extended beyond the boundaries determined by Enlightenment logic and made for a critical tradition thoroughly American: "Hybridity, cultural mixing and symbiosis make the American Baroque a bizarre, fanciful, colorful and popular art that, far from reflecting the experience of submission presupposed by Acosta, in fact constitutes a vigorous sign of New World originality."[68]

The New World Baroque, thus, managed to generate critical motifs and strategies outside of Enlightenment standards of reason. In the Baroque imagination of the New World, fragments of European history were stitched together with the ruins of indigenous and African traditions to make something strange and peculiar but indisputably American. This sort of American art did not need Kant in order to think for itself; it announced itself with every bit of daring and danger as some of the best critical thinkers of Europe, but without the same degree of overweening confidence. In other words, the New World Baroque had a critical tradition, but with a dark, tragic component, which carried all the heavy burdens of Latin American histories—the defeats, the miseries, the insecurities.

The Baroque, in short, has become a welcome alternative to the hubris of some Enlightenment accounts of Western history. The excess and obscurantism that was so distasteful to classic Protestant and Enlightenment perspectives has become cherished by our own age, which sees itself and all human understanding with chiaroscuro brush strokes, as obscure and uncertain. With its taste for shadows and ambiguities, allegories and myths, theater and ceremony, the Baroque was everything that the Enlightenment sought to shine its light on and, in the process, defeat or, at least, explain in rational terms. Not only was the name of God something of this kind, but tragedy, too, was handled with impatience, in a rush to prove that reason could finally explain it all, leaving no room for shadows and mysteries, dark thoughts and dark skins.

As a kind of poetic justice, then, this tradition that was disfavored and even despised by the Enlightenment became its nemesis, carrying within its own Trojan horse an army of strategies and images that would dismantle some Enlightenment prejudices. What were empty shells for some became precious and valuable for others, shells that carried hidden pearls. New World artists would gather these shells from the various corners of the earth and combine them with their own experiences and worldviews, all in the hope of shoring themselves up against the ruins of New World history.

The Hidden God of the New World Baroque

It is hard to imagine any other form of theology taking root in a continent so saturated with these sorts of ruins and defeats than a theology of the cross. New World theology was born, as William Faulkner once said of children of the U.S. South, with its "arms spread on the black crosses" of slavery.[69] With their arms spread out, feeling alienated and exiled from God, while somehow close to God, at the foot of the cross one might say, Baroque New World artists achieved greatness.

I have already suggested that the New World's understanding of the horror vacui was determined much more by the traumatic effects of colonialism than by the new science of the time. Representations of "void" or "abyss" in the New World may have had European parallels, but in the New World these metaphors were tragic symbols suggestive of the voiding of natives peoples or the abysmal nature of suffering; they were burdened by the terrors of history more than the terrors of infinite space famously described by Pascal. In Latin American religion, therefore, the most revelatory of religious images were those that captured the horrors of its history while still offering tender assurances. The New World Baroque, for this reason, turned theologically to symbols and allegories that captured the tragedies of history and the seeming absence of God. Images of Christ crucified and the sorrowful mother of God, or images of suffering saints, would relieve and console the anxieties of a crucified people. While many of these traits could be found in earlier art forms—the Renaissance, Mannerism, and others—the Baroque took things further and gave us exaggerated forms of pain. The art historian Arnold Hauser describes the Baroque in this way: "This emotionalism and sentimentalism, this wallowing in pain and suffering, wounds and tears, is Baroque, and has nothing to do with the intellectualism, spiritual aloofness and emotional remoteness of Mannerism."[70]

Colonialism brought to the shores of the New World this kind of dark iconography, this wallowing in wounds and tears, but it would take on new significance impossible to disentangle from the effects of the Conquest. In Mexico, the Baroque was deliberately incorrect and aberrant, as if these distortions were necessary to capture the extent of New World tragedies.[71]

In these aberrations, the New World Baroque gave us an art that had the hidden God exploding onto the Latin American scene.

Writing about seventeenth-century piety, Mariano Picón-Salas has shown us the theological component of this aberrant and exuberant art. He mentions the famous epic poem, written in 1610 in Lima by a Dominican, Diego de Hojeda, *The Cristiad* (a work Menéndez y Pelayo called the best sacred epic in Spanish literature). It is impossible not to detect an anguished form of piety in this epic, one that resonates with the tortured soul of the Americas: "The Calvary scenes and the Dominican's skillful depiction of the metamorphosis of the gentle Mary into the sorrowing Mother transfixed by grief have the vitality and pathetic realism of the best Spanish painting of the time. . . . The Oriental solemnity of the Biblical metaphor contrasts with the dramatic action in which one can sense the suffering, thirst, sweat, blood, and tears of the God who was made man."[72]

As disturbing as many of these images appear in our contemporary world (especially among triumphal versions of Christianity that prefer images of resurrection over those of the cross), they must have spoken a hard truth to individuals and communities reeling from the blows of empire. Throughout the centuries, the image of an innocent man put to death in the figure of Christ would be widely embraced by oppressed communities. Think of the importance of theologies of the cross among Latin American Liberation theologians: in their case, the Christian story is a tale of God's response to the griefs and miseries of oppressed communities, of communities that recognized the blood, sweat, and tears of Christ in the sorrows of their own lives. Instead of triumphs and conquests, Liberation theology saw the disappointments, failures, and hopes of afflicted peoples as the heart of the Christian story. If oppressed communities turn to the figure of God in the lowly Jesus of Nazareth, it is because he knew so well the bitter taste of human tragedies and still produced courage and faith out of tribulation.

My point is, the New World Baroque bequeathed this heritage of a theology of the cross to later Latin American Liberation theologians. To be sure, the Baroque age generally did not politicize these images the way later Latin American Liberation theologians would (under the influence of Enlightenment ideas). If we compare Liberation theology with the Baroque depiction of suffering in *The Cristiad*, for instance, we notice something quite different from an indulgent wallowing in pain. Liberation theology is deeply dissatisfied with a straightforward portrait of suffering, however poignant and consoling it might be. Instead, to avoid the accusation of being an opiate, they focus on change, indeed, change of the most radical sort, one that will cause widespread upheaval and turmoil in order to prepare the way for a new age of justice. This is a theology as radical as they come, a return to the roots for the sake of a new and startling future, for the kingdom of God.

And yet, with this significant caveat in mind, it is impossible to miss the presence of Baroque images of suffering in Liberation theology. The great Peruvian theologian Gustavo Gutiérrez makes these parallels clear in discussing one of his homeland's figures of Christ, "El Señor de los Temblores," the Lord of the Terrified. Gutiérrez turns to José María Arguedas to describe the image: "The face of the crucified Christ was dark and gaunt, like that of the *pongo*. . . . Blackened, suffering, the Christ maintained a silence that did not set one at ease. He made one suffer; in such a vast cathedral, in the midst of the candle flames and the daylight that filtered down dimly, the face of the Christ caused suffering, extending it to the walls, to the arches and columns, from which I expected to see tears flow."[73]

This is not a theology based on the resurrected Christ, but on the figure of Jesus abandoned on the cross. Latin America produced a figure of God—whether in Jesus or Mary—that shared the wounds and sorrows of mortal man. "All the Mexican Christs are dead," writes Fuentes, "or at the very least in agony. Whether in Calvary, on the cross, or laid out in a glass bier, the Christ that one sees in Mexico's village churches is bleeding, prostrate, and lonely."[74] The cult of fragments in the Baroque is extended, then, to include religious representations of Christ: his body in pieces, contorted and grotesque, fractures that release a profusion of blood, his face wearing a tortured expression, God in ruins. All of this is enough to produce vertigo in the eye of the beholder, dizziness from an excess of suffering. The Mexican Christ is in ruins like so much of Latin American history.

In this instance, at least, a Baroque consciousness is present in Liberation theology.[75] Though the prophets may be the most prominent voices in Liberation thinkers, the histories of injustice and misery made the tragic vision of the Baroque a natural ally in confronting the vexing problem of evil. In Liberation theology, in fact, the question of evil is the fundamental crux of the problem (and not, for instance, the problem of God's existence), one that was far more difficult to avoid than were theologies in other more privileged and affluent contexts.[76] Wrestling with the darkness meant doing theology, doing theology as a matter of life and death, doing

theology as a soulful agon. This is existential, gut-level theology, meditation on God from the ghettos and gutters, from the slums and squalor.
Out of desperation, this kind of theology desires God the way Lazarus
desired the food scraps from the rich man's table.

In many of these desires and hopes in Liberation theology, therefore,
one can hear the mournful echoes of Baroque anguish—and the laments
of the hidden God. The face of the hidden God in New World Baroque
established a pattern of belief and piety, popular religion and theology, art
and drama that survives to this day throughout the Americas, including
among Latino/a religion in the United States (Roberto Goizueta's wonderful book *Caminemos con Jesus* is a good example of this heritage in North
America).[77] Travelers to Latin America will recognize the contours of this
sensibility. It is evident in the "high" and "low" culture of Latin America:
in the abundance of saint's days and festivals; in celebrations of Marian
apparitions; in the art and music; in celebrations commemorating the dead;
and, of course, in the tragic features of Christ hanging from the cross in
churches and homes. These are all allegories of a spirituality that is restless
and uneasy, an image of the Baroque's enthusiasm for movement over stillness, for excess over moderation. If there is a tone of tragedy in all of this,
it is because this darker vision captures best the feeling of exile and strangeness at the heart of the Americas. It is this broken image that shaped Latin
America's mutant identity and the continent's art of displacement. This is
precisely how Carlos Fuentes interprets the significance of the New World
Baroque: "The Baroque is the art of displacements, similar to a mirror
in which we are constantly able to see our mutant identity."[78] In the New
World Baroque, wonder keeps getting stranger and stranger.

Or else, wonder is wounded, as I suggested earlier, but rises time and
time again and becomes an instance of the contradictory impulses inherent in the tragic beauty of the Baroque: both the obsession with death
and the love of fiesta. Though the Baroque welcomes and succors death, is
both fascinated and repulsed by death, it does so with revelry and aesthetic
abandon, with the spirit of fiesta and celebration. The Baroque artist re-
fashions the art of dying of older ages and comes at death with dance and
laughter as much as dread, something it learned, according to Octavio Paz,
from Burgundy: "In the area that interests me here, that of sensibility, it
is enough to recall two inseparable and hostile urges that dwell in our
souls: the fiesta and our obsession with death. Two tragic forms of excess
and dissipation that are the legacy of Burgundy. This legacy took root in
the sixteenth century in the valley of Anahuac, similarly a land of dance

and sacrifice, laughter and penance. . . . The Baroque festival is a representation in which even death is extravagantly attired and masked" (OP, 145–47).

"Even death is extravagantly attired and masked": to put death on the stage, to dramatize it, to mourn it, laugh at it, mock it, are features that come from the depths of Baroque soul. Baroque culture adds exotic flavor and vibrant color to the pale face of death. Though the crosses of Ash Wednesday are indelible marks on Baroque man and woman—like the ash crosses inscribed on the foreheads of the seventeen sons of Colonel Aureliano Buendía—the Baroque detested dismal and morose displays of death, preferring, instead, death with pageantry. The blank stare of death would suddenly come alive in the tragic theater of the time, in the religious procession and festivals, in the poetry and music of the period. There is something like a defeat of death—however fleeting—in these dramatizations. Joy and laughter would dethrone death's grim posture and overcome it by a strategy of carnivalesque play. The deep-seated bitterness and melancholy of the period, the disillusionment and pessimism, thus goes hand in hand with a celebration of life. However tragic it might be, the New World Baroque also believed in the joyful overcoming of death; it believed in resurrection.

And these facts remind us that tragedy is neither simply equivalent to suffering (that would be pathos) nor always at odds with the hope for redemption. Instead, tragedy is the creation of art that arises from the struggle with suffering, the poetry of resistance and defiance in the face of suffering. Tragedy is the poetry forged through the crucibles of history, the poetry that is born through the collision of words and events, the poetry come from the conflicts and calamities of the human experience. The New World Baroque gave us art of this sort, filled to the brim, overflowing in fact, with the contradictory impulses of life, the disillusionments and hopes, the tragedies and wonders, the sorrows and ecstasies.

The subjects of our next chapter, Cervantes and Sor Juana Inés de la Cruz, are artists in this Baroque mold, and they put on exuberant display the tragic beauty, or the mutant art of displacement in Fuentes's words, that is essential to the Baroque in Spain and the New World.

FOUR

BAROQUE ARTISTS IN EXILE

Cervantes and Sor Juana

And wonder, dread and war

have lingered in that land

where loss and love in turn

have held the upper hand.

—*Sir Gawain and the Green Knight*

In the prologue to *Don Quixote*, the author makes a gesture toward the classic epic when he invokes the muses. He tells us that under the right conditions, even the most barren muses can bring "forth a progeny to fill the world with wonder and delight" (*DQ*, prologue). For everything else it might be, literature seems to have a special, magical power to produce wondrous progeny. Books have this reproductive potential, the power to engender new, unexpected possibilities in our lives and, thus, to re-create, define, and mold us. They are midwives to our most cherished beliefs, values, narratives, myths, legends, and practices. This fact is clearly apparent in Cervantes's masterpiece *Don Quixote*. Don Quixote is a devoted reader of books with an extraordinary capacity for wonder. He is a dreamer with an unbridled imagination who has fashioned his life in accordance with the heroes of his library. He is the flesh and blood incarnation of the books he reads, or rather, devours and imbibes so that they come alive in his flesh and blood. As Don Quixote leaves his village to begin his exploits and adventures, his life becomes an open book, a fiction and fantasy that has escaped the pages of a book.[1]

As different as the great Mexican poet Sor Juana Inés de la Cruz is from Don Quixote (and their differences are crucial to this chapter), they do share this obsession with books. Sor Juana's own life story cannot be told without emphasizing how deeply books shaped her, beginning as a child with the books of her grandfather's library to her adult years when she owned her own vast and impressive library. Her books must have had the same value and importance to her as Don Quixote's library; or else, the same value as Dulcinea in Don Quixote's love-crazed imagination. Indeed, Sor Juana's devotion to wisdom is every bit as mad and romantic, fierce and uncompromising as Don Quixote's devotion to Dulcinea. The objects of their desires may have had different names, but the two converged in madness for reading—*lectura* was *locura*.[2] Though these desires would remain forever unfulfilled and unrequited (what human desire isn't?), it is also true that their romantic cravings allowed their minds to wander and soar to new heights, far beyond the confines of the convent or the plains of La Mancha. Their books propelled them on distant journeys into new worlds, and this made possible discoveries and insights unimaginable if they had remained confined to the limiting borders of their places of birth.

In considering the motifs of wonder and exile in the Baroque age, we would be well served by concentrating on Don Quixote's wandering. It is a good image that captures the restlessness and impetus for exploration in this age that gave rise to the early modern period. In subtle or explicit ways, the aspirations and ideas of Cervantes and Sor Juana would capture all the wonders and all the disasters that accompanied the "discovery" of the New World.[3] In this sense, cognizant of these impulses for movement and discovery in the wake of 1492, I want us to notice in this chapter the traces and echoes of the New World in the work of Cervantes and, conversely, the traces and echoes of the Old World in the poetry and art of Sor Juana.

By joining these two authors, I want to emphasize the shared world that Spain and the Indies inhabited and, yet, at the same time, recognize the distinct and diverse possibilities of the Baroque imagination vis-à-vis Cervantes the great novelist and Sor Juana the great poet. Both of them took very different paths—from the life of a nun to that of a soldier—and this resulted in quite different forms of art and life. But then again, they both lived in interesting times (a Chinese curse, we should note) of exploration, discovery, and conquest, and these historical realities forced their way onto the stage of their artistic achievements. With one eye on the effects of conquest and exile, then, our other eye in this chapter will hopefully see with greater insight the new, more broken and fragmented nature of wonder in this age of unprecedented discoveries.

The configuration of wonder changes, to say it another way, when haunted by the anxiety of the grave—this much is certain in the age of Cervantes and Sor Juana. Toward the end of her life, Sor Juana would be forced to relinquish her books upon pressure from the Archbishop of Mexico, Francisco de Aguiar y Seijas. Though she said very little about this sacrifice, part of her must have been in mourning like Don Quixote when the priest and barber burn the books of his library, or like Prospero in *The Tempest* when he announces that he will drown his books of sorcery (5.1.57). With his books now cast into the deep, Prospero's thoughts would turn to matters of the grave instead of the world of spells and magic. The same can be said about Don Quixote and Sor Juana: the abjuration of the source of their art and imagination (books) results in a gradual loss of power and a steady march toward death. And this is a lesson that we cannot miss about wonder in the age of the Baroque: it wears the grief-stricken mantle of death and is always oppressed by the weight of exile. So, for all the liberating and magical impulses that their books kindled, inspiring and urging them to venture forth, the blaze soon turns to a smolder, suffocated by the shadow of death. In the Baroque, these oppressive shadows had various faces, from the conquering impulse of the Spanish Empire (now in decline, decrepit like Rocinante) to the dark specters of the Inquisition. Both of these forces would influence and disrupt the dreams and ideals of many artists of the age, including Cervantes and Sor Juana.

The wonder of literature—the novel in Cervantes and poem in Sor Juana—is only part of the story I want to tell in this chapter, therefore. I want to pick up where I left off with the Baroque and explore the impact of exile on the literature and religion of this period, and specifically what this has to teach us about the configurations of wonder after the force of exile is felt. This chapter will also mark the transition and passage in my book to twentieth-century literature and religion in Latin America in the following chapter. Beginning with Cervantes will help us understand his impact in Latin America and why, for instance, Carlos Fuentes once called Cervantes the "founding father of Latin American fiction."[4] It will help us appreciate the echoes of the New World, particularly on the themes of wonder and exile, in the work of the modern world's first major novelist.

Cervantes and Sor Juana in Exile

In the case of *Don Quixote*, the signs of exile are fundamental to Cervantes's creation of this new genre, the novel. We are given a clue of this right away in the prologue with the description of the particular conditions in which *Don Quixote* was born: in prison. This alone signals to us that we are in a very different (Baroque) world from anything that has gone before (the epic poem, pastoral and chivalry romances, medieval ballads, the picaresque). These genres are not exactly discarded by Cervantes, but instead reformed and reconstituted in light of the new exigencies and threats of the early modern period—the wars and conquests, the expulsions, the unprecedented scale of imprisonments. Like someone recently released from prison, now disillusioned and hardened, familiar with the humiliations and miseries of captivity, he will use his tongue in bolder, more profane ways. Though Cervantes will continue to use and invoke older literary genres and speech styles, he puts away the childish things of past styles—the innocence and optimism—to create something more heartbreaking. The achievement of this pluralistic and hybrid mosaic that is his novel is awesome and it owes much not only to the author's prodigious mind, but to a sense of exile that haunts the pages of this new invention.

And this experience was not simply a Baroque motif for Cervantes. It was all too personal. As is well-known, even in childhood, thanks to a father who spent time in a debtor's prison, Cervantes would personally know the shame of poverty and delinquency. Later as an adult, he would follow in his father's ignominious footsteps and spend time in prison himself. And regardless of whether these experiences hardened him, none of this would prepare him for the experience of captivity he would endure for five years in North Africa, between 1575 and 1580, after being taken prisoner by Algerian pirates. This experience was a deadly serious and agonizing one for thousands of Spaniards and left a deep mark on the soul of Cervantes.[5] Américo Castro has said that this captivity was the "most transcendental event in his spiritual career," and Juan Goytisolo that it is the "void—hole, vortex, whirlwind—in the central nucleus of the great literary invention."[6] If Cervantes's imagination sails into new virgin territory in this great novel, we should always remember that it was by navigating the voids and whirlwinds of his past that he achieved artistic excellence.

The same might be said of Sor Juana Inés de la Cruz. By sailing against the tides of her age and from the marginal position of exile in the Americas, she reaches undiscovered regions of poetry and art, beauty marked by struggles and brawls. I follow Octavio Paz in seeing her poetry as stained by the marks of her illegitimacy (the absence of her father), her insecurity as a criollo writer of the Indies, and, of course, the fact that she is a woman poet and theologian in a deeply patriarchal world. If these are the blemishes of her poetry, they are also the source of great artistry and inventiveness.

The dream of Sor Juana's poetry (*First Dream* is perhaps her greatest work) is altogether different than Don Quixote's chivalrous dreams, but Cervantes and Sor Juana, these two Baroque, Catholic authors, do come together on some matters of significance, especially on a portrait of wonder and mystery after their encounter with exile. The Golden Age is irrecoverable, this much Cervantes knew well. We live in the age of iron, and if there is any hope in literature filling the world with wonder and delight it is only after they have gone through a purgation of fire, after being subject to a process of disillusionment and critique. For both Cervantes and Sor Juana, the experience of wonder is recoverable only in the ruins of exile.

The Theater of Life

Michel Foucault begins his reading of *Don Quixote* by calling attention to the pervasive force of exile in the book, first by concentrating on the language itself. For Foucault, the words of the novel themselves suffer the humiliation of exile, where language breaks its ties with the Renaissance and appears in an alienated and Baroque form, no longer a mirror of nature. Language is now exiled from "things" and is held captive in a cage of fiction and dreams, illusions and deceptions. In this estranged condition, the task of disentangling truth from falsehood, illusion from reality, is impossibly difficult. Don Quixote's wandering, then, is emblematic of the wandering of words off the pages of reality, a movement further and further away from language as participation and resemblance. We are entering the modern experience of literature, an experience inseparable from the predicament of exile.

> *Don Quixote* is a negative of the Renaissance world; writing has ceased to be the prose of the world; resemblances and signs have dissolved their former alliance; similitudes have become deceptive and verge upon the visionary madness. . . . Words wander off on their own, without content, without resemblance to fill their emptiness; they are no longer the marks of things. . . . The signs of language no longer have any value apart from the slender fiction which they represent. . . . *Don Quixote* is the first modern work of literature, because . . . in it language breaks off its old kinship with things and enters into that lonely sovereignty from which it will reappear, in its separated state, only as literature.[7]

Literature emerges at this point of loneliness and separation, for Foucault, when reality itself has become fictional, including the author and readers themselves.

Like a great spinner of yarns, Cervantes's web of fiction is spun so broadly that it catches and traps everything close to it. The effect is the gradual erosion of the borders between the fictional world of the book and reality outside. Besides the numerous references to the author throughout *Don Quixote*, part 2 of the novel, written in 1615, ten years after part 1, is the most obvious development of this motif, where fiction is reality and reality, fiction.[8] Many of the characters in part 2 have actually read part 1 and soon become participants and actors in the drama of Don Quixote and Sancho Panza. These readers, like the Duke and Duchess—bored and decadent aristocrats, quick to abuse and ridicule others for their amusement—are thrilled by the opportunity to play a role in this fantastic narrative, and they soon take their place as actors on the stage of Don Quixote's and Sancho Panza's lives. Cognizant of his fictional fame, Sancho Panza introduces himself to the Duke and Duchess with this in mind: "I am that squire of his [Don Quixote] who plays his part or ought to play his part in that there history and who's called Sancho Panza—unless they changed me when I was in the cradle—by which I mean, at the printing press" (*DQ*, part 2, 30).

Like the Duke and Duchess, almost every character in the novel takes up the mask or disguise of an actor. The galley slave Ginés de Pasamonte becomes Master Pedro, the puppeteer; Sansón Carrasco plays the part of the Knight of Mirrors, then later, Knight of the White Moon; Dorotea adopts the role of Princess Micomicona; the priest dresses as a damsel in distress; Sancho's friend, the exiled Moor, Ricote, also takes up a disguise, but in his case, the disguise is a matter of life and death—he and his family have been exiled from Spain by the order of expulsion in 1609 and, thus, he is forced to play a tragic role as a hunted fugitive. With this kind of revelry and carnivalesque festivity, no wonder Mikhail Bakhtin regarded *Don Quixote* as one of the "greatest and most carnivalistic novels of world literature."[9]

Playing with the theatrical motif (recovered by the Renaissance from the ancient world), Cervantes gives us a very modern portrait of the world as constituted and formed by illusions and dreams, a world made of human hands (Don Quixote: "Everything in this world is trickery, stage machinery"; *DQ*, part 2, 29). The fact that the author becomes a character in his own work, and readers enter into a fictional realm by becoming characters themselves cannot but make us wonder—the millions of readers since its publication—if we, too, belong to this fictional realm. Is reality composed of a vast library in which we are all characters, all players on a stage? Jorge Luis Borges suggested as much: "In 1833, Carlyle observed that the history of the universe is an infinite sacred book that all men write and read and try to understand, and in which they are also written."[10]

Although Borges mentions Carlyle in 1833, he was quite conscious of this tradition going back to the Baroque and that it began, above all, with *Don Quixote*. The Baroque nature of the *Quixote* is evident at so many points, but it is no more obvious than when the characters remind us that we are all actors that have come to this "great stage of fools" (*King Lear*, 4.6.183). Don Quixote makes this point to Sancho:

> Actors and dramatists . . . hold up to us at every step a mirror in which we can see the actions of human life most vividly portrayed; for there is no more realistic representation of what we are and what we are going to be than plays and players. . . . One actor plays the pimp, another plays the liar, this one the merchant, that one the soldier, another the fool who is wise, another the lover who is a fool; but once the play is over and they remove their costumes, all the players are equal. . . . Well, the same happens in the play of this life, in which some act as emperors, others as popes and, in short, all the characters that there can be in a play; but when it is over, in other words when life ends, death strips them all of the costumes that had distinguished between them, and they are all equals in the grave. (*DQ*, part 2, 12)

In his wise madness, Don Quixote tells us that the theater is a mirror that reflects back to us the strange variety and vanity of human behavior and, above all, the evanescence and impermanence of human life. The mirror that Don Quixote holds up for us here is a vision of life from the grave where everyone occupies the same and equal plot of dirt, finally stripped of all costumes and masks. From this vantage point, we are all nothing but insubstantial reflections vainly pretending to be something greater, or as Macbeth has it, "a walking shadow, a poor player that struts and frets on the stage and then is heard no more" (*Macbeth*, 5.5.24–26). The condition of our lives is equivalent to being thrown onto a great stage of fools that we cannot quite fathom or comprehend. We are confined to the stage, forever unable to remove our masks to see what lies behind it. The essence of the real eludes us.

In Cervantes, the theme of exile is so pronounced because his sensitivity to the cruelty and anguish of his times is so acute. Regarding his age as a postlapsarian age, the age of iron, he is perfectly aware of his age's distance from Eden, or from anything resembling the garden-like contexts of pastoral and chivalry romances. The fact that Cervantes gives Don Quixote a home in the arid and austere plains of La Mancha (in Spanish meaning "stain") is crucial in this regard: in addition to resembling the sad and lonely wandering of a *pícaro*, Don Quixote's sojourn echoes the biblical diaspora of the Israelites, or the exile of Dante, both situated in the desert of exile. There is no doubt that Don Quixote is a man in exile, so far from the world he knows from his books and tries to resuscitate. Cervantes is no different. He is identical with the deepest desires of Don Quixote: he wants to recover a world that has been lost, a world in which justice, beauty, and love are cherished above all.

In this regard, Cervantes has Platonic inclinations. His novel is filled with a profound spiritual yearning for transcendence, and every failure and heartache endured by his tragic heroes dramatizes his epoch's estrangement from the Good—and, at the same time, his epoch's infinite, vast spiritual hunger. By the end of the novel, we know that Cervantes is closer to the disillusioned Don Quixote than to his previous persona at the beginning of the novel; like Don Quixote, he has been disheartened and coarsened by the failures and distresses of history, making it impossible for him to believe in the realization of justice, beauty, and goodness, but whether he retains a faith in the effort and struggle is one of the questions that has been debated for centuries. I will return to this later.

In the meantime, we are left with a thorny problem concerning the depth of human estrangement from reality or truth. If words are now alienated from reality in *Don Quixote*, then is it even possible to disentangle truth from illusions and dreams? As we saw in the last chapter, the Baroque age was obsessed with this dilemma, and in *Don Quixote* the confusion is extended in many directions, but particularly with regard to the question of madness. Neither the readers nor the characters in the novel, for instance, can resolve the question of whether Don Quixote is delusional or wise in his madness. Just when we think the answer is with the former— as in his experience in the cave of Montesinos—Don Quixote shocks us with his luminous insight. After describing his fantastic visions in the cave of Montesinos, sounding crazier than ever, he suddenly has this mystical lesson to impart: "Now indeed I have understood that all the pleasures of this life pass away like a shadow or a dream, wither like the flowers of the field" (*DQ*, part 2, 22).

The fact is that the readers—and characters of the book—have a hard time deciding on Don Quixote's sanity because there are traces of wisdom and foolishness both. The difficulty of this decision is the same for anyone living in "detestable times," where truth is always scrambled and confused with falsehood. There is real anxiety felt by the Baroque artist in trying to distinguish between the real and the imaginary, and Michel Foucault put his finger on it by describing it as the peculiar madness of the Baroque: "Madness preserves all the appearances of its reign. . . . It plays on the surface of things and in the glitter of daylight, over all the workings of appearances, over the ambiguity of reality and illusion, over all that inde-terminate web, ever rewoven and broken, which both unites and separates truth and appearance. It hides and manifests, it utters truth and falsehood, it is light and shadow. It shimmers, a central and indulgent figure, already precarious in this baroque age" (*MC*, 36).

Foucault's account of madness is a brilliant way of describing the anxiety of the Baroque age—the interplay of light and shadow, truth and appear-ance, all entangled with the maddening frustration of how to sort them out. I will discuss the question of madness in greater detail below, but at the pres-ent I want to mention Sancho's response to these issues. He, too, shares Don Quixote's belief that we live in fallen, detestable times: "But we'd better leave it all in God's hands, because he's the great knower of everything that's going to happen in this vale of tears, in this wicked world of ours where there's hardly a thing that isn't besmirched by evil, deceit and villainy" (*DQ*, part 2, 11). God is God and man is man; like a Barthian, the distance of man from God is the most pronounced element of Sancho's theology. God is clearly not absent for Sancho or Don Quixote, but signs of his pres-ence are increasingly difficult to discern "in this vale of tears." God is hid-den. This seems to be the gist of Sancho's theology—or his "theorology."

According to György Lukács, the world Cervantes gives us reflects a pro-found sense of homelessness, a world in which God has withdrawn: "The first great novel of world literature stands at the beginning of the time when the Christian God began to forsake the world; when man became lonely and could find meaning and substance only in his own soul. . . . Cervantes, the faithful Christian and naively loyal patriot, creatively ex-posed the deepest essence of this demonic problematic: the purest heroism is bound to become grotesque, the strongest faith is bound to become madness, when the ways leading to the transcendental home have be-come impossible."[11] Although I have my reservations about the tone of the passage—Baroque Spain, much less the New World, is clearly not Lukács's culture of twentieth-century atheism—it does capture well the anguished spirituality of the period, when heroism became grotesque and faith madness. As argued in chapter 3, a sense of divine hiddenness (not absence) intensely preoccupies the Baroque artist and has left him lonely and homesick, distraught by his inability to find his way to his transcendental home. In this, Lukács is right. But, then again, he is too quick to conflate divine hiddenness with atheism. It seems to me, on the contrary, that the age's peculiar spirituality emerges, oddly enough, from a feeling for God's presence through absence, or better yet, through divine nothingness. And, as I've said before, this is nothing like nihilism—there remain traces of divine presence, though nebulous and shadowy, throughout creation.[12] Thus, the great Baroque paradox: as God's withdrawal/hiddenness is escalating in all its existential depth, the age was furious, dynamic, and spirited in representing—through drama, ritual, festival, art, dance, music, literature— God's presence. This Catholic sensibility of divine immanence did its best to allay (without curing) the dread and anxiety of the period and to prevent the world from assuming an extreme condition of dereliction and abandonment at the hands of God. God is hidden, not absent.

Cervantes in Exile

For Cervantes, the struggle with the hidden God left him with gaping wounds never more visible than in his experience in the prisons of Algiers. With exile as our theme, consideration of Cervantes's years of captivity in North Africa will be important to understand some of the historical events and circumstances of his age. It gives us a window not only into the production of *Don Quixote*, but into the fate and experience of hundreds of thousands of exiles in the Baroque age. In this case, we would do well to keep in mind Henry Kamen's reminder that Spain has the dubious honor of "being the only European nation to have systematically dispossessed of house and home hundreds of thousands of its own citizens."[13] In the effort to consolidate its empire, Spain turned to a particularly Roman form of punishment, exile. Spain was to create a nation by the expulsion of its minorities. While the Moors of Spain were not expelled in 1492 with the Jews, they were, nevertheless, expected to relinquish their religion and culture. The large-scale burning of Arabic books in 1501 (in Granada) is representative of this mood of intolerance and militant Christianity. Castilians would increasingly show disdain toward the conquered cultures and religions of its lands. A letter sent by the Moorish leaders of Granada in 1501 to the Sultan of Turkey expresses well the fact that they had now become exiles in their places of birth: "Peace be with you in the name of the slaves who remain in al-Andalus, in the West, the land of exile. . . . We complain before you, my Lord, of the injuries, shame, and enormous calamity which befell us! We have been betrayed and converted to Christianity, breaking with our own religion; we have been oppressed and dishonoured."[14] It is this spirit of protest that later led—in 1568, for instance—to widespread rebellion in Granada. The leaders of Spain would react to this event, first, by the expulsion of thousands of Moors in 1569 and eventually, in 1609, with the expulsion of all Muslims from Spain.

Miguel de Cervantes (1547–1616) lived during these tumultuous times of mass expulsions and conquests, all the effects of the epoch-changing year of 1492. His great novel shows the effects of the suffering and violence of the times, from the events in Spain to the affairs of the New World. Indeed, it seems to me that his own experience of suffering and captivity in Algiers captures in allegorical form many of these misfortunes.

After his military service in Lepanto (1571) Cervantes continued his life as a soldier until 1575, when he was taken prisoner aboard a Turkish Algerian ship. He spent the next five years in captivity along with thousands of other Christian captives. After trying to escape several times—and risking his life in doing so—Cervantes was eventually ransomed by a Trinitarian priest in 1580. Soon after his release he wrote a play, *El trato de Argel*, and contributed an affidavit of his experience in Algiers in a piece titled *Información de Argel*.

As María Antonia Garcés has shown, these works give us a very vivid and tragic image of the abuses and suffering in Algiers. In *El trato de Argel*, the character Aurelio describes his life in captivity in these troubled lines:

> Sad and miserable state! Sad and bitter enslavement!
> Where the sorrow is as long as the good is short and abbreviated!
> Oh Purgatory in this life, Hell placed in this world,
> Evil that has no equal, strait that has no exit.[15]

Aurelio goes on to describe a torment so overwhelming as to confound his ability to express himself. His tongue falters before the horror: "Be silent here, my torment, which, since it is my enemy, what I say will not approximate what I feel."[16] Another character, Per Alvarez, enters the picture and turns to *La Virgen de Montserrat* to be a refuge for his fears and sorrows:

Blessed and beautiful Virgin, comforter of the human race,
Be thou here the star that in this insane sea guides my poor boat
And protects me from so many dangers! Virgin of Montserrat,
Send me a ransom, take me out of this sorrow.[17]

And a chorus of captives turns to the Virgin in the same way:

Turn your eyes, Saintly Virgin Mary, which give light and glory to
    heaven,
To the sad ones who cry night and day, and who water the ground
    with their tears.[18]

These passages from Cervantes's play resound with his own personal experience in Algiers. Later on these anguished sentiments would make new appearances in the pages of *Don Quixote*. In fact, Cervantes waters the ground of his great novel with a copious amount of tears, so much so that the result is a curious mixture of tragedy and comedy. On the theme of captivity, for instance, Cervantes tells us a beautiful tale of captivity, exile, and love in the episode known as the Captive's Tale. If one is careful to notice here, the tortured appeals to the Virgin Mary in *El trato* surface in the captive's devotion to the beautiful Moorish woman Zoraida. Zoraida is clearly identified with Mary in *Don Quixote* and shares with her a redemptive purpose. She refuses the name Zoraida, for instance, and insists on being called "Maria." She makes constant allusions and references to Mary in her letters, and in her first visit to a church in Spain it is Mary that she recognizes. She also first enters the novel riding a donkey, with the captive walking by her side. It's hard to miss the references to the Mary and Joseph story, especially since Mary and Joseph follow the bright star and, in the mind of the captives and Baroque Catholicism, the Virgin Mary is the star of liberty. This motif is present in one of Cervantes's other works about his experience of captivity in Algiers, *Los baños de Argel*: "I have the Hail Mary," the child captive Francisquito remarks, "hammered into my heart and she is the star that guides me in this sea of affliction."[19]

Most significantly in *Don Quixote*, though, Zoraida is referred to as *señora de nuestra libertad*, a title that is surely connected with the image of Mary adored by Christian captives in Algiers, *Nuestra Señora de la Libertad*. In the Captive's Tale, it is the initiative and courage of this Moorish woman that is responsible for the salvation of the captives. Here Zoraida/ Mary represents more than a tender and compassionate mother figure. She appears as a liberating prophet, one who "proclaims liberty to captives and sets the oppressed free" (Luke 4:18–19). From the captive's perspective, she is a "goddess from heaven who had come down to earth for my delight and deliverance" (*DQ*, part 1, 41).

If Zoraida is an incarnation of this liberating image of the goddess, she, too, shares in redemptive qualities; she is a heavenly force. Zoraida is for Cervantes what Beatrice is for Dante. Recall the words of the pilgrim in exile about his beloved Beatrice: "O lady, you in whom my hope gains strength, you who, for my salvation, have allowed your footsteps to be left in Hell. . . . You drew me out from slavery to freedom, by all those paths, by all those means that were in your power."[20] And it is important to remember that when the exiled Dante was lost in the "dark woods" at the beginning of the *Inferno* (Canto II), it was the Virgin Mary entreating St. Lucy and then Beatrice to rescue the lost pilgrim.[21]

The fact that redemption comes through a feminine figure is only part of what is startling about Cervantes's portrait, however. Zoraida is a Moor from North Africa, after all (possibly based on a real, historical person, the daughter of Hajji Murad, one of the richest men in Barbary). And salvation comes through her, this impure hybrid of Moorish and Christian traits. She is the "borderline between the Christian and Muslim worlds," a liminal figure on the threshold of a new heterogeneous identity.[22] In her exotic and syncretic beauty, she is a microcosm of Spain's mongrel history of miscegenation, the product of a history that began with Islam's migration into al-Andalus in 711. To Cervantes, Zoraida is an echo of happier times in Spain, when love forged unions among a barbaric motley of peoples, when love prevailed over divisiveness and discrimination, when Eros triumphed over Thanatos.

We might also see Zoraida as the concrete embodiment of the language that was spoken by the captives in Algiers, a "bastard" language neither Arabic nor Castilian, a mixture of various tongues (*DQ*, part 1, 41). Leo Spitzer interprets her significance in this way and suggests that she represents a polluted, heterodoxical grace, universal and inclusive, catholic and pluralistic.[23] She is a graceful bastard, an allegory of a once pure faith that now has been contaminated. Zoraida's faith is a curious and strange manifestation of a form of grace that has crossed the borders of sameness and found a resting place in this adulterated and dark-skinned Moorish beauty. God's grace has become grotesque and shattered the cultural and theological versions of purity and sameness. In Cervantes's hands, the traditional practice of "baptizing the pagans" has become a theology of impurity.

We might see this impure goddess of Spain's Christian and Moorish past as the mother of another hybrid goddess, this one of the New World, the Virgin Guadalupe. In the sixteenth century and thereafter, the image of Guadalupe from Spain assumes a new identity in the Americas, an identity that is a bridge between the Christian and Indian worlds. She is a hybrid of European and Indian traits, just as Zoraida/Mary is a mestiza of Christianity and the Middle East. "The Virgin of Guadalupe was a point of union among criollos, Indians and mestizos," writes Octavio Paz, "the answer to their triple orphanhood": "Indians, because Guadalupe-Tonantzin was the transfiguration of their ancient female deities; criollos, because the Virgin's apparition made the land of the New Spain more of a real mother than Spain had been; mestizos, because the Virgin did and does represent reconciliation with their origins and the end to their illegitimacy" (OP, 44).

As Guadalupe comes to the aide of American orphans—Indians, criollos, and mestizos—Zoraida, too, in *Don Quixote*, becomes the tender redeemer of the captive. Like *La Morenita* of Mexico, Zoraida is on the side of the oppressed and downtrodden.

In *Don Quixote*, Zoraida/Mary quite literally redeems the captive from his nightmare of imprisonment and possible death. The captive describes to us his destitution in the following passage. Given Cervantes's own experiences as a captive and his escape attempts, these lines are packed with autobiographical details:

> The hope of my gaining freedom never forsook me, and whenever what I dreamt up and put into practice didn't have the intended result I would immediately, without despairing, seek out or invent some other grounds for hope, however feeble they might be, to sustain me. . . . And although hunger and lack of clothes might have distressed us at times—in fact, nearly always—nothing afflicted us as much as hearing and seeing, all the time, my master's unimaginable cruelty to the Christians. Every day he hanged one, impaled another, cut the ears off a third, and all for such petty causes, or without any cause at all. (*DQ*, part 1, 40)

We notice a similar grief in the character Saavedra in *El trato*—who in *Don Quixote* is described by the captive as a prisoner in Algiers—as he recounts being overwhelmed by tears when he first catches a glimpse of the city:

When I arrived as a captive, and saw this land, ill famed in all
the world, whose bosom conceals, protects, embraces such a throng
of pirates,
    I could not keep from weeping, so that, in spite of myself,
    without knowing what it was, I saw my gaunt face bathed in
water.[24]

As much as it evokes laughter, as I've suggested, *Don Quixote* is also
bathed in these kinds of tears and traumas. We are never sure if the tears
evoked by the narrative are the effects of laughter or tragedy. As Don
Quixote is put in a cage and forcibly carried back to his village in part 1,
for instance, we are not sure if we should laugh or cry. It is naturally amus-
ing to imagine this "Knight of the Sorrowful Countenance" confined to
a cage, but as he sounds this painful lament it elicits in the reader compassion and pity. The innocence and goodness of Don Quixote comes through
in his prayer as well: "Forgive me, beauteous damsels, if, quite inadvertently,
I have done you any mischief, for I have never harmed anyone willfully
or consciously; and I pray to God that he deliver me from this captivity"
(*DQ*, part 1, 47).

And if Don Quixote acknowledges the pain, Sancho never tires of reminding Don Quixote and the reader of the marks and bruises of their
adventures. In Sancho's mind, none of his suffering is an enchantment at all,
"but real bruises and real misery" (*DQ*, part 1, 37). Not all of this is a joke.

Yet again we are reminded how different the genre of this novel *Don
Quixote* is from anything that went before, especially the chivalry romances.
As I discussed in the prior chapter, the social conditions and histories of
criminals and prostitutes, pirates and exiles, make their way into the novel
(one glaring difference from Sor Juana's poetry). We enter a world in which
the author's hand is clear and discernible, and hence we know that we are
in a made-up scene, but we also know that not everything is enchantment
and that human beings are made of flesh and blood, vulnerable to the
bruises of history. Sancho does not let us forget that; Cervantes, the former
exile and captive in Algeria, does not let us forget.

In this sense, the "history" of Don Quixote combines the realism of
historical events and circumstances with a poetic, fictional imagination.
The problem is, however, that we are not exactly sure where one ends and
the other begins. Bruce Wardropper explains this element of *Don Quixote*
in this way: "*Don Quixote* does not disentangle the story from the history,
but points its telescope at the ill-defined frontier itself. . . . This awareness

of the ill-defined frontier between history and story, between truth and lie, between reality and fiction is what constitutes Cervantes's *Don Quixote*, is what constitutes the novel as distinct from the romance."[25]

I have already been exploring this intersection of reality and fiction in the Baroque, but I want to insist here how much the realities of history make their impact felt in Cervantes's novel. *Don Quixote* records the dark moments of history in many ways. A host of social problems appears throughout *Don Quixote*, especially in part 2, as Roberto González Echevarría explains: "The expulsion of the moriscos, the problem of Catalan brigandage, the excessive influence of the church in state affairs, the irresponsibility of the aristocracy, and corruption in government. Among those of international policy there are the Turkish threat, piracy in the Mediterranean, Catalan separatism, and the pressing problem of the state's finances."[26]

Thus, the kind of fiction that Cervantes is inventing combines the marvels of the imagination with an attention to the particularities and concrete uniqueness of human history, including all of these social problems described by Echevarría. In what might be seen as a forerunner of the genre "magical realism," the canon describes the nature of fiction in this way: "Fictional stories should suit their readers' understanding and be written in such a way that, by making impossibilities seem easy and marvels seem straightforward and by enthralling the mind, they amaze and astonish, gladden and entertain, so that wonder and pleasure go hand in hand; and none of this can be achieved by the writer who forsakes verisimilitude" (*DQ*, part 1, 47).

Later generations (e.g., the Latin American "boom") will take up many of these suggestions and compose novels that are both wondrous and amazing and equally close to the truth of history, close to the violence and nightmares of history. *Don Quixote* is the beginning.

Expulsion of the Moors from Spain

We are reminded how close *Don Quixote* is to the violence of the times when part 2 relates the circumstances and effects of the 1609 exile of Muslims from Spain. The episode of Sancho's neighbor Ricote and his daughter Ana Felix dramatizes the tragedy of the expulsion. With sensitivity to their plight—though missing a clear repudiation of the order of expulsion—the novel describes the horror that these exiles would have to endure. Ricote describes to us the pain of separation from Spain: "You well know, Sancho Panza, my dear friend and neighbor, how the proclamation that His Majesty commanded to be published against those of my race filled us all with terror and dismay; or at least it terrified me so much that I do believe my children and I were feeling the rigors of the prescribed punishment before the time allowed for us to leave Spain had elapsed. . . . Wherever we are we weep for Spain—after all we were born here, it's our native country" (*DQ*, part 2, 54).

Ricote informs us that the terror began to grip them long before their exodus. They must have known something like this was coming. Ricote goes on to describe the consequent diaspora of these Spanish citizens, their scattered existence throughout the world, their dismay at being uprooted. He mentions wandering through various lands, North Africa, France, Italy, Germany. He is sure of nothing, a confused and disoriented refugee. His language is fraught with this uncertainty. He is the embodiment of a life of errantry familiar to all persecuted and expelled communities throughout history. He says that he is on his way to find his wife and daughter in Algiers and then has plans on moving on to France or Germany, but he confesses that "we shall wait and see what God decides to do with us" (*DQ*, part 2, 54).

Ricote describes their sojourn as a kind of labyrinthine wandering, without a clear direction or purpose except to stay alive. Ricote and his people are lost and hesitant, drained of purpose. Dwelling in a labyrinth seems to suggest something like this, something akin to being caught in a puzzling web, not sure of the goal or telos of one's movement, a wanderer to no purpose.[27] Ricote's experience is evocative of an exodus into the desolate and disorienting terrain of the desert. Indeed, to bring us to our contemporary world, this experience of disorientation is quite common among immigrants crossing desert landscapes. The scorching heat of the desert sun has lethal effects and within hours can cause a person to lose their sense of direction and eventually consciousness. In this condition, the desert is not only a confusing labyrinth, but a potential gravesite. The desert of the U.S.-Mexico border is littered with the graves of immigrants and refugees of this sort, and the Jews and moriscos of Spain must have experienced a similar distress upon expulsion.

I cannot speak for every reader, but I, at least, study *Don Quixote*, or any great classic of literature for that matter, in the hopes of understanding my own age, if not my own self and its deepest desires and dreams, fears and anxieties. I want literature to help me understand the human drama and, if this proves too much for mortal man, to know its mysteries and wonders. I read the tragic events of *Don Quixote*, therefore, with an alert attention to the atrocities of our own times. Echevarría encapsulates this approach in the following way: "With the twentieth's century's ethnic cleansing, the Holocaust, mass murder by fascist and communist regimes, and exiles provoked by religious and political persecutions still so fresh in our memories, Ricote's ordeal has a distressingly familiar air. The expulsion of the moriscos, which began in 1609, like that of the Jews in 1492, shows that the consolidation of a modern state was not brought about without depredations and atrocities that would become common, and much worse, in centuries to come."[28]

Don Quixote gives us, in other words, a kind of genealogy (or archaeology) of the modern world, one with numerous allusions and warnings about the disastrous effects and entanglements in the business of empire building. And the events surrounding the various decrees of expulsion by Spain stand in Cervantes's novel as a baleful portent of worst atrocities to come in the modern period, of harsher exploits that European nation-states would visit on others in the pursuit of imperial dreams. Cervantes's great novel gives us grief in all its tragic manifestations, and it educates our soul in the lessons that only suffering can impart.

Sancho goes on to tell us about the widespread anguish and grief caused by the exile of the Moors in his own village. He even admits that it made him cry, "and I'm not normally a cry-baby." He mentions the urge that many felt to hide Ricote's daughter, but says their fear of the king's punishment prevented them from resisting the order of expulsion (*DQ*, part 2, 54). Sancho is compassionate, but not a prophet. There is no trace here of the fierce and condemnatory tone of Las Casas in facing injustice. Las Casas philosophizes with a hammer and Cervantes with the brush of an artist; Las Casas burns, Cervantes simmers. He is markedly more cautious and ironic—in a word, Baroque.

Madness and Wonder

Notwithstanding this irony, it is impossible for Cervantes's portrait of wonder to remain unaffected by the satirical criticism at the heart of *Don Quixote*. In Cervantes, the motif of wonder must endure the same deconstruction as the genre of chivalry romances—it must come tumbling to the ground (one of the last lines of the novel). Fantastic and amazing things happen to knights-errant, and at least one reason for the popularity of the chivalry romances (including or especially among adventurers in the New World) was that it fed a hunger for the marvelous and magical. If *Don Quixote* is, however, a destructive satire of these romances, then it is also a critique of the uses and abuses of wonder. Unlike the fate of chivalry, however, wonder is both deconstructed and rescued. For Cervantes, wonder has a legitimate place in the post-critical genre of the novel, but not in chivalry.

Since the publication of Michel Foucault's *Madness and Civilization*, histories of Western knowledge and reason are forced to consider the role played by madness. This approach would be rather embarrassing to Enlightenment portraits of knowledge—with their confidence in reason's purity and transparency—but to the Baroque, the human soul was a seething cauldron of strange, dark forces. Portraits of the human soul that repressed the madness were, thus, not sane in an age that felt unhinged and out of joint. Foucault knew this and saw the Renaissance and Baroque as kindred ages to his own.

In his study of madness, Foucault reminds us that the fate of the mad in the late Middle Ages eventually took the part once played by lepers. By the fifteenth century, the threat of leprosy disappeared from European consciousness and was soon replaced by a new crop of outcasts: the mad, the criminals and vagabonds. The same process of exclusion would hold for the latter: "Poor vagabonds, criminals, and 'deranged minds' would take the part played by the leper, and we shall see what salvation was expected from this exclusion, for them and for those who excluded them" (*MC*, 7).

In fact, there was an actual "ship of fools" that would carry its insane cargo from town to town. While madmen were not invariably expelled from cities, there was, in fact, a practice of exiling the mad to a wandering existence. If Ricote is exiled to a condition of homelessness in desert terrains, the mad would find their homeland on the abyss and chaos of the sea. Foucault argues that the mad come to represent the pilgrim or passenger par excellence: "Confined on the ship, from which there is no escape, the madman is delivered to the river with its thousands arms, the sea with its thousands roads, to that great uncertainty external to everything. . . . He is the Passenger *par excellence*. . . . He has his truth and his homeland only in that fruitless expanse between two countries that cannot belong to him" (*MC*, 11).

For Foucault, the mad are images of human exile, cast into the sea and its innumerable roads and currents. They perfectly represent the predicament of an age that is unmoored and adrift. There is no place for them on shore, where only the reasonable and healthy belong. The mad share with the vast sea the uncertainty and volatility of nature's violent disorder, like the chaotic turbulence of mighty waves. Or they share with Jonah the experience of being vomited from the whale and cast overboard. Their own psyche is subject to the same disorder and turmoil. A madman is no safer than a small boat caught in a tornado, cast away and lost in the vastness of the abyss.

While Don Quixote is never confined to a boat, he wanders the roads of La Mancha the way fools aboard ships once wandered the ocean, the way migrants today wander the desert. And he becomes a fugitive the way so many of them did in the Baroque period. In part 1, his freeing of the galley slaves, his killing of the sheep, the attack of the funeral procession, all result in a warrant for his arrest by the Holy Brotherhood. Now Don Quixote is more of a pícaro than he is a knight-errant. He is a criminal on the run. His companions are now the characters he runs into on the road and at the inns—galley slaves, migratory prostitutes, pícaros like the innkeeper, gangsters like Roque Guinart. The inn is a symbol of transience (especially given the holes in the dilapidated roof) and it is a refuge of transients. The mad and criminal Don Quixote is one of them.

In part 2, the themes of madness and death begin to escalate in significance and put the novel at even greater distance from the courtly love and chivalric traditions. This subtle transition marks the border (admittedly a porous one) between the Renaissance and Baroque. Foucault makes note of the changes, especially in emphasizing the growing obsession with both death and madness in the early modern periods. For Foucault, the motif of madness announces a similar anxiety felt by a culture saturated with images and experiences of death. The emptiness of the mind in madness is not altogether different than death's blank emptiness and, for this reason, much of the iconography of the period would portray the fool in company with death (Hans Holbein's piece "The Idiot Fool," for example, is part of his *Dance of Death* series). Foucault describes eloquently the intersection of these themes: "Death's annihilation is no longer anything because it was already everything, because life itself was only futility, vain words, a squabble of cap and bells. The head that will become a skull is already empty. Madness is the *deja-la* of death. . . . The substitution of the theme of madness for that of death does not mark a break, but rather a torsion within the same anxiety" (*MC*, 16–17).

Madness and death are manifestations of the same anxiety, the same emptiness threatening the coherence and stability of life. They both reveal us to be—all of us—unstable, fragile, neurotic creatures. Foucault reads madness as one of the greatest allegories of the late Middle Ages, one that sees the insanity of a world nearing a catastrophic end. Madness, thus, signals the advent of the apocalypse with all its grotesque, contorted, and monstrous images. Apocalypse describes to us a world in pieces, whose center cannot hold. The noble achievements of reason and culture are a heap of vanities and delusions; the world of society and politics, absurd. Reason and knowledge are engulfed by the night: "This is the great witches' Sabbath of nature: mountains melt and become plains, the earth vomits up the dead and bones tumble out of tombs; the stars fall, the earth catches fire, all life withers and comes to death. . . . It is the advent of a night in which the world's old reason is engulfed" (*MC*, 23).

For Foucault, however, there is a reason for this obsession with unreason and death. The Baroque artists are fascinated by madness because it is another case of an esoteric and hermetic truth that they so avidly adore. They see it as an occasion for learning—there is wisdom hidden beneath the mask of madness. The mad see what no one else wants to acknowledge: the dark and beastly ghosts within the human soul: "By an astonishing reversal, it is now the animal that will stalk man, capture him and reveal him to his own truth. . . . Animality has escaped domestication by human symbols and values; and it is animality that reveals the dark rage, the sterile madness that lie in men's hearts" (*MC*, 21).

And if madness is rampant and uncontained, it has consequences beyond the moral realm. What would this mean for knowledge? The mad sees what no philosopher or humanist wants to believe, that knowledge is empty, futile, absurd (Ecclesiastes: "He who increases knowledge, increases sorrow"; 1:18). Again, in Foucault's words, "If madness is the truth of knowledge, it is because knowledge is absurd" (*MC*, 25).

The Madness of Empire

Much of this assessment of madness in the Renaissance and Baroque appears in the pages of *Don Quixote*, but the madness was never greater and more dangerous than in the imperial imaginings of Spain. It has long been suggested that Cervantes's denunciation of chivalry masked a criticism of Spain's mad imperial project, the nation's dream of world domination. In his *Persiles y Sigismunda*, his last novel, for instance, Cervantes suggests that the defining feature of a "barbarian" is the impulse to conquer the world (*Los trabajos de Persiles y Sigismunda*, ed. Carlos Romero [Madrid: Cátedra, 2004], part 1, ii). It seems incredible to imagine that Cervantes never saw traces of barbarism in the country of his birth.

In fact, *Don Quixote* is littered with such evidence. Its most obvious manifestation is in the hopes and dreams of Sancho of becoming a governor of an island. In this scenario, Don Quixote appears in the role of conquistador in winning new worlds for Spain, and Sancho as one of his soldiers to receive land for his services (Columbus did this for his soldiers). Sancho fantasizes of owning black slaves and then selling them in Seville: "All I'll have to do is ship them over here to Spain, sell them for hard cash, buy myself a title or some official position or other, and live at my ease for the rest of my days. . . . And they can be as black as they like, I'll soon turn them into yellow gold and white silver" (*DQ*, part 1, 29).

To produce gold out of black bodies: pure madness, but a madness that is a real blight on the historical record. With this kind of nefarious business, the science of alchemy assumes a sinister purpose, now with human bodies in place of base metals. The end is strangely similar, though, to transform something ordinary into gold and silver. Here Sancho's dream of dominion is a frank and unabashed acknowledgement of the benefits of abduction and conquest. In Sancho's growing disillusionment and eventual renunciation of his role as governor, however, we see the novel's disapproval and censure for the insanity and inhumanity of world domination and conquest.

There is no doubt, indeed, that Cervantes was disillusioned and troubled by Spain's imperial designs. In a short play of his, *El retablo de las maravillas*, or "Pageantry of Marvels," Cervantes satirizes the "purity of blood" ideal in relation to Spain's budding nationalism. In *Don Quixote*, Master Pedro's puppet show (a *retablo de las maravillas*) becomes a similar farce and allegory for the novel's critical sally against the empire's madness.[29] Master Pedro's puppet show dramatizes a Spanish ballad recounting the ancient strife between Christians and Muslims in Spain. Don Quixote then recalls the role of Santiago Matamoros (St. James the Moor-Killer) as one of Spain's first great knights (*DQ*, part 2, 58). He celebrates this "great" moor-killer and it becomes clear that the ballads and chivalry romances are acting in collusion with the violence and intolerance of early modern nationalism. Here Don Quixote's madness is equivalent to the madness of Spain's imperial-colonial project. The romances provide the inspiration and allure for energizing and uniting Christians in both the Reconquista of Andalusia and the Conquista of the New World. The marvelous invoked in these histories is contaminated with violence.

All of this reminds us of the intersection of feudal traditions of chivalry with imperialism in the New World, and, consequently, the novel's criticism of both. In the course of the novel, in other words, Don Quixote resembles not only the knight of chivalry, but the conquistador of the Americas.[30] And, thus, if these two figures are conflated in *Don Quixote*, we are able to recognize the more contemporary criticism that is the novel's target. This is a crucial point that Diana de Armas Wilson emphasizes: "The satire of *Don Quixote* is aimed not at medieval chivalry—such a retrograde target *would* be quixotic—but at its early modern revivals, at the mimicry of chivalry displayed by both Don Quixote and the conquistadors."[31] As she suggests, the parody at work in *Don Quixote* is far more timely and pertinent to the events of his day, including the matters of the New World, than has often been appreciated.

According to Echevarría, Alejo Carpentier recognized these echoes of New World affairs in *Don Quixote*. When Carpentier wrote his novel about Columbus, *The Harp and the Shadow*, for example, he had in mind the Master Pedro puppet show in *Don Quixote*, and Cervantes's *El retablo de las maravillas*. In *The Harp and the Shadow*, "Columbus" sets up a show for the king and queen with his captives, the Taíno Indians, as his actors. He calls it the *gran compania de retablo de las maravillas de Indias* ("Spectacle of the Marvels of the Indies").[32] Carpentier describes Columbus's entire life as a great performance with the Indians as his buffoons:

> When I search through the labyrinth of my past, in this my final hour, I am astonished by my natural talents as an actor, as the life of the party, as a wielder of illusions, in the style of the mountebanks in Italy who, from fair to fair, brought their comedies, pantomimes, and masquerades. I was an impresario of spectacles, taking my Pageant of Marvels from throne to throne. I was a promoter of a sacred representation, carrying out, for the Spaniards who came with me, the great act of the Taking Possession of Islands that did not even consent to be known. (*HS*, 122)[33]

Columbus took his part on the stage of world history, this impresario of spectacles, by directing his own comedies and delighting his audiences with his new possessions at hand, not only new lands, but also new bodies. It did not occur to him, as it did to Las Casas and Cervantes, that this spectacle was more tragic than comedic.

So, Cervantes's great novel, thus, is a guide through the tragic conditions of history that helps us sift through and separate harmful marvels from that which is enriching, like sifting fool's gold from something more authentic. Cervantes is a miner of the myths and wonders of literature, but the novel first takes us through a path of demythologization and disillusionment before anything precious can be recovered. He wants to demolish the reader's naive attachments to the fool's gold of destructive dreams and desires in order to advance authentic portraits of wonder. He warns us of the danger of losing ourselves (and our minds) in a world of pure speculative ideas or, worse, of losing our souls in fantasies of world conquest.

A Theology of Failure

It is with Don Quixote's great failure at the end of the novel that we are given the clearest allusion to Cervantes's disillusionment with Spain's empire, both at home and abroad. Frederick de Armas sees this failure as the most obvious difference from chivalric romances (Ariosto's *Orlando Furioso* in particular). Don Quixote fails to achieve his chivalric dreams, and this failure is a mirror of Spain's own ruin. In glaring contrast to the heroic portrait of the triumphal knight (as in Titian's painting of *Charles V at Mühlberg*, for instance), Don Quixote is the antihero, the abortive and bungled knight: "The decorum and triumphal grandeur of Titian's painting are turned into the transgressive and comic-melancholic defeats of Cervantes' novel."[34] De Armas points to Titian's depiction of Charles V's powerful jaw in the painting and contrasts it with the jaw of Don Quixote (one of his first names in the novel, Quijada, means jaw). Charles V's jaw is that of a champion boxer; Don Quixote's is made of glass, infinitely fragile and decrepit. I like this observation, but I would have us devote more attention to Charles V's horse in contrast to the old, broken-down Rocinante. Or better yet, consider Sancho's beloved donkey as the extreme opposite of Titian's rendition of Charles V's powerful steed.

Strangely enough, the Renaissance and Baroque were fascinated with the image of the donkey. Frances Yates's studies of sixteenth-century Hermeticism show us how prevalent the symbolism of the ass was in this period. As an image of our protagonists, the donkey is a humiliated, stubborn, and vulnerable creature—no giant of an animal to be sure. And recall that in the biblical texts, there are many occasions when a donkey becomes a revelatory symbol. I have already mentioned the donkey that Mary rides with Joseph to the humble inn of the Nativity, but we should not forget that Jesus also rides a donkey upon his entrance to Jerusalem before being arrested and crucified. In Christian thought this has often signified the complete reversal and undoing of traditional expectations of the Messiah, empty of all pomp and circumstance, without the display of power and might. Instead of a powerful and mighty king (a Charles V), the Messiah comes in the guise of a humble and lowly peasant, on a donkey no less. The Messiah of Christianity is more like Don Quixote and Sancho Panza than the Caesars of the world.

For Cornelius Agrippa and Giordano Bruno, however, there is more to it. In their efforts to develop a hermetic philosophy, they advocate the cultivation of asinine qualities. Agrippa refers to himself as a "philosophical ass," with no pejorative meaning intended! The ass, for them, is an arcane and esoteric symbol accessible only to those armed with the mystical logic of foolishness. Bruno actually associates the symbol of the ass with two of the Sefirot of the Jewish Kabbalah, Hokmah (Wisdom) and Ayin (Nothingness).[35] In the words of Bruno, "Certain Talmudists . . . [say] that the Ass is the symbol of Wisdom in the divine *sefirot* since he who wishes to penetrate into the secret and occult recipes of it [Wisdom] must necessarily be by disposition sober and patient, and have the mustache, head and back of the Ass: he must have a humble soul, contained and squat and lack the sense to distinguish cabbage from lettuce."[36]

This passage does read as a fairly accurate description of our Sancho Panza (Don Quixote actually calls him a "beast" and "ass" in the novel). Sancho Panza is made in the mold of Bruno's ass: humble, patient, senseless, ridiculous, a cabbage head. And yet, Sancho is capable of shrewd and astute observations. He embodies both Hokmah and Ayin: wisdom disguised as ignorance, wisdom disguised as an empty head. The meeting of "wisdom" and "nothingness" in the symbol of the ass represents for Bruno a form of learned ignorance, with Ayin here indicating the negation of intellectual forms of knowledge (the nothingness of human learning). The ass represents an enlightenment that negates and destroys the logic and presumptions of cultured elites, a language of unknowing. For Bruno, it is the symbol of negative theology.[37]

In the New Testament, there are many parallels to this sensibility, especially in St. Paul (e.g., God chooses the foolish of the world to humble the mighty and proud), but one of the most striking is in the gospel of Mark, where it is the mad who recognize Jesus as Messiah while the ruling and educated classes have eyes but they do not see. The mad and poor, the lepers and blind: in the Gospels these outcasts of society are portrayed as having a privileged insight into the kingdom of God.[38]

Don Quixote and Sancho Panza are part of this tradition, where God is acquired on horses and donkeys, on roadways and inns, in wandering the wide world of human experience. In the eyes of Don Quixote, the sacred is everywhere and the world is saturated with mystery. He sees things with the eyes of a poet, or a child, where everything is fresh and extraordinary, astonishingly new. What to others is ordinary, dull, and ugly is transfigured in his imagination into something wonderful and unfamiliar (e.g., the peasant girl becomes the princess, Dulcinea; dilapidated inns become castles; windmills are giants). He represents a rupture of worn-out, tired, and hackneyed perceptions of reality. In this sense, he is an incarnation of the Baroque poet's love of the surprising. Nothing is predictable in his mind because his mind is not normal after all: it is mad.

If there is wisdom to be had in *Don Quixote*, then, it can only be achieved by appreciating the *mania* of the poetic imagination. And books are not enough in this endeavor: we need the same kind of daring of Don Quixote and Sancho Panza, the willingness to break with the familiar, to explore with abandon, to venture with courage. Eric Auerbach reminds us that if Don Quixote had not gone mad he would have never left his home. His errant lifestyle made possible his interaction and dialogue with a great diversity of individuals and communities, from aristocrats to rogues, bandits, and prostitutes: "It is on the very wings of his madness that his wisdom soars upward, that it roams the world and becomes richer there."[39] And this passion for movement and wandering in Don Quixote (as in Baroque architecture) returns us to the theme of exile, for what else is this roaming disposition but an emblem of exile? By leaving the *place* of his birth, Don Quixote enters the transitory space of *displacement*. And in this transient condition, through the ordeals and trials of life on the road, Don Quixote and Sancho Panza become somehow wiser for it.

The mad roaming of Don Quixote and Sancho Panza becomes, in fact, the occasion for them to encounter wisdom in the most odd and peculiar of individuals and circumstances (as we saw earlier with Sir John Mandeville and Cabeza de Vaca). In his short story "The Dogs Colloquy," Cervantes makes a case for the value of travel by calling to mind the great wanderer Ulysses: "Travel and meeting different people teaches men wisdom [remarks Berganza]. Scipio: That is very true. Indeed, I remember hearing a very clever master I had say that the famous Greek called Ulysses gained a reputation for prudence simply because he had travelled a lot and met various peoples from different nations."[40]

In *Persiles y Sigismunda* Cervantes makes a similar claim but now with the interesting suggestion that that the pluralism inherent in travel is a model for the writing of a novel. The variety and diversity of the novel mirrors the variety of long journeys: "Long journeys always bring with them diverse events; and since diversity is composed of different things, the events, too, are different. This is well demonstrated by our story, whose diverse events cause us to lose the narrative thread, putting us in doubt where to retie it" (part 3, 10).

In this regard, the novel, as distinct from philosophy, gathers its narrative threads from the variety and peculiarity of human experience encountered on the roads of life. The sources and material are the same for the novelist as for any intelligent and curious traveler seeking to understand life in all its idiosyncrasies. The novelist and philosopher both share the passion for wisdom, to be sure, but the novelist seeks companions among historians, ethnographers, and legal minds, for the light they shed on the singularity of human behavior. For Descartes, at least, philosophy can do without the travel experience, without ethnography and history. Philosophy is to build its castle on a foundation of general and rational principles. The specificity of history is irrelevant in this enterprise. Stephen Toulmin explains this element of Descartes well: "Early in the *Discourse on Method*, Descartes confesses that he had had a youthful fascination with ethnography and history, but he takes credit for having overcome it: 'History is like foreign travel. It broadens the mind, but it does not deepen it.'"[41]

If the historian is like a foreign traveler for Descartes, the philosopher, it seems, is content with remaining in place, secure and established where he is, not needing to take to the highways, happy with his immobility and sedentary ways. Descartes's immobility and condescension regarding the place of history in human understanding—it "broadens the mind, but it does not deepen it"—gives us an image of philosophy threatened by the confusion and uncertainty of historical becoming. Descartes wanted to build his house on firm foundations, and history must have seemed far too shaky and inadequate to support philosophy's heavy truths. Even Hegel noticed that "history" is a problem for reason. History is the sandy, desert terrain that would erode the philosopher's certitude, like termites infesting a once solid home.

In choosing the form of the novel instead of philosophy, Cervantes would tolerate the plurality and ambiguity of history, and he would, it seems to me, come to terms with the dissolution of absolute certainty, eroded in the sand by the force of the ocean's waves. *Don Quixote* would resemble a travel narrative more than philosophy, and it would capture history's fables and enigmas, its violence and madness, its sadness and laughter. The labyrinthine movement of Don Quixote is the drama of history in all its disorienting confusion, but told specifically from the perspective of failed actors. Cervantes's great novel is the voice of the failed and shunned in the age of the Baroque, the voice of those who had remained invisible in the Renaissance: exiles, criminals, vagabonds, prostitutes, madmen. Cervantes incorporates these disgraced lives into his novel the way Walt Whitman would embody American roughs in his poetry:

> Through me many long dumb voices,
> Voices of the interminable generations of slaves,
> Voices of prostitutes and of deformed persons,
> Voices of the diseased and despairing, and of thieves and dwarfs. . . .
> And of the rights of them the others are down upon,
> Of the trivial and flat and foolish and despised. . . .
> Through me forbidden voices, . . .
> Voices indecent by me clarified and transfigur'd.[42]

Cervantes already prefigured Whitman's inclusion of such disreputable voices into poetry. Cervantes's novel gives expression to an unruly and shoddy variety of sacred and profane experiences without clamoring for perfect harmony. The novel joins together a host of miscellaneous and despised truths like a wedding feast that brings together the poor, blind, and uninvited with people of privilege (Luke 14). For Cervantes to capture the ambiguity and disillusionment of the Baroque, to be, in other words, the genius of his age, along with Shakespeare, he had to choose images and scenarios of failure and depravation more than success, none more glaring and failed than his dear Knight of the Sorrowful Countenance.

As the novel approaches the end, Don Quixote returns to his village a defeated man, humbled by the Knight of the Moon (Sansón Carrasco). Upon returning to his village, Don Quixote has an ominous feeling that he will never see his beloved Dulcinea. She will remain forever absent the way Spain's empire will remain forever separated from its dreams of imperial domination. Regardless, Don Quixote's failure instigates a process of disillusionment (*desengaño*) that leads him to regain his sanity. When back in his own bed, he falls into a deep slumber. When he awakes, he is in a condition of perfect mystical lucidity and he tells his niece that God's infinite mercy has been revealed to him (*DQ*, part 2, 74). Now he tells us that he is no longer Don Quixote de la Mancha, but Alonso Quixano the Good. Now he is an enemy of Amadis of Gaul and all those profane histories of knight-errantry. His eyes have been opened and he now exemplifies Christian goodness.

Don Quixote has awakened from his long, errant dream. If Don Quixote's previous life can be explained by the enchantment of the written
word, his current condition has epiphany written all over it—he has awakened from a dark night of ignorance. His conversion is the fruit of a hard-
fought combat with the variety of life's disappointments and heartaches,
but it has given him a brief taste of peace in his restless and anguished life.

I agree with Otis Green that his conversion recalls many biblical motifs.
"*Desengaño*," writes Green, "is related to the sort of awakening to the
nature of reality that the Prodigal Son must have experienced: 'I will arise
and go to my father.' This waking to true awareness is called *caer en la
cuenta*: to have the scales fall from one's eyes, to see things as they are."[43]
The scales begin to fall from Don Quixote's eyes just as our hero falls off
his horse after being defeated by the Knight of the Moon. He later awakes
a different person, more humble and uncertain, infinitely more gentle and
good. His name change is an obvious indication that he is no longer the
same person, like Jacob becoming Israel after being wounded by God in a
wrestling match. His failure is a lesson that success could have never equaled.
Don Quixote is now a wounded soul. His experience of disillusionment
may share some features of the Platonic metanoia ("turning of one's soul"),
but the Baroque accent is apparent in Alonso Quixano's melancholy and
tragic sense of failure. And, of course, the shadow of death now darkens
Alonso Quixano's room and we know we are in the black, doleful night of
the Baroque.[44]

In other words, Don Quixote's failures bring us closer to a Christian narrative than a Platonic one. In any plain reading of the Gospels, it is almost
impossible to overlook the fact that death and failure threaten everything
in the narratives. The central characters are the failures of Rome's empire
(close to death in their poverty, sickness, and oppression), and Christ himself fails more than he succeeds. He is regularly misunderstood, denied,
mocked, and abused, and, of course, he is killed. Whatever one thinks
about Don Quixote's madness, it is hard to deny that he knew the burdens
of a cruel fate, not unlike the figures of Job or Christ. Don Quixote comes
to see himself through a mirror of misfortune and suffering: "I was born
to be a model of misfortune, the target and mark for the arrows of affliction" (*DQ*, part 2, 10).

Don Quixote may not have lived the same life, nor died the same death,
but affinities with Christ are not incredible and have been noticed by a host
of commentators throughout the centuries, from Dostoyevsky and Graham
Greene to Rubén Darío and Miguel de Unamuno.[45] In these readings, the

quest of Don Quixote is the quest of all dreamers from Jesus of Nazareth and Las Casas to Martin Luther King Jr. Their dreams are every bit as quixotic as that of Don Quixote and their hopes every bit as mad and impossible. With their desires as infinite and fierce as the sea, they sought to create rivers and streams where there were only deserts, so that righteousness would pour forth like an overflowing fountain and justice like a mighty stream. These are mad dreams for the kingdom of God, but ones deserving of our warmest sympathy, to quote Ramón Menéndez Pidal: "Don Quixote ennobles all his ridiculous life with profound mystical sentiment. . . . Don Quixote always places his hopes in God, even though he always finds his expectations frustrated. He wishes to 'improve this depraved age of ours' and to restore to it the purity of chivalry though the whole world be ungrateful to him for it. . . . The heroes' noble madness assumes a bitter, tragicomic meaning. It is a madness sustained by an ideal which, although never realized, is deserving of humankind's warmest sympathy."[46]

The ideal is still worth defending. Don Quixote's passion for justice— to free the oppressed, proclaim liberty to captives, to succor widows and orphans, defend the weak, humble the mighty—survives the experience of his disillusionment. It is evident in Don Quixote's words of advice to Sancho when he was to assume his governorship. Be merciful and humble, he tells Sancho, "possess all as if you don't possess," feed the hungry, visit the prisoners, fear God (*DQ*, part 2, 51).

Thus, as scarce as it is, and difficult to recognize in an age that witnessed so many rampant acts of injustice, Cervantes's great novel is suffused with a resilient faith in justice, in an ethic of dispossession.[47] Indeed, "faith" is the correct word here if we take it as a trust in things unseen.[48] What is more unseen in this age of the hidden God than justice? In a world in which God is hidden, justice must be accordingly hidden, wandering unknown among the nations, subject to the actual ruler of world affairs—might.[49]

Indeed, justice is as scarce in Cervantes's age as the law is ubiquitous and extensive. And Cervantes is unmistakable in this distinction—the law is not always the handmaiden of justice. He knew that the law was more like its unruly and capricious cousin, not someone that can always be trusted. In Cervantes's time as in our own, most of his readers "would have equaled justice with the world of lawyers, judges and other men of the law," writes Richard Kagan.[50] Cervantes himself, however, like his idealistic hero, answers to higher laws, to a vision of the kingdom of God. Given the current state of earthly affairs—where we dwell in lonely exile here—Don Quixote's dream of justice is naturally absurd, foolishness to the learned and wise, comprehensible only to the humble and lowly. Even when his intentions misfire—as they do throughout the novel—Don Quixote's dream of justice, this knight of faith, is part of the great heritage of Cervantes's masterpiece.

In short, though there are forms of madness—unrestricted marvels, delusional curiosities, imperial dreams—that are finished along with chivalry in *Don Quixote*, the hope of justice does not suffer the same fate. In the end, *Don Quixote* demonstrates that there are certain wonders that can be preserved and defended if only first they are subject to critique and made to travel through the fires and purgations of history. The wonders of Don Quixote's imagination—his defense of lofty, ancient values, his poetic capacity to turn plain and ugly things into precious and beautiful ones—must, in other words, be sifted through Sancho Panza's realistic filter, through his hard and unadulterated vision of human struggles in a cruel and unjust world. The tears of Sancho are symbols of this realism and they remind us how perceptive he was of the traumas of his age. And they remind us that Don Quixote's wide-eyed vision of life's wonders is flawed and unbelievable without Sancho Panza's worldly, material wisdom.

The journey of wonder in *Don Quixote*, then, is from a pre- to post-critical position. Cervantes's awareness of the nightmares of history made it impossible for him to believe in the marvels of chivalry romances or anything like them (call them New Age spiritualities in our own time). But this doesn't stop him from seeing reality as fantastic and wondrous. He will continue in this vein with his last novel, *Persiles y Sigismunda*, a novel even more fantastic and magical than *Don Quixote* (though not better). Even through his failures, or because of them, Don Quixote succeeds in reminding later generations of the wonders of reality: "In truth, ladies and gentlemen, if we reflect upon it, those who belong to the order of knight-errantry behold the most extraordinary and wondrous sights" (*DQ*, part 1, 37). Cervantes could have said the same thing of an artist like himself who imagined and brought the novel into being.

If *Don Quixote* displays Baroque pessimism, it is also a celebration of what elevates life, joy and laughter, wonder and goodness. Cervantes succeeds in joining a tragic sense of life with a carnival spirit. In this sense, the twilight of Don Quixote's life is like a fantastic sunset that surprises us with color and splendor even as night is fast approaching. Nietzsche would later embrace this tragic circus of life in the figure of Zarathustra. Zarathustra would try to teach the philosophical pessimist how to laugh and dance, to sing and love. Perhaps this is closer to what Cervantes is teaching us: "You ought to learn how to laugh, my young friends, if you are hell-bent on remaining pessimists. . . . Or, to say it in the language of that Dionysian monster who bears the name of Zarathustra: 'Raise up your hearts, my brothers, high, higher! And don't forget your legs! Raise up your legs, too, good dancers; and still better: stand on your heads!'"[51]

Sor Juana Inés de la Cruz

At the beginning of this chapter I suggested a parallel between the book-crazed Don Quixote and Sor Juana Inés de la Cruz. Though the scope of her learning is far more expansive than chivalry romances, Sor Juana exhibits a similar madness as our knight-errant. Sor Juana's passion for learning is so vehement and uncompromising that it reminds one of Don Quixote's devotion to Dulcinea, as I mentioned earlier. In Sor Juana, Dulcinea has become the figure of wisdom; Sophia has replaced Dulcinea, and Sor Juana pursues her with such a dogged and resolute will that there is madness in it—and plenty of eros. Indeed, Sor Juana invests the love of learning with such erotic intensity that it is hard not to think of her devotion as subli- mated sexual yearning. Neither Don Quixote nor Sor Juana would ever know married love and this solitary existence turned their books and imag- inations into their most steadfast companions. In Sor Juana's life, learning became a substitute for falling in love and it must have made her feel some of the same emotions—thrilling anticipation, insatiable craving, electrify- ing madness. The joy of learning must have made her feel genuinely and truly alive. In lieu of the wedding bed, then, Sor Juana blossomed with the light that flooded her eyes from the pages of books and gave her a taste of the enlightenment that was her soul's deepest desire. She discovered herself through the world of letters.

Given her historical context, it would be impossible to consider Sor Juana's peculiar kind of madness without taking into account her gender. She was quite cognizant that this fact transformed her into a strange crea- ture in the eyes of her age: "Unless it be that my sex, so peculiar, could or would be the cause for the extraordinary to be accepted as perfection."[52] Of course, what is peculiar for her age is the fact that this *female* mind and body is endowed with such a monstrous hunger for knowledge: "From the moment I was first illuminated by the light of reason, my inclination to- wards letters has been so vehement, so overpowering, that not even the admonitions of others . . . have been sufficient to cause me to forswear this natural impulse that God placed in me" (SJ, *PPD*, 11). And so we have here her own frank admission of this overwhelming devotion to letters, this madness for knowledge. For her daring refusal to succumb to the reprimands and warnings of the powers that be, Sor Juana followed Kant's maxim, "Dare to know." The result was Sor Juana's own version of "critique," a version that combined diverse genres (philosophy, theology, mythology, music, poetry, dance) into an original concoction that would challenge her epoch's laws and morals.

It must have been a rather curious muse that moved and inspired Sor Juana, a bold and risky spirit like the mysterious duende that carried Federico García Lorca to poetic heights. Sor Juana would discover quickly that the price of such daring, as Don Quixote knew, was exclusion, persecution. Sor Juana became a similar fugitive as Don Quixote, hunted and pursued for her transgressions, her refusal to keep her place and remain silent. Her mind was too restless and boundless, too gifted to remain still. When she tells us that she could not have done otherwise, she reminds one of the prophet Jeremiah, who likened the word of God to an uncontrollable fire, exploding and bursting forth. He tells us if he had been able to contain it—this flood welling up within him—he would have gladly done so to avoid being the object of scorn, persecution, and even imprisonment. No matter, he couldn't repress it however much he tried.

Sor Juana's search for knowledge will lead to similar consequences. Sor Juana is flirting with the forbidden. She will pay for her transgressions, for trespassing onto foreign lands protected and guarded by patriarchal society. She knows that she must be stealthy and cryptic in her approaches. In an age that delighted in masks and deceits, it is not surprising that as a child she would choose to disguise herself as a boy in order to pursue her love of letters. She would use Baroque strategies to subvert Baroque constraints: artifice, cunning, and concealment were her weapons of choice. She would use her wiles to pursue her forbidden love affair like a sly and wanton lover. She was, in short, a walking allegory and mystery in the New World Baroque, a strange, alien creature in this male-dominated world of learning.

Octavio Paz explains Sor Juana's alienation, in part, in terms of her illegitimacy. It is almost certain that Sor Juana was born out of wedlock and she probably never knew her father. She rarely mentions him, except to make note of her Basque ancestry. Sor Juana's father is a ghost that haunts her more from his absence than any direct presence.

Paz sees in the mythology of Hercules, so popular in the Baroque, an allegory of this illegitimacy—and, specifically, an allegory of her illegitimate hunger for knowledge, where knowledge becomes the substitute to fill the gaping void in her life. In the description of the birth of the Milky Way, described in an account by Baltasar de Vitoria, Hercules is portrayed as the illegitimate son of Jupiter and Alcmene (wife of Amphitryon). In order to confer full divinity on him, Jupiter waited until his wife, Juno, was asleep and brought Hercules to be breast-fed. Upon waking, Juno angrily pulled her breast away from the child's mouth, thus spilling her milk across the sky, forming the Milky Way (OP, 83).

In Paz's account, Sor Juana is this illegitimate child desperately grasping at this sacred milk of learning. As much as Hercules, she wants the dignity that would come from being a child of God and she saw learning as the nourishment for this possibility, for her entrance into a more dignified and, yet, forbidden world. She would be forced to use trickery and subterfuge to break through the walls of prejudice that kept her and other talented women from joining the feast of letters and erudition. Sor Juana is a thief and fugitive in this regard, but she sees in the world of learning a palliative for her illegitimacy. The world of books was a balm to her, in other words; it would heal and cleanse her of her bastardy, or, perhaps, like Don Quixote, of her loneliness. If Hercules seeks a more complete divinity, Sor Juana yearns for a dignity of the feminist sort: a vision of complete humanity for herself and for women throughout history.

As a female with such a monstrous hunger for knowledge, it is not surprising that she would endure a wide range of responses, from persecution and envy to wonder and awe at this woman with such prodigious talents. She had become one of the great marvels that the Baroque age sought to collect and display for profit. She entered center stage to play a part in another Baroque *retablo de las maravillas* (show of marvels) not unlike Master Pedro's in *Don Quixote*. In the words of Sor Juana, "What would the mountebanks not give to seize me and display me, taking me round like a monster, through by-roads and lonely places in Italy and France, which are so fond of novelties, where the people pay to see the Giant's head. . . . Not that! Your fortune you'll not find with that Phoenix, you merchants; for this is why it is confined behind thirty locks, in the convent."[53]

Sor Juana protested this commercial use of the marvelous, of becoming a demeaning character in some minstrel-like show. She will not stand for being this object of amusement and entertainment—it's degrading and dehumanizing. In her own poetic way, she suggests to us that this approach represents a monumental failure of imagination in which a caricature and stereotype precludes recognition of the full complexity and range of the female gender. Neither beast, nor clown, nor angel, the female persona plays a variety of roles, just as difficult and complex as any male persona.

And the same could be said about the demeaning representations of Indians in her age, in which natives would be assigned the inferior roles— as allegories of the passions and instincts lacking in intelligence, of the sensual without soul, of the manifold manifestations of vice. Thus, the critique of these perverse portraits of the marvelous (as in Cervantes's satire of the marvels of chivalry) is advocacy for the full humanity of the other. Whether it is Columbus's display of Indians in chains or the exhibition of Sor Juana like a freak object in a traveling circus, the effect is equally humiliating and exploitive. She will not play Caliban to Europe's desire for amusement and wealth (recall that in Shakespeare's *The Tempest*, Trinculo dreams of putting Caliban on display in Europe for financial profit; 2.2.26– 31). Like Cervantes, Sor Juana wants to see these wonder shows come tumbling to the ground.

If she is a monster, it is not of this kind. Instead, she is something like her own description of Abraham in her work *The Divine Narcissus*: she describes him as a "monster of faith" (SJ, *SW*, 108). Abraham is a monster because of his transgression of reasonable behavior, his mad willingness to sacrifice his son. Though Sor Juana was always devoted to the possibilities of reason, her life is riddled with behavior that can be described only as unreasonable and bold—again, this immoderate and savage devotion of hers, come what may, to God's gift of knowledge implanted in her soul. Her madness is her heterodoxical, errant ways, originality under the guise of tradition. Paz describes this beautifully: "She was contradiction itself, the epitome of her world and its negation. She represented the ideal of her ear: the monstrous, the unique, the singular example. She was a species in herself. Nun, poet, musician, painter, errant theologian, embodied metaphor, living conceit, beauty in a wimple, syllogism in a gown, a creature doubly to be feared: her voice enchants, her arguments kill" (OP, 274).

There is still more to the monster in her, however. It appears in the pages of her writings devoted to the native "monsters" of the Americas. Her poetry, she tells us, is infused with the spells of the Indians of her land: "What are these magical infusions of the herbalist Indians of my land that spread their spell through all the letters of my pen?" (OP, 303). In this way, she is the orphaned poet of New World orphans, the magical voice that brings to life—from a state of disrepute and neglect—the indigenous and hybrid voices of her land.

Sor Juana was one of the first poets of the New World, for instance, to experiment with native ballads written in Nahuatl (known as *tocotines*).

These ballads were accompanied by dance and had the Assumption of Mary as their theme. One of these ballads is a mixture of Spanish and Nahuatl and the other is entirely in Nahuatl. It includes black and Indian characters who express their sorrow and pain at the thought of God (through Mary) leaving them in darkness: "If you go now our beloved Lady, do not, our Mother, forget us" (OP, 317). One of the black characters, Heraclito, expresses his fear at the thought of her absence: "Let me cry. She is going and leaving us with all the work."[54] When the Indian characters enter the stage, they, too, express their sorrow at the departure of their beloved *tonantzin* (the indigenous goddess of Mexico). The ballad attempts to reassure these characters that Mary will continue to intercede on their behalf as she departs the earth. But the key consolation comes in the form of Mary's brown skin: the ballad reminds the characters that she shares their dark countenance. "Doesn't she say," Democrito remarks, "I am *morena* because the sun has shone upon me?"[55]

The reference in this line is to the Song of Songs. On many occasions, Sor Juana associates the bride of the Song of Songs with Mary. She delights in emphasizing Mary's dark skin as in this *villancico* for the Feast of the Conception of Mary:

> Black is the bride. The sun shines on her face. (Song 1:5–6)
> Ebony against a red sky. She calls herself black not for being in the
>   shade,
> Rather constantly her purity is fired in the furnace of the sun.
> Black is the bride. The sun shines on her face. . . .
> No horror of sin could have had such an effect,
> Rather the cause of her radiant color is such, she claims,
> It adds to her grace.
> Black is the bride. The sun shines on her face.
> (SJ, *SW*, 49–50)

Note that the hue of blackness in this poem is nothing like blemish or sin, but becomes a sign of radiant grace, of a purity that was fired in the furnace of God's fire/light. While the tone of these ballads is festive and cheerful (they are composed, after all, for occasions of fiesta), they also express bewilderment and confusion at the seeming absence of God, a theme more pronounced in other poems, as we shall see below. At this point, however, it is enough to notice the intersection in her poetry of Indian, African, and Spanish themes. Sor Juana's novelty is increasingly felt in this strange mixture of various cultures in her poetry. Her defiance of the pure and uncompromising borders established by the Spanish crown in the New World has an American accent to it. Sor Juana transforms the poetry of the New World into Mexican poetry. In some cases, her poetry captures the rural speech and popular dialects of Mexico:

> God bless you, my little beauty, off on your way to see God!
> I think you're just as pretty as a picture from Michoacán. (OP, 318)

Or in another case, Sor Juana sings about the untamed variety of spices in Mexico. The poem exalts Baroque diversity and multiplicity and includes a warning about cultural presumptions of purity and pride:

> Because I am so spicy, I like to bring salt,
> Five hundred varieties my voice will exalt.
> You may have a fine voice, but don't be conceited,
> For the salt of Mexico is *tequesquite* [saltpeter]. (OP, 318)

The poet's description of herself as spicy is perfectly fitting for Sor Juana, not only for the association of fiery spices and Mexico, but also as an adjective of Sor Juana's piquant, saucy, biting personality. And, of course, in this poem it also can be seen as a symbol for the delightful and delicious variety of human flavors and cultures. Regardless, Sor Juana's trial with these genres and themes (rural and popular dialects) represents an artistry that prefigures the birth of Mexico. The spell of the Indians in her poetry is the inspiration for an American consciousness. Her poetry represents the contamination and impurity of various cultures—Indian, Iberian, African— that is a defining feature of the Baroque in the New World. The Baroque strategy of gathering diverse and contradictory cultural fragments found a new voice in Sor Juana. She found her own voice, ironically, by imitating Old World figures and by translating them into a colonial context—and this by the hand of a woman. Sor Juana transformed her status as a colonial woman poet into a virtue and advantage.

Loss and Disillusionment in Sor Juana's Poetry

In his famous work, the *Solitudes*, Góngora describes a particular character, the goatherd, as "someone overwhelmed by loss."[56] This simple line captures well the particular anguish of the Baroque. As we have already seen, the Baroque is an age in mourning, overwhelmed by loss. The melancholy of the period is the response to a widespread pall that shrouds the age in a sentiment of bereavement, like a black cloth over a coffin. Consider the great Spanish poet Quevedo and his poem about the experience of desengaño. Like Don Quixote, Quevedo dreams of possessing his beloved only to late realize that what he was pursuing was nothing but a phantom: "Ah, Floralba, I dreamed that I . . . shall I say it? Yes, since it was a dream: that I possessed you, but I awakened from that sweet confusion and saw that living, I was there with death, and saw, although with life, that I was dead" (OP, 290). His eyes have been opened, only to see staring at him not Floralba but the only beloved he can be sure of, death. The man awakes from a long dream to realize, in the infinitely sad words of Don Quixote, "I was born to live dying" (DQ, part 2, 59).

These dark sentiments in Baroque Spain eventually made their way across the wide ocean to arrive in the New World, and Sor Juana received them like the mother of orphaned children. This is one of her best-known poems:

> Stay, shadow of contentment too short-lived,
> illusion of enchantment I most prize,
> fair image for whom happily I die,
> sweet fiction for whom painfully I live . . .
> 'Tis no triumph that you so smugly boast
> that I fell victim to your tyranny;
> though from encircling bonds that held you fast
> your elusive form too readily slipped free,
> and though to my arms you are forever lost,
> you are a prisoner in my fantasy.
> (SJ, PPD, 183)

This is a perfect Baroque sentiment. Like Quevedo, Sor Juana clings to her fantasy like a pleasurable dream, but writes with a lucid mind of the impermanence of love. The poet sees with clarity the sweet illusions and fictions, the ephemeral pleasures of our lives, and yet there is persistence in Sor Juana's lines to not relinquish so soon the fantasy, to stay with the dreams and myths that make it easier to bear reality (and we know, with T. S. Eliot, that humankind cannot bear too much of it). The poet is perfectly aware of the absence of the beloved, forever lost, but still clings to love's fiction. In the same poem, she calls love a "taunting fugitive" because it is forever on the run, ever elusive and obscure. We desire its presence and taste only its absence.

In this sense, Sor Juana's poetry follows the tradition of "exalting the superiority of absence over possession" (OP, 224). In some cases, she is speaking of unrequited love, as in her poems to the Countess of Paredes de Nava (Maria Luisa), where she writes of a bliss that "neither can be deserved nor dreamed of being achieved"; or of a lovesickness that forever remains unfulfilled and far removed from the object of love:

> I approach and I retire: who could find, were it not I,
> in what is absent to the eye a presence in what is afar? . . .
> I must now go, and not remain, to live far from your radiance
> where even my love-malady will serve to foster your disdain.
> (OP, 224)

This expression—"a presence in what is afar"—is a theme I have clung to in my study, and it articulates beautifully the mood of the entire age. Sor Juana is after spiritual fullness in an age that felt deeply the threat of emptiness. Her poetry expresses a profound longing for a meaningful presence even in the throng of illusions and fictions. What is absent to Sor Juana's eye (the beloved, God) is kept a prisoner of her spirit, deep in the recesses of her soul.[57]

It seems to me that this Baroque dialectic between presence and absence affects Sor Juana's theology as much as it does her secular poetry. Sor Juana was bold enough to describe God's absence in terms that echo her meditations on human love. She is coming to grips with an age that was in crisis, and this surely included the theology of the times.

Her play *The Divine Narcissus*, for example, captures the same anguish in the experience of God's absence as in her poems on human love. Recalling the language of absence in the Song of Songs, the poem describes her desolation in seeking her lost love (reminiscent of her Nahuatl ballads):

> Oh, how many days have I examined the forest, flower by flower,
>   plant by plant, as I wasted away in anguish, my heart constricted
>   with pain
> and my feet exhausted, stumbling on through time become centuries,
> through woodland become world?
> Let the ages be my witness to regions I have traveled,
> to sighs uttered, to tears in torrents shed, to labors,

shackles, prisons, suffered on many occasions . . .
O nymphs living in this flowery and pleasant meadow,
earnestly I entreat you, should you perchance encounter
the one my soul desires, tell him of my passion,
of the yearning with which love has made sick my soul.
(SJ, *SW*, 117–18)

For this exhausted and wandering soul, the context of the garden in the Song of Songs is no longer paradise, but rather the point of expulsion. The lover is in exile and estranged from her beloved. She is sick with passion, disoriented, stumbling through the vast regions of the world. Her suffering mirrors the experiences of forced labor, imprisonment, slavery. She is inconsolable. Later in the poem, the anguish felt by this outcast lover is finally soothed by the intervention of Christ (the Divine Narcissus). Sor Juana sounds these laments in the face of the death of God:

Air is cloaked in clouds. Earth shudders.
Fire flames up in agitation. Water seethes and churns.
With open mouths the dark graves now reveal
that even the dead can feel.
Respond, respond to my anguish. Bewail, lament his death!
(SJ, *SW*, 157)

While much of this may sound like a conventional account of the Christian story, Sor Juana invests it with a Baroque accent, with the feeling of loss and the weight of the world's suffering. Many of her poems resound with this tone of tragedy. Even in the midst of God's presence, she experiences an abyss of suffering. At the same moment that she ascends to the heavens by the working of grace, she is laid waste by an immense storm, as in this beautiful poem:

While by Grace I am inspired, 'tis then I near the precipice,
I would ascend unto the Sphere, but am dragged down to the
    abyss . . .
My thinking often is obscured, among dark shadows ill-defined,
then who is there to give me light when reason falters as if
    blind?
Of myself I am the gaoler, I, executioner of me,
who can know the painful pain, who can know the tragedy? . . .

I love and find myself in God, but my will His grace transforms,
turning solace to a cross, quitting port to seek the storm.
(SJ, *PPD*, 145)

The dialectic between presence and absence has many forms in this
poem: ascent/descent, heavenly sphere/abyss, light/darkness, reason/shad-
ows, grace/suffering. As much as this philosopher-poet was devoted to reason, she admits a profound confusion here, reason groping in the dark and
obscured by dark shadows. The light of reason has been extinguished and
she is dragged down to the abyss. She confesses her faith—"I love and find
myself in God"—and yet tragedy pushes her over the precipice. Her solace
wears a crown of thorns and her soul sails away from the port to the storm,
a boat tossed about by riotous waves, marooned by the deep. If grace
comes to her at all, it comes violently, in a way that echoes Greek tragedy.

Other poems escalate the sense of grief, as when she stops to consider
the vanity of physical beauty and the damaging effects of time:

> This that you gaze on, colorful deceit, that so immodestly displays
>   art's favors,
> with it fallacious arguments of colors is to the senses cunning
>   counterfeit,
> this on which kindness practiced to delete from cruel years
>   accumulated horrors,
> constraining time to mitigate its rigors, and thus oblivion and age
>   defeat,
> is but an artifice, a sop to vanity, is but a flower by the breezes
>   bowed,
> is but a ploy to counter destiny, is but a foolish labor, ill-employed,
> is but a fancy, and, as all may see, is but cadaver, ashes, shadow,
>   void.
> (SJ, *PPD*, 169)

Like a disillusioned poet, Sor Juana peels away the colors and sensual
indulgences of Baroque pageantry to discover the ashes and void behind
it all. The cruel years march on, accumulating horror on horror, soon to
defeat all efforts to lessen the force of time's destruction. It is easy to hear
many echoes of other Baroque poets in these lines, as when Góngora
reminds the young to enjoy their bright gold hair, red lips, and graceful
necks, "enjoy them all . . . before the gold and lily of your heyday, the red

carnation, crystal brightly gleaming, are changed to silver and withered violet, and you and they together must revert to earth, to smoke, to dust, to shadow, to nothing."[58]

Another poem of hers on the "malady of Hope" is particularly surprising given the belief in Christian theology that hope is one of the chief theological virtues. Sor Juana refers to it as "disguised cruelty" instead:

> Oh, malady of Hope, your persistence sustains the passing of my
>   weary years,
> while measuring my wishes and my fears your balances maintain
>   equivalence . . .
> Still Murderess is how you must be known, for Murderess you are,
> when it is owned how between a fate of happiness or strife my soul
> has hung suspended far too long; you do not act thus to prolong
>   my life
> but, rather, that in life death be prolonged.
> (SJ, *PPD*, 177)

In this account, hope dangles in front of the poet the dream of contentment and satisfaction, perhaps the fantasy of being united in love (with one's beloved or God), but the dream is forever deferred, forever unrealized—thus the pain and weariness. The anguish is deepened, not lessened, by the hope that it might be realized. The growing realization of this melancholic spirit is that this day will never come, that the force of absence holds at bay any fantasy of oneness, and that death is only more pronounced in clinging to the illusion of hope.

For sure, it is quite clear that the image of death runs through the poetry of this great Mexican dreamer. In one of her ballads, she describes sleep and dreams as practice for death: "Let him lie asleep, for he who sleeps is, in his dream, practicing for death" (OP, 323). This is an appropriate line to remember when we consider her greatest poem, *First Dream*. It is only natural that the poem begins at night, when darkness and shadows descend on the earth. It is a poem devoted to the moon goddess rather than the sun, to the experience of blindness more than light. It is a poem about dreaming, about the limits of knowledge, about poetic creativity, about wonder and awe. It is a mystical poem about an ecstatic journey (*ek-stasis*: to go beyond oneself) into the heights of the cosmos. And yet, it is about the consequent failure and descent from such a flight. In the poem, Sor Juana's soul resembles a daring yet wounded bird pulled to the earth by gravity. If the poet sets out during the night in an effort to understand the universe and God, then it is a poem about the defeat of this purpose, the dispossession of knowledge. Sor Juana, in this case, does not strike me as too different from Don Quixote. As Don Quixote is vanquished by the Knight of the Moon—thus instigating Don Quixote's disillusionment—Sor Juana is defeated by the dizzying variety and infinity of the universe. Sor Juana's spiritual journey in *First Dream* is the narrative of a wanderer and wonderer, a travel narrative of the mysterious and strange labyrinths of God, the cosmos, and the human self.

First Dream

Many have already noted some of the possible sources for Sor Juana's journey in *First Dream*. The usual suspects are Scipio's "Dream" in Cicero's *De re publica*, the *Corpus Hermeticum*, and Athanasius Kircher's *Iter exstaticum coeleste*. Though Sor Juana may have read Cicero directly, it is unlikely that she ever had her hands on the *Corpus Hermeticum*. Thus, if there is a hermetic element in Sor Juana's poem—and I think there is—it most likely came to her through the Jesuit Kircher, whom she read with care and enthusiasm (like many of his generation, Kircher was enthralled by the exotic mystery of Hermeticism). Although this tradition was believed to be Egyptian in origin, the *Corpus Hermeticum* was written in the second and third centuries in a syncretistic atmosphere of Neoplatonism, Stoicism, and other Greek schools of thought.[59]

The most obvious trace of the *Corpus Hermeticum* in Sor Juana's poem—I repeat, through Kircher's reading—concerns the motif of revelation during sleep.[60] In Kircher's "Ecstatic Journey to the Heavens," for instance, he describes the sudden appearance of a beautiful, winged angel after being overcome by drowsiness and sleep: "I am Cosmiel, minister of the God of Heaven and earth. Arise, do not fear. . . . Your desires were heard and I have been sent to show to you, insofar as may be permitted to mortal eye, the supreme majesty of the God Optimus Maximus, who shines in splendor in all his works" (OP, 364).

Although Sor Juana will be shown similar glimpses of the majesty of the universe and God, in her case there is no divine or angelic mediator (an angelic mediator is a central part of Hermeticism). In this case, her solitude is more reminiscent of Christian mysticism than Hermeticism (largely ignored by Paz).[61] Whatever the case, it seems clear that bits and pieces of these diverse fragments make their way into Sor Juana's "dream" but always with a Baroque inflection. Thus, she begins her poem under the light of the moon goddess as she describes the various creatures of the night, especially owls and bats. The poem then invokes several mythologies of metamorphoses: "humiliated, poor" Nyctimene turned into an owl as punishment for incest; three sisters turned into bats for lack of faith in Bacchus's divinity; the sorceress Alcyone turned into a fish for her treatment of suitors (she would transform them into fish); Actaeon turned into a deer for seeing Artemis in the nude. Heavily influenced by Ovid and Petrarch, the Baroque artist delighted in these mythologies of beastly transformations.

At the beginning of the poem, Sor Juana also mentions the god of silence and night, Harpokrates (the son of Isis, "Horus"). St. Augustine had called Horus the "great god of silence," and Sor Juana will find great significance in this name as the poem progresses. As the body gradually falls into a slumber, the soul ("made in His image and treasuring the spark of the Divine she bears within") is freed from its corporeal chains and begins to soar (SJ, *PPD*, 93). The soul is now ascending like an eagle toward the sun, observing the various heavenly bodies, noticing the smallness and lowliness of the earth. Although the soul dares to penetrate further into the heavens, the "wings could not breach the impregnable" (SJ, *PPD*, 95). The soul is defeated and plunges earthward, exhausted and overcome with awe. The "sun-baked" traveler is now dazed and confused, punished for "having ventured to give vision wings" (SJ, *PPD*, 97). The poet tells us that no consolation has thus been won. The first mystical voyage ends in defeat.

Sor Juana now introduces the Egyptian pyramids and describes them as material symbols of the soul's desire, a desire that she likens to a "striving flame," burning upward, toward the heavens, climbing upward toward the "First Cause" (SJ, *PPD*, 99). Thus, after the first failure, now recovered from its dizziness, the soul dares again to follow the "pyramid of the mind" in soaring to new heights.

> At this near immeasurable pinnacle, joyful, but marveling,
> marveling, yet well content, astonished,
> the supreme and sovereign Queen of all the earth—
> free of the obstacle of spectacles, the vision of her beautiful and
> intellectual eyes unclouded by any fear of distance

or resistance of opaque obstructions—cast her gaze across all
  creation;
this vast aggregate, this enigmatic whole,
although to sight seeming to signal possibility,
denied such clarity to comprehension, which (bewildered by
  such rich
profusion, its powers vanquished by such majesty)
with cowardice, withdrew.
(SJ, *PPD*, 101)

The vision she describes here begins with the seeming possibilities of
the intellect, but ends with its limitations when confronted by the impossible. She is stunned by what the soul encounters. As in the work of many
Christian mystics, it is a pure vision, up close, without mediation ("free of
the obstacle of spectacles"). It is joyous, marvelous, astonishing. As much
as this vision signals mystical immediacy, however, she is quick to stress
the vanquishing of this purpose. Bewilderment and awe is the result of
this second failure. Sor Juana compares this failure to Icarus's attempt to
ride the chariot of the sun only to find himself cast down, "drowned in the
sea of his own tears" (SJ, *PPD*, 103). Sor Juana describes the soul as observing everything, but in fact seeing nothing, "so awestruck that, surrounded
by such bounty, afloat upon the neutrality of a sea of wonder, indecisive,
it feared that it might founder; by observing everything, it saw nothing"
(SJ, *PPD*, 103).

"Afloat upon the neutrality of the sea of wonder": Sor Juana invokes
the language of wonder (*asombros*) here to illustrate knowledge's failure.
The poet had set out with the intent of growing in knowledge, but she is
so overwhelmed by the "incomprehensible variety" of the cosmos to leave
her at a loss, humbled, her mind silenced by the stunning infinity (SJ,
PPD, 103). The experience of wonder and awe is the response of the poet
to a blinding light that leaves one without vision ("It saw nothing"). It
seems to imply an a-gnostic experience, marvelous yet outside the boundaries of what can be known and comprehended.

Indeed, to recover from this dazzling vision, the soul has recourse to the
shadows to let her eyes gradually adjust. Then, yet again, heedless of her
previous failures, the soul dares to gaze directly into the light once more.
She regains her concentration "although . . . unable still to rid herself of the
prodigious awe that had paralyzed her reason, admitting only, of a blurry
concept, the hazy embryo, ineptly formed, sketching the disorienting chaos

of the confusing images her eyes beheld" (SJ, *PPD*, 107). This time her description of the soul's failure is more pronounced and tragic-sounding:

> In that tempest, the Soul's ship, sails furled,
> heedlessly subject to swirling winds and tossing,
> storm-whipped waves . . . ran hard aground, to her dismay,
> stranding her upon the mental shore, rudder shattered,
> mast badly splintered, battered keel kissing . . .
> innumerable grains of sands
> (SJ, *PPD*, 107–9)

The soul is shipwrecked and marooned, her reason paralyzed. In this stranded condition, with her sense of direction shattered, sand in her mouth, she beholds, at best, blurry and hazy concepts. Her soul is dazed and confused. The disorienting chaos of the world proves too much for reason to organize and assess. Reality is, thus, opaque and obscure. The poet-philosopher in Sor Juana is mystified, then, measuring her spiritual journey thus far only in terms of her failures. In fact, it seems to me that she does more than measure her own journey—she measures the spiritual disquiet and unease of her entire age, one that saw itself as shipwrecked, or else in drift, on the wide expanse of the sea.

To not concede defeat yet, however, the soul considers a new strategy, an Aristotelian one. Instead of beginning with the universal, she will try an inductive and empirical way, a science that begins with human experience. Indeed, the soul will begin with the "least of the inanimate" and gradually rise to the vegetal and animal worlds. "It seemed advisable to narrow her attention to one theme," to assign a more modest role to the mind's faculties (SJ, *PPD*, 109). Perhaps confidence can be achieved thus. The poet begins by considering a simple flower:

> And what of one still ignorant of why the fragile beauty
> of a flower is sometimes limned in pearl, yet others, robed—
> like streaks of carmine in the dawning sky—
> in fragrant scarlet, why it exhales its sweet perfume,
> why it unfurls its petals to the breeze, bloom upon bloom,
> each exquisite, a frilly ruff, a gorget edged in gold,
> that . . . unfolds to bare, with boastful ostentation,
> the red of Venus' blood . . .
> For if before a single object reason ignobly flees . . .

comprehension turns away, dismayed . . .
then how could one deliberate on the complexities
of a mechanism so immense.
(SJ, *PPD*, 117–19)

Even now, before a single object of the natural world, reason is dismayed. For Sor Juana, a simple flower is fragrant with mystery and is as immense and inexhaustible as the universe's most majestic parts—the sea, the stars, the mountains, a lover's body. The poet heightens our consciousness of mystery, now only deeper and more intense when confronted with the particular uniqueness of a flower. Sor Juana allows us to see the flower as a piece of nature's rarity and strangeness, its exquisite colors, stimulating scents. Before this ostentatious display of a singular flower—so proud that it unfurls its beauty to the wind—the human spirit is so exhilarated that its breath is taken away. Reason, at least, loses its breath in the face of this innocent flower and, thus, as it gasps and pants, cannot grasp or comprehend it. In meditating so closely and attentively on a simple flower, Sor Juana captures the wonder and magic of poetry: the ability to see the cosmos with youthful eyes opened for the very first time, eyes that are not yet weary, not yet tired, complacent, colorless.

Sor Juana's poem now turns its attention to the strangest and most unique creature of nature, the human being. The dialectic of ascent and descent, success and failure in the poem's spiritual journey becomes a metaphor of the human condition. She describes the human person as a creature of God, formed by the hand of Almighty Wisdom, *Sabia Poderosa Mano* (note the feminine noun for wisdom), but this creature is awfully fragile and weak. The Wondrous Maker created a being "that in its heavenward thrust seals its return to dust" (SJ, *PPD*, 113). This one line can alone be taken as the theme of the entire poem: we are a contradictory mix of angelic and beastly elements, both stellar qualities and dust—something like stardust. Sor Juana appeals to the book of Revelation for the following metaphors of human nature: "The mighty angel whose feet of fire trod earth and star alike, or the towering statue whose haughty brow gave forth a golden glow but, as we know, stood uncertainly upon two feet of clay that crumbled with the slightest trepidation. Man, in sum, the greatest marvel posed to human comprehension, a synthesis composed of qualities of angel, plant, and beast, whose elevated baseness shows traits of each" (SJ, *PPD*, 115).

The "elevated baseness" of the human condition describes for the poet the duality and ambiguity of human desire. Its "elevated" dream is nothing less than the infinite desire of the human soul to be one with God, and yet human "baseness" reveals our tragedy, how distant we remain from God. The poem tells us in classical mystical language that the purpose of humankind is to "join with the Divine through loving Union," but equally emphasizes how rarely this purpose is realized (SJ, *PPD*, 115). Humankind is meant for union, but separation and estrangement from God is what is most familiar. Human beings are failed mystics.

The emphasis Sor Juana places on this failure again reminds us how different the Baroque artist is from the Renaissance artist. As much as Renaissance Hermeticism is present in Sor Juana, there is a clear difference between figures like Pico della Mirandola, Marsilio Ficino, and Giordano Bruno. In a more pronounced way than these scholars, Sor Juana's writings include a very Jewish and Christian sensibility of human limits and fragility, impermanence and mortality. Her confession that we are "dust" serves as a perfect illustration of her distance from Renaissance gnostics. In this sense, her poetry is anti-gnostic, with a heavy dose of perspectives inherited from the Renaissance (e.g., skepticism) as well as the Reformation and Counter-Reformation (e.g., finitude, sin).

The last figure she introduces in the poem before she awakes is the bold charioteer who tried to ride the chariot of the sun, only to be struck down by Zeus. Phaethon is the bastard son of Apollo and the nymph Clymene. For Sor Juana, he is an allegory of the desires and dreams of her own soul. His daring and brave attempt, if also foolish and hapless, inspired her to persevere with a similar kind of audacity. Phaethon is the model of spiritual brazenness, of risks taken in the face of dangers and sure failures:

> Neither the watery tomb—blue sepulcher to his ill-starred ashes—
> nor vengeful, lethal, lightning flashes deter, despite their warning,
> the haughty spirit that, scorning life, rashly will seek his doom
> in order to immortalize his name. Instead, that figure serves
> as perilous exemplar, kindling in an ambitious spirit ardor to soar
>   again
> and, making of fear a form of flattery to nurture courage,
> transcribes glory from letters that spell out tragedy.
> (SJ, *PPD*, 121)

Sor Juana's biography is written all over this poem. Phaethon is a prophecy of Sor Juana's secret name and identity, one made of "letters that spell out tragedy." Sor Juana adopts the bastard Phaethon for his tragic excess, his mad and bold dreams. She would let neither the lightning flashes nor fear of falling into the watery abyss deter her from risking flight into prohibited regions of the world. She was capable of a hawk-like daring. For Octavio Paz, Phaethon is the hieroglyphic symbol of the rebel in Sor Juana: "To learn is audacity, violence: the library is transformed into open space, like the mental sky of *First Dream,* from whose height plummets the over-reaching youth, struck down by Zeus. . . . The figure of Phaethon falling from the heights, one of the most intense and least abstract images of *First Dream,* is a metaphor of her transgression: the audacity that prompts the admonition of her elders" (OP, 83).

While this is put so well, Octavio Paz misleads us in his final evaluation of the poem: he contends that it is a poem that "denies revelation. More precisely, it is the revelation of the fact that we are alone and that the world of the supernatural has dissipated" (OP, 367). Besides the fact that the imprint of God is all over the poem (as the First Cause; or the Wise and Powerful Hand; or more tenderly, in the goddess images of Diana and Isis; or Thetis, who offers the world of vegetation her "fertile maternal breasts"), this conclusion says more about Octavio Paz than about Sor Juana. There is, in fact, revelation in the poem and it comes in the form of a "presence of absence" instead of a complete lack of revelation as Paz claims. I agree with Paz in suggesting that *First Dream* is a modern poem and, thus, evocative of tragic loss and emptiness, but there is also spiritual meaning and theology in the work. Paz minimizes how profound and alluring the divine is for Sor Juana even amid experiences of God's absence. Her theology maintains a very Baroque mixture of both divine presence and absence. Paz has eyes only for the latter.

Again, the image of Phaethon speaks to us in this regard. Sor Juana's poem is filled with mystical yearnings, with an infinite desire to know and experience God. If she is disappointed and disillusioned, distraught and confused by her inability to realize this end, she does not, nevertheless, concede any final defeat. She dares again and again. Sor Juana gives us poetic images of an insatiable hunger to soar into the heavens despite human failure. Her poetry does not imply a kind of atheism in which the search for God is no longer compelling or worthwhile. The pursuit remains something sacred and meaningful for Sor Juana despite her recognition that knowledge of the cosmos and knowledge of God is endlessly beyond us. Like other Baroque artists, Sor Juana may be a traveler forever removed from the final destination, but the path she travels is still hallowed ground.

Spiritual Exercises

In fact, when Sor Juana appeals to the language of wonder, she is marking the journey toward something beautiful and alluring of this sort, something sacred that beguiles without full disclosure. Instead of repressing it, Sor Juana's skepticism (that there is no definitive, absolute knowledge) intensifies her capacity for wonder. Sor Juana turns to metaphors of wonder and awe at the precise moment when the mind is paralyzed. In this state of paralysis, when language falters, the soul's journey begins and, as we've seen, has the potential to reach unimaginable heights. This can be a moment in and out of time, an epiphany of truth outside the boundaries of reason. In this regard, if Sor Juana embraces logical contradictions and paradoxes, it is because they get us close to this timeless dimension, to the sacred territory where language cannot reach. In venturing into these lofty regions, the mind risks madness without totally succumbing to it, like a shaman who has seen the other side but returns with his ordinary faculties intact, wiser perhaps, but not deranged. No wonder Sor Juana calls paradox a "sane frenzy" (OP, 78). Paradox startles and surprises to such an extent that the mind risks losing control and becoming unhinged like a moonstruck lover in a frenzy. Baroque poetry is almost always moonstruck in this way.

Sor Juana's indulgence in paradoxes of this sort resembles Nicholas of Cusa's description of "learned ignorance": "Not a knowledge by which someone believes one knows what is unable to be known, rather such ignorance is that in which knowing is knowing that one is not able to know."[62] It seems to me that Sor Juana's own delight in paradox and her account of reason's failures call to mind many elements of Nicholas of Cusa's mystical thought—knowing that one is not able to know—especially his descriptions of the "coincidence of opposites" and learned ignorance. The Baroque poet in Sor Juana is much closer to Nicholas the Cusan than Octavio Paz would want to allow (this would ally her too closely with Christian theology!).

In Nicholas, as a case in point, wonder shares with ignorance a certain emptiness of understanding, and yet wonder has a certain fullness, or overfullness, that distinguishes it from plain ignorance. Wonder is somewhere between knowing and unknowing, the half-uncharted territory of the world, as Emily Dickinson saw perfectly:

> Wonder—is not precisely Knowing
> And not precisely Knowing not—

A beautiful but bleak condition
He has not lived who has not felt.[63]

To feel wonder is to be truly alive, to be moved by life in all its beauty and sorrow. For both Dickinson and Nicholas of Cusa, wonder and ignorance somehow belong together: they both indicate what happens when the mind reaches an impasse that it cannot think its way through, when it approaches something it can neither decipher nor fathom. If ignorance— like Foucault's madness—is the symbol of an empty head, devoid of knowledge and incapable of comprehension, wonder is the response to an emptiness that is spiritually saturated with reality, like the awe felt by a Buddhist when contemplating *sunyata*. In this sense, wonder appears on the lips of a poet when reality is so remarkable and astounding as to stun the efforts of the mind. Wonder is the signature of learned ignorance.

Make no mistake about it, however, for both Nicholas of Cusa and Sor Juana, these two great intellectuals, wonder is inconceivable without the intellect's activity. A theory of learned ignorance is not anti-intellectual. The intellect is stimulated and deepened by the passion of wonder, so that it realizes its fullest potential before it immolates itself in the face of the Unknown. Nicholas of Cusa describes it in this way: "For our intellectual spirit has the power of fire within it. It has been sent by God to earth for no other end than to glow and to spring up in flame. It increases when it is excited by wonder, as if wind blowing on fire excites its potency to actuality."[64]

Wonder is the oxygen breathing life to the fire, intensifying it, building it higher and higher to the point that the fire overwhelms the intellect and burns it up. Wonder is the negation of presumptive claims to knowledge, of the universe or God. For the Cusan, it is thus related to negative theology: "Consequently, negative theology holds that God is unknowable either in this world or in the world to come, for in this respect every creature is darkness, which cannot comprehend infinite light, but God is known to God alone."[65]

Because God cannot be known by anyone, no matter how intelligent and wise, Nicholas argued that there are lessons to be learned by the most unlearned and ordinary of individuals, wisdom to be found in lowly places. As a crushing and shameful blow to philosophers and theologians puffed up like toads, Nicholas, in fact, placed himself with the camp of the *idiotae*.[66] Negative theology, in this way, is the handmaiden of simple and humble folk, the Sancho Panzas of the world.

But the question has to arise of why would humans be given such a fierce desire to know if God is unknowable? Nicholas of Cusa considers this question with serious determination. Indeed, Nicholas takes it for granted that Aristotle's first sentence of the *Metaphysics* is convincing ("A remarkable thing: the intellect desires knowledge"), and yet he is most overwhelmed by the intellect's futility in arriving at knowledge of God. Nicholas had already begun to foresee the emergence of a form of skepticism that would give up the search for God altogether (e.g., if God is absolutely inaccessible and absent, as negative theology claims, then why continue the quest if total ignorance is inevitable?). For the Cusan, however, the search remained profound and marvelous despite the intellect's failures; indeed, it became more alluring and seductive because of its incomprehensibility, like the moon when it is hidden during an eclipse. For Nicholas, God is forever shrouded from the mind in this way, but continues to enthrall and beckon.

While Nicholas of Cusa's mystical theology does not give us the anguish of an outsider and exile—as in Cervantes and Sor Juana—the apophatic moment at the core of his writings is an extraordinary prophesy of what will come to be commonplace in the modern age: exile from truth. Karsten Harries's book *Infinity and Perspective* has very intriguing suggestions in this regard, how the feeling of exile and wonder in Nicholas—especially in light of Nicholas's ocean journey (it was in the middle of the ocean that his discovery of "learned ignorance" came to him)—describes other philosophical positions of our age:

> As Nietzsche knew so well, distance from what we take to be terra firma lets us wonder about just where we are and should be going. Thus he lets his Zarathustra address his doctrine of the eternal recurrence first to sailors, to those who, finding themselves at sea, have left behind the familiar and readily taken-for-granted. Related is Wittgenstein's observation in the *Philosophical Investigations* that philosophical problems have the form, "I do not know my way about," a remark that refers us back to Aristotle who locates the origin of philosophy in wonder. Philosophy has its origins in dislocation, in a leave-taking from what normally orients and grounds us, from the everyday world and its concerns.[67]

Throughout this book, I have been insisting on this kind of travel experience, an experience of wonder and exile that has its roots in dislocation.

In imagining ourselves in the middle of the abyss (desert or ocean), we no longer belong to our familiar homeland. When uprooted from our cultural and cosmic centeredness in this way, we become strangers to everything and everyone we once knew (including ourselves). By being displaced in this way and no longer occupying solid, secure ground, we are forced to unlearn all that we have known before and somehow tolerate or negotiate this newly discovered uncertainty and ignorance.

And this process can be painful, like drifting on the ocean if not experiencing total shipwreck. No wonder, then, that Gonzalo Fernández de Oviedo, in a perfect succinct summary of this attitude, once exclaimed, "To sail is to suffer."[68] In the Baroque, sailing is, indeed, suffering, and it is accompanied by the terrifying possibility that one may never find the port again, that one may remain adrift in the thick fog of the deep.[69] If, however, one is brave enough to enter the fog without clamoring for final answers, there can be something revealing of this condition, something like Nicholas of Cusa's "learned ignorance" or Sor Juana's vision of Infinity.

In this sense, though Sor Juana's own capacity for wonder has much of the confused ocean experience I have been describing, there is also a positive dimension to her experience of the great unknown. She does not hesitate, for instance, to call this moment—when human vision is stunned and blinded by the unknown—blessed ignorance:

> How blessed is the ignorance of one who's wise, naively so;
> he finds, in what would seem a flaw, he's blessed for what he does
> not know. . . .
> Let us learn to be ignorant.
> (OP, 298–99)

While Sor Juana's wisdom is surely not of the "naive" sort, her writings describe to us a mounting feeling of reason's shortcomings and of the limits of the philosopher's search for knowledge. In her *Respuesta*, she reminds us that though she studies with such dedication and passion, she knows nothing. My discussion of Nicholas of Cusa should make clear that I see Sor Juana's spiritual travels as describing for us a similar perspective, especially in the following way: for both of these great failed mystics, infinity has positive attributes that overwhelm the capacities of human language and understanding. There is something about infinity that draws and allures the soul to itself, a magnet whose gravitational pull is as irresistible to the soul as a fallen apple is to the earth. For the two of them, the encounter with infinity is an experience of a transcendent ultimate reality that is entirely unthinkable and yet redemptive, totally other yet beautiful.

In the wake of the intellect's conundrums (thinking the unthinkable), both Nicholas and Sor Juana envision other strategies in the search for God, especially through forms of spiritual training. A split between theory and practice, reason and spirituality, would be as foreign to Nicholas of Cusa or Sor Juana as it would be to any Hindu or Buddhist philosopher. If learned ignorance is a silencing of the mind, then, it is also an activity of the body and spirit. Its fundamental purpose unfolds in the life of the philosopher; it is an art of living before an art of thinking. As H. Lawrence Bond argues about Nicholas, learned ignorance is a *therapeia* and *cura animarum* more than the exercise of logic.[70] Hans Blumenberg describes it this way: "The language and system of metaphor that he developed for *docta ignorantia* do not represent a state of knowledge but a praxis, a method, a path to a certain sort of attitude. They draw intuition into a process in which at first it is able to follow linguistic instructions. . . . But at a certain point, the instruction passes over into what can no longer be executed."[71]

As an illustration of this path of learned ignorance, Nicholas introduces the image of the "hunting dog on the trail" and the metaphor is clear: we are always on the hunt through the trails of our lives and God is the prey that we never capture, the target our arrows never reach. We are always in the middle of the search, never to rest and arrive, but we press on, hunting with everything we have, body and soul, a total commitment. Even when theory reaches an impasse, Nicholas pushes his readers forward on the hunt and journey.

What I am suggesting about Nicholas on this matter holds for Sor Juana's writings as well: they do not represent merely a state of knowledge, but therapies of the soul, spiritual exercises. The fact that many of her writings are meditative exercises and devotional poems should be enough to confirm for us the importance of both theory and practice among her vast and diverse intellectual productions.[72] While these exercises do not have the aesthetic value of her poems or other writings, they do serve to illustrate the liturgical, meditative, and communal value of her work. In her *Respuesta*, furthermore, Sor Juana herself insisted on the importance of spiritual training and purity of life in the pursuit of knowledge: "There is one condition [in the pursuit of understanding] that takes precedence over all the rest, which is uninterrupted prayer and purity of life, that one may entreat of God that purgation of spirit and illumination of mind necessary for the understanding of such elevated matters: and if that be lacking, none of the aforesaid will have been of any purpose" (SJ, *PPD*, 21).

Perhaps to Octavio Paz, such a sentence is insignificant or irrelevant in understanding her work, but in my mind to read Sor Juana with this hermeneutical key is to see her with fresh eyes, through a seaman's eyes like Nicholas of Cusa, as one of Nietzsche's sailors, or perhaps as one of Foucault's fools, and this could open up an entire new window into her life and thought.[73]

In this sense, Sor Juana gave us not merely a body of knowledge but spiritual exercises. She gave us something that would draw the reader's soul on a journey similar to hers, one filled with life's wonders and tragedies, beauties and agonies. In the body of her work she bequeathed to us a cathedral of her vast learning, a place where secular and religious alike can gather and pay homage. Despite the failures of her life, she gave us powerful images of the joys and pains of the intellectual hunt for wisdom. Though a feeling of Sophia's absence haunts her poetry, her response is never one of despair but instead of daring and transgression. Her faith in a "presence in what is afar" inspired this resistance as much as did the examples of Icarus and Phaethon.

And, nonetheless, this daring also caused her suffering. When we consider how much her poetry and prose is disrupted by the assaults on her person and work, we realize that beneath her (widely acknowledged) physical beauty rested a troubled and unhoused soul. Her writings bear the traces of the bruises of history, of never feeling at home, of being the alien American artist she was. The Baroque motifs, particularly the sense of exile and alienation that is pervasive in the age, clearly separate Sor Juana from Renaissance thinkers and account for her ambiguous account of infinity: infinity wears two masks in her poetry, positive and alluring, and at times, confusing and fearful. Sor Juana may not have suffered the kind of exile and imprisonment experienced by Dante or Cervantes, but she writes from a similar experience of estrangement and loss, from the same well of sorrow. She lived in a world that could be as unforgiving and punishing to women poets and theologians as Dante's Florence or Cervantes's Spain.

Thus, her drive "to know" may have begun as the experience of wonder in her childhood, but it soon matured into a more disillusioned form of understanding, one that joins the infinite yearning for wisdom with a tragic sense of human failure and loss. For the contemporary reader to understand this great Mexican nun, we must follow the directions of Nicholas of Cusa, or be like one of Nietzsche's sailors and leave the terra firma behind.

Sor Juana's poetry demands that we recognize that the center cannot hold and that reason cannot secure a firm foundation. When we begin to view the earthly condition from a decentered position and from the vantage point of the other shore of Sor Juana's beloved Indies, of Don Quixote's roads and inns, of Nicholas of Cusa's ship of fools, of Dante's desert experience, then we begin to approach the learned ignorance of Sor Juana. It is at this point, lost in the middle of the desert or cast without rudder in the vast ocean—when we do not know our way about, as Wittgenstein put it—that wonder becomes our guide.

FIVE

MYSTICISM AND THE MARVELOUS IN LATIN AMERICAN LITERATURE

> From my fourth-floor room overlooking infinity, in the visible intimacy
>
> of the falling evening, at the window before emerging stars, my dreams
>
> are journeys to unknown, imagined, or simply impossible countries.
>
> —Fernando Pessoa, *The Book of Disquiet*

So, fast-forward a couple of centuries from the age of the Baroque to the twentieth century. The final piece of our story about wonder and exile in the New World concerns the emergence of a distinct style of literary representation in the twentieth century widely known as magical realism. As a child of the Baroque, magical realism carries on the fascination with the marvelous that it inherited from its parent. In magical realism, Baroque wonders assume the modern look of the novel, but the same wild and excessive desires are at play. We recognize magical realism when wonder appears so extravagantly that it has "broken its chains and gallops wild and feverish, permitting itself all excesses," to borrow from Mario Vargas Llosa.[1] Or it emerges, now with Angel Flores, when the "common and everyday" is magically transformed into the "awesome and unreal"; it is an "art of surprise."[2] We might say, then, that magical realism is the poetic version of alchemy: it takes what is base, ordinary, and predictable (what has been stripped of mystery)—love, sexuality, death, beauty, science, God—and transforms them into something golden, fantastic, astonishing. The prosaic and trivial planes of existence are interrupted by a revolution in perception and awareness. Suddenly, one is jolted out of the ordinary and you come before a new world, a world saturated with transcendence and charged with sublimity. Whatever else is meant by this term, then, magical realism is a map for the wildest sort of journeys, journeys to unknown, imagined, or simply impossible countries. It is about the discovery of remote and transcendent lands not miles away, but here and now, in front of us if not within us. For all the apparent fascination with magic, magical realism is most truly about these infinite journeys and dreams.

For this reason, the *New York Times Review of Books* got it right when first reviewing *One Hundred Years of Solitude*. The novel by Gabriel García Márquez, the reviewer wrote, "forces upon us at every page the wonder and extravagance of life." More than any other piece of literature in Latin America, this book has been synonymous with the term "magical realism," a concept that is as mysterious as the realities and events that occur in the fictional town of Macondo. As the reader enters this fantastic world, we would do well to listen to the narrator describe how the patriarch of the novel, José Arcadio Buendía, intends to educate his children: "In the small separate room, where the walls were gradually being covered by strange maps and fabulous drawings, he taught them to read and write and do sums, and he spoke to them about the wonders of the world, not only where his learning had extended, but forcing the limits of his imagination to extremes" (*OHYS*, 16).

So much of the beauty and power of magical realism is described there— magical realism is a fabulous map of uncharted terrain. It stretches the imagination to new and impossible limits. It has the same feverish fascination with the "other side of things" that José Arcadio Buendía possesses in Baroque-like abundance (*OHYS*, 6). Again, Mario Vargas Llosa explains it in this way: "In Macondo, as in the enchanted territories where Amadis and Tirant rode, the boundaries separating reality from unreality have gone to pieces. Everything can happen here: excess is a rule, beauty enriches life and it is as truthful as war and hunger."[3]

No rules, boundaries, or borders are respected in Macondo, only the rule of extravagance. *One Hundred Years* transgresses the bounds of reality in order to get to the "other side," and then it returns—like a man now acquainted with the secrets of the grave—to educate us in the very real and material fabric of our being, to make us feel down to the marrow of our bones the painful realities of hunger and war. So, in this sense, the motif of exile is as significant to magical realism as the prodigal displays of women. As much as magical realism elevates the soul and imagines marvelous journeys, the component of realism pulls us, like the gravity of suffering, like the weight of Sancho Panza, back to the earth, into the realm of history and society, culture, and politics. In this sense, magical realism is about crossing borders and undermining dichotomies: myth and history, the fantastic and political, the imaginative and realistic, faith and skepticism. Because the poetic word is loaded with prophetic power for Latin American writers, magical realism never is simply an object of beauty, never an aesthetics missing an ethics. With one hand, it exalts and extols beauty, and with the other, it recalls the tortured voices from the Latin American past. Magical realism is so valuable to my study because it is yet another example of the liminal space, the border territory between the mystical and prophetic, wonder and exile.

With this frame of mind, Lois Parkinson Zamora and Wendy Faris explain the significance of magical realism in their invaluable text *Magical Realism: Theory, History, Community*: "The essays generally agree that magical realism is a mode suited to exploring—and transgressing—boundaries, whether the boundaries are ontological, political, geographical, or generic. Magical realism often facilitates the fusion, or coexistence, of possible worlds, spaces, systems, that would be irreconcilable in other modes of fiction. So magical realism may be considered an extension of realism in its concern with the nature of reality and its representation, at the same time that it resists the basic assumptions of post-enlightenment rationalism and literary realism."[4] By inhabiting regions in-between, magical realism conjures, with wand in hand, the wonder of life while still concentrating attention on the injustices and agonies of history. If it delights in stories of metamorphosis (a feature that we saw in the Baroque), it is because it revolts against hardened and intransigent borders, ontological or geographical. Magical realism moves and shifts, mutates and migrates, the way postcolonial communities move in order to stay alive. Magical realism is the narrative rendition of the transmigration of bodies and souls, constantly shifting and negotiating identity, reincarnating itself in new circumstances, new languages, new worlds.

The fact that some of the major figures of magical realism (Alejo Carpentier, Miguel Ángel Asturias, Gabriel García Márquez) each experienced the unenviable plight of exile also gives them a unique vantage point for clarifying the dichotomies and dualities I have noted about magical realism. Living in exile can, indeed, be the occasion for a unique perspective, potentially more heterogeneous than the perspective of one who has known only one space and location. A duality and hybridity of consciousness is almost inevitable for an exile, thus making his or her consciousness a perfect model for the contradictions of magical realism. The place of exile in the work of these writers makes possible forms of thought that are nomadic, unsystematic, and decentered; forms that wrestle with the complexities and contradictions, the aporias and mysteries of human life. A consciousness of exile can make possible originality of vision by breaking down barriers and prisons of thought. Edward Said puts it in these terms: "Seeing the 'entire world as a foreign land' makes possible originality of vision. Most people are principally aware of one culture, one setting, one home; exiles are aware of at least two, and this plurality of vision gives rise to an awareness of simultaneous dimensions. . . . Borders and barriers, which enclose us within the safety of familiar territory, can also become prisons, and are often defended beyond reason or necessity. Exiles cross borders, break barriers of thought and experience."[5]

Magical realism nurtures a creativity that follows Said's description of exiles, and in doing so it meets F. Scott Fitzgerald's test for a creative intelligence: "The test of a first-rate intelligence is the ability to hold two opposed ideas in the mind at the same time."[6] Besides seeing in magical realism the kind of intelligence that Fitzgerald admires, this chapter hopes to call to mind a neglected feature of some literary accounts, namely, the theological, transcendental elements in magical realism. To neglect this element would risk incurring the denunciation of Borges when he complains of the neglect of the masters of the genre of theology in the study of fantastic literature (see chapter 1). To rectify this negligence, I follow Roberto González Echevarría and Fernando Alegría in their insistence on understanding magical realism in light of a continent saturated with religious feeling. "The magic of Carpentier and Asturias," writes Alegría, "can be a genuine metaphysical experience, that is to say, a personal commitment not only to the kingdom of this world, but also to the other world."[7] And Echevarría insists that "Carpentier's concept of the marvelous or magic rests on an onto-theological assumption: the existence of a peculiar Latin American consciousness devoid of self-reflexiveness and inclined to faith."[8] The preference I have for Carpentier's term, *lo real maravilloso*, for this reason, is clearly related not only to the theme of wonder in my study, but also to the place and influence of religious sentiments in the New World.

Magical Realism in the Latin American Literary Tradition

Magical realism did not emerge in the late 1940s and 1950s out of a vacuum. As we have already seen, the fascination with wonder permeates the continent from the time of the Conquest forward, so there are many forerunners of this movement: the narratives of the early chroniclers and missionaries of the New World, Baroque poetry and art, travel writing and anthropological reports, and literary movements such as *modernismo*, literary realism, and the avant-garde (to not confuse *modernismo* in Latin America with European and North American modernism, I will leave the term in Spanish as I go along).

According to Octavio Paz, *modernismo* developed in Latin America in the late nineteenth century as a response to the growing spiritual drought felt by many in an age when positivism and scientific empiricism reigned absolute. In the effort to be modern and Western, some of the intellectual elites of Latin America embraced a version of the Enlightenment that was even more inflexible and hostile toward religion than was its European ancestor. Religion would go into hiding and with it a host of spiritual sentiments. Thus, *modernismo* "answered spiritual needs," writes Paz. "Only because it answered needs of the soul could it be a true poetic movement. . . . Among us *modernismo* was the response needed to contradict the spiritual vacuum created by the positivistic criticism of religion and metaphysics."[9]

On many key points, *modernistas* are heirs of the Romantics, and this filiation is never more obvious than in the reverence they show for the poet and artist. The poet is the spiritual guide for the modernistas, as Cathy Jrade remarks: "As a result, the poet emerges as savior, a savior that finds transcendence in eroticism, spirituality in art, and profound knowledge in both."[10] For the modernistas, the poet is a "priest of the eternal imagination," a prophet of the divine word, mystic of radiant beauty.[11] The poet is a seer who finds harmony and rhythm in the earth and stars, a lover who feels the cosmos throbbing with erotic energy. Indeed, the cosmos is mystically, erotically charged for the modernistas and, for those who have the eyes to see it, the seductive beauty of the cosmos beckons exiled man and woman back to the source, back to our mythical origins.

As in Aristophanes's famous mythology of human origins described in Plato's *Symposium* (that primordial humans were once androgynous and perfectly whole before our fall and exile into materiality and separateness), many of the modernistas describe eros as a mystical force that can return us to our prelapsarian condition of oneness. Eros is mysticism, it draws us upward into the heavens and heals our fragmented nature by returning us to our original condition of wholeness and unity. It returns us to our source. In our end is our beginning. On this, modernistas are heirs of Neoplatonic conceptions that go back, at least, to the Renaissance, if not to the ancient world.[12]

Octavio Paz considers this insatiable, mystical yearning to lie behind so much of Latin American culture and literature:

> The history of Mexico is the history of a man seeking his parentage, his origins. . . . What is he pursuing in his eccentric course? He wants to go back beyond the catastrophe he suffered: he wants to be a sun again, to return to the center of that life from which he was separated one day. (Was that day the Conquest? Independence?) Our solitude has the same roots as religious feelings. It is a form of orphanhood, an obscure awareness that we have been torn from the All, and an ardent search: a flight and a return, an effort to re-establish the bonds that unite us with the universe.[13]

The suggestion that the sense of orphanhood has its source in religious sentiments well captures the world of many magical realists, including Asturias, Carpentier, and Márquez. Magical realism navigates in search of union with the All, but like a boat caught in a storm, it is disoriented and confused, pursuing an eccentric course that carries it farther away, lost and adrift. Think of the eccentric courses plotted by the Buendías: some characters seek the All through a fascination with esoteric and magical wonders (brought to them from the mysterious "East" by the gypsy Melquíades); or through sexual prowess and virility; some through innocence and virginity; others by the lust for power and violence; still others by religious means.

On this latter purpose, for instance, José Arcadio Buendía envisions a modern method to solve one of the oldest questions on the face of the earth: can God be seen by mortal flesh and blood? José Arcadio turns to the daguerreotype to solve this ancient query that echoes throughout the centuries, from the biblical Moses to the Greek Psyche. Like Moses and Psyche—Moses is denied the request to see the face of God and Psyche is banished from her beloved, Eros/Cupid, and forced to wander the earth after she sees the awesome face of her husband—José Arcadio Buendía's desire is frustrated, and he, too, like all the Buendías, will wander the earth without rest, without love. José Arcadio's quest is identical to that of the classic mystic: he desires the face of God, but, of course, he fails like every other character in the book. No one sees the face of God, no one finds their source, no one achieves wholeness. We are all orphans, desperate in our solitude. The mystical impulse in magical realism is, thus, impossible to disentangle from the catastrophe of exile. Amid the cruel and anguished histories of Latin America, the magical realists write of the mysteries of beauty and wonder, love and justice, without diluting the nightmares of history.

Like a migrant's journey, however, their fiction crosses the desert of exile in search of new beginnings, when "the world was so recent that many things lacked names," as *One Hundred Years of Solitude* puts it (*OHYS*, 1). Perhaps every poetic purpose has to begin here, when things lack names, so that they can be re-named, re-created, re-born. The magic of poetry starts here and brings things to life from the void, beauty out of loss and estrangement, order out of chaos. In furthering this end, modernistas preferred analogy as the proper vehicle for representing the relatedness and correspondence of all things. Like a handmaiden of beauty, analogy would serve the aesthetical imagination and strengthen the bonds that join humankind with the cosmos and the cosmos with God.

Beauty, in this sense, is the incarnate form of analogy, when analogy is embodied and arrayed in a vibrant variety of forms: the body of creation, the body of a beloved, the rapture of music, the sensuality of dance. Indeed, to keep with the last image, dance is one of the most telling analogies: dance is analogy come alive, in full animation and seductive visibility. In capturing the rhythms of the earth, dance is the perfect emblem of a harmonious cosmic order. It is through the dance of the cosmos that T. S. Eliot would find the still point (though he is no modernista, mind you):

> At the still point of the turning world.
> Neither flesh nor fleshless; neither from nor towards;
> At the still point, there the dance is.[14]

The dance is there, in the soulful footsteps of man and woman, joined arm in arm, circling round and round, keeping the time of the seasons and the constellations in their dancing. In dance, we belong to the earth, participate in its rhythms and patterns. Dance is the human counterpart of nature's harmonies, and poetry is the dance of language. Poetry moves to the beats and tempos of the turning world, to the music come from the heavenly bodies. The modernistas saw the cosmos throbbing and alive in these ways, and nothing captured this cosmic energy better than poetry.

Of course, religious rituals, liturgies, and festivals are also rhythmic movements of cosmic harmonies, but the modernistas preferred the liturgy of the word, of poetry, above religious rites and sacraments. Poetry had sacred significance. Modernistas affirmed the value of poetry in an age that esteemed only what is economically and technologically useful. To the modernistas, the modern age had harmful consequences, soul-deadening consequences. They would embrace Nietzsche's diagnosis of the modern age: "Modern man has a small soul."[15]

On the question of mystery, for instance, they charted a path far removed from the positive sciences. While positivism sought to explain and solve all mysteries, the poets of modernismo sought to make mystery more palpable, radiant, and pervasive. Modernistas pitted their own science of the human spirit over and against the hard sciences. Thus, if the goal of many late nineteenth-century governments in Latin America was to modernize their countries and to revolutionize their economies and major industries—to make their citizens (mainly, in fact, the ruling classes) wealthier and more powerful—modernistas dreamed of making their readers more soulful.

Although some of these aims and features of modernismo would appear in magical realism (especially the fascination with the wondrous and exotic, the esoteric and mystical), in Latin America the emergence of avant-garde writers, the *vanguardia*, in the first half of the twentieth century signaled an important change and disruption of the modernista project that would have importance consequences for the emergence of magical realism. The vanguardia turned the dreams of modernistas into nightmares replete with ghostly signs of death, broken images, and bloody spirits. With the avant-garde in Latin America—like modernism in Europe and the United States—the spirit of skepticism and uncertainty, of anguish and brokenness, came galloping into the picture like the horses of Picasso's *Guernica*. Instead of a celebration of beauty, harmony, and unity, modernist writings are parables of human fragmentation and incompleteness. They opted for experimental styles of writing, ones that were iconoclastic and shocking, ones that revitalized language and pushed it to new imaginative extremes, beyond ordinary rules of logic and reason, closer to dream images than ordinary consciousness. Since they view modern society as a heap of ruins and fragments, they preferred language that captured the same sentiment.

Octavio Paz argues that the shift from modernismo to the avant-garde is parallel to a transition in signs: from analogy to irony. While the modernistas saw meaning and intelligibility in nature—nature is a book that can be deciphered with the right spiritual insight—the avant-garde poet and writer is blind to such order. Nature does not communicate. The universe is silent. Paz explains the transition to irony in this way:

> Irony is the wound through which analogy bleeds to death; it is the exception, the fatal accident. . . . Irony shows that if the universe is

a script, each translation of this script is different, and that the concert of correspondences is the gibberish of Babel. The poetic word ends in a howl or silence: irony is not a word, nor a speech, but the reverse of the word, non-communication. The universe, says irony, is not a script; if it were, its signs would be incomprehensible for man, because in it the word death does not appear, and man is mortal.[16]

Paz regards irony as the avant-garde's prized possession. It is the bomb that disrupts and shatters the harmonies of the Romantics, the howl of analogy as it bleeds to death, the word becoming gibberish. Dissonance, negation, and doubt replace the trust and confidence of the modernistas. After Babel, human language has suffered dispersion and left us all in a state of vertiginous confusion. The concert of words and sounds has turned into a riotous cacophony, as if a school of children picked up a musical instrument for the first time and played at their whim—clashing cymbals, rowdy shouts, disharmonious noises. Ironic knowledge, according to Paz, is this music of disruption, not the "contemplation of otherness from the vantage point of unity, but the vision of the breaking away from unity. . . . Irony reveals the duality of what seemed whole, the split in what is identical, the other side of reason; it is the disruption of the principle of identity. Anguish shows that existence is empty, that life is death, that heaven is a desert; it is the fracturing of religion."[17]

For the vanguardia, in this light, the most appropriate images are the ones that capture the emptiness and anguish of the modern age—hence, desert, wasteland, abyss. For avant-garde writers, Romantic and modernista poetry failed because it clung too tightly to images of unity and harmony while the world (especially in the context of the world wars of the early twentieth century) decomposed into a valley of ruins—the world had become a cemetery. The avant-garde, thus, spoke to a generation well acquainted with failure and disillusioned by claims of triumphal greatness. The specters of alienation, estrangement, and fragmentation haunted the vexed souls of the avant-garde.

The avant-garde must have spoken in a convincing tone in naming the anxieties and fears of the age, because their nocturnal vision eventually found a large audience. Even the great modernista Rubén Darío would be affected by this growing uncertainty and anguish. As Jrade points out, in his later years, especially in his poem titled "Nocturno," Darío comes close to the spirit of the avant-garde. Consider this famous poem:

"You that have heard the heartbeat of the night . . . will know how to read the bitterness in my verses. I fill them, as one would fill a glass, with all my grief for remote memories and black misfortunes, the nostalgia of my flower-intoxicated soul and the pain of a heart grown sorrowful with fetes. . . . All this has come in the midst of that boundless silence in which the night develops earthly illusions, and I feel as if an echo of the world's heart had penetrated and disturbed my own."[18]

Even this modernista and his flower-intoxicated soul feels the deadening silence, the bitterness accumulating in the dark hours of the dead. The flowers have withered and turned to ashes. Darío gives us a night vision, an anguished expression of art. He insists that only those who share this grief will know how to read the bitterness of these verses. The description of the poet in this condition reminds me of the famous lines of Borges describing the writer Leopoldo Lugones, a major figure associated with the avant-garde in Latin America. Borges describes Lugones as a "man who controlled his passions and industriously built tall and illustrious verbal edifices until the cold and the loneliness go to him. Then, that man, master of all the words and all the splendor of the word, felt within his being that reality is not verbal and may be incommunicable and terrible, and went, silently and alone, to look, in an island's twilight, for death."[19]

Reality is incommunicable and terrible: this sentiment runs through much of the avant-garde like a river that snakes through the infernal underworld. As much as it receives the wonders of the New World, magical realism also inherits this legacy. This transition from magic to terror is perfectly illustrated in a key moment in *One Hundred Years of Solitude*, when the fantastic and miraculous events surrounding the life of Remedios the Beauty are interrupted by an apocalyptic destiny that replaces amazement with horror. As much as the reader is enthralled and awed by the spiritual power of Remedios (the people light candles and pray novenas in her honor), the novel abruptly returns us to the tragic realm of history where magic is wizened and powerless. After the reference to the novenas in her honor, the very next sentence in the novel is the following: "Perhaps there might have been talk of nothing else for a long time if the barbarous extermination of the Aurelianos had not replaced amazement with horror" (*OHYS*, 255). Indeed, with this sentence the sense of exile gathers momentum in the novel to eventually eclipse earlier courtships with fantasy. The seventeen sons of Colonel Aureliano Buendía are all scattered into exile and marked for death, with a cross of ashes on their foreheads. The banana company hires assassins with machetes to hunt down and kill the Colonel's sons. The apocalyptic comes to shatter mystical tranquility. There is no repose.

This transition from modernismo to the avant-garde, from analogy to irony, is not unlike what I am suggesting about the dialectic between wonder and exile, the mystical and prophetic, both key elements of magical realism. The appearance of irony in the community of the beautiful (where everything is analogically related and, finally, one) is something like, to appeal to David Tracy's theology, the sudden appearance of the prophetic-ethical-historical voice in a community of mystical aesthetes. Dynamite has the same explosive effect. The feeling of unity, harmony, and radiant beauty among the mystics is now deconstructed and fragmented by the alienating and distancing proclamation of the word: "This prophetic word comes also as stark proclamation, as kerygma, to disconfirm any complacency in participation, to shatter any illusions that this culture, this priesthood, this land, this ritual is enough, to defamiliarize us with ourselves and with nature, to decode our encoded myths, to inflict its passionate negations upon all our pretensions, to suspect even our nostalgic longings for the sacred cosmos."[20]

In the early and mid-twentieth century, the most inspired version of this alienated theology, "crisis theology," was the work of Karl Barth.[21] He exploded on to the scene and reduced to rubble all the liberal, optimistic theologies of modernity (those of Schleiermacher above all). He adopted a tone that mimicked the cries of anguish, dread, and anxiety heard throughout the world in the age of the world wars. He theologized with a hammer, demolishing and smashing any theologies that ignored the negativities and crosses of history, the mass deaths and catastrophes, past and present. He held in contempt philosophies, theologies, religions, cultures, and nation-states that would presume to be divine, anything that touted human progress and moral conceit. He noticed only decay and wreckage, within and without. The apocalyptic sensibility had suddenly come into fashion, but this for an obvious reason: the age was so menacing and dark. Theologians took notice and returned to rethink the Christian story in light of new historical tragedies.

In all, Barth saw plenty of irony in the Christian story and he introduced his age of theology to the language of negation and estrangement, to the experience of exile that the avant-garde had embraced and consumed like a medicine that is also a poison. If it is wonder that had captivated the modernistas—key to their fondness for myth, ritual, nature, and heterodoxical spiritualities—Barth sounded like the vanguardia of Latin America, filled

with existentialist agony. In speaking of modern man's solitude and estrangement, he spoke their language. In describing displaced persons and wanderers, he expressed their fears and anxieties. Barth developed a theology
of failure that would prove so prophetic and germane in an age and nation
(Barth is German) that gave birth to a pagan ethic of the strong and
mighty, and that crushed the weak and poor into the dust of the earth. For
Barth, God is hidden and infinitely other, but when he appears, it is to
gather the failures of history together, like the gathering of fallen fruit that
was never allowed to ripen.

For Barth and the avant-garde, the implications of this sensibility for
mystical desire are plain and simple: the prophetic word is the language
of estrangement not union, of proclamation not participation, negation
not belonging. All mystical searches for origins and unity are forever disrupted, and homecomings always deferred dreams. We inhabit the desert,
and our promised land is far away. Life is exile.

In examining this historical and theological context, I am suggesting
that magical realism echoes many of these themes. Like Baroque *mestizaje*,
magical realism would not be satisfied with any one tradition. It would
gather many of the fragments discussed above with promiscuity and excess,
and without any concern for logical consistency. If its children resemble
features from modernismo, there are also clear visual resemblances with
other parents, like the avant-garde just described, or else the trend toward
realism in both literature and art, to which I now turn.

History of "Magical Realism"

The concept of "magical realism" had its origins in the European world of
art criticism. It was the German art critic Franz Roh who first coined the
term in 1925 to describe the trend in European painting after Expression-
ism. Roh associated magical realism with the Post-Expressionist "recuperation of the objective world," with the artistic rendition of the world in its
most humble, common, and mundane forms.[22] This recuperation of the
ordinary dimensions of life did not, however, forsake the fantastic and
exotic; it only added to it by juxtaposing these different ways of seeing the
world. In Roh's portrait, magical realism aimed for an inclusive spirit, one
that represented transcendence through immanence, and conveyed a sense
of magic and wonder in and through the ordinary objects and experiences
of human life, not beyond them.

In making the invisible shine through the visible, the artist in this mold would revolutionize our understanding of ordinary objects. The artist would lead us to rediscover the world and, no less, ourselves in the process. "It is the discovery of a whole new world," writes Grethe Jürgens. "One paints pots and piles of rubbish and sees these things in a completely different way as if one had never before seen a pot. One paints a landscape, trees, houses, vehicles, and one sees the world anew. One discovers like a child a land of adventure."[23] Ordinary objects of this sort—garbage, trees, landscapes—are carefully scrutinized to reveal the mystery at the heart of things. Every artistic endeavor is an exploration of the depths and thickness of reality, a venture into the unknown lurking in the most familiar objects. The artist is diviner and visionary, then, one who uncovers truths and destinies in everyday things, the flight of a bird or the leaves of trees. He sees things with clairvoyance and visualizes a reality pulsating with mystery. Franz Radziwill describes the purpose of the Post-Expressionist artist in this simple line: "Art should attempt to interpret the greatest wonder of all—reality."[24] And the Italian painter Giorgio de Chirico calls to mind the ghostly contours of reality in this explanation: "Every object has two aspects: the common aspect, which is the one we generally see and which is seen by everyone, and the ghostly and metaphysical aspect, which only rare individuals see at moments of clairvoyance and metaphysical meditation. A work of art must relate something that does not appear in its visible form."[25]

To grasp the ghostly, metaphysical aspect of things is the purpose of art. Magical realists—painters and writers alike—seek out the traces and footsteps of the supernatural in our everyday lives. Their art has proved so successful and enduring because it fills us with "astonishment before the magic of Being [Franz Roh]."[26]

In Latin America, there would be many artists adept at evoking the magic of Being. Long before the term magical realism was transplanted to Latin America, Jorge Luis Borges showed signs in this direction. As early as 1926, in an essay titled "Tales of Turkestan," he described a literature in which the "marvelous and the everyday are entwined. . . . There are angels as there are trees: they are just another element in the reality of the world."[27] Literature that adhered to these principles would soon dominate the Latin American literary scene. Though Borges would never use the term "magical realism," he inaugurated approaches that would be recognizable in later Latin American literature: philosophical interrogations of what constitutes reality; metaphysical and mystical desires; labyrinthine quests;

the permeable borders between fantasy and reality, dreams and consciousness, the supernatural and empirical. Without saying much about "magical realism," Borges gave us wonders to tease the mind into deep thought, to keep us from neglecting the transcendent and uncanny dimensions of the human experience. He would follow the metaphysicians of Tlön in this regard: "They do not seek for the truth or even for verisimilitude, but rather for the astounding. They judge that metaphysics is a branch of fantastic literature."[28]

In fact, the stories of Borges do nothing if not astound. Like a mystical theologian, Borges turned the purpose of literature into a spiritual odyssey through the mazes and conundrums of human life, into a mad search for ultimate reality, be it God or some other unnamable source behind the universe. Borges would use the genre of detective stories to dramatize a search more elusive and irresolvable than that of a murder mystery. Like the character in his story "The Secret Miracle," the Jewish translator of the *Sefer Yetzirah* and author of a study of Jakob Böhme, his search is esoteric, mystical: "I am looking for God."[29] He gave us stories with magical objects—like the coin in his story "The Zahir"—that would disclose to us the dark mysteries of the universe, a microcosm or icon of the invisible truths of the cosmos. The Zahir would point us to God: "Perhaps behind the coin, I shall find God" is the last sentence of this short story.[30] Theological enigmas of this sort define him as a writer, though they are always unresolved and marked by a spirit of equivocation and indeterminacy ("perhaps"). It couldn't be any different in his universe, cloaked as it is by misty and foggy conditions, impossible to see with any clarity and precision. Rather than quelling or stifling his mystical desires, however, these obscure conditions seemed to escalate and swell them. As late as 1971, he would speak in no uncertain terms about the centrality of these subjects to his short novella that he considered his masterpiece. *The Congress*, he wrote, is about a "mystical experience I never had, but maybe before I die I'll be allowed to have it."[31]

There is no doubt, then, that Borges had a special affection for "extravagant theologies," in his words, and turned these themes into the subject of many of his stories.[32] He bequeathed to later generations of Latin American writers these obsessions with recondite, metaphysical, and mystical themes, appealing to traditions like idealist philosophy, Kabbalah, Sufism, and Buddhism. And Dante: Borges was haunted by Dante's masterpiece and he would make the final mystical vision of the pilgrim in *Paradiso* his own desperate quest. The fact that this supernova of Latin American writers would eventually go blind seems a fitting fate for someone devoted to the night, to the black magic and dark mysteries of life. He had the seer-like vision of the blind prophet Tiresias and the intuition of the anonymous mystic of *The Cloud of Unknowing*, and went looking for God in the shadows and dark clouds. At least in this way, he was a disciple of the Dark Ages more than the Enlightenment, a proponent of unknowing over knowing.

Although Borges set the tone for many twentieth-century representations of the marvelous in Latin America, it was Carpentier who explicitly adopted the term and transformed it into something genuinely American. (The first figure, however, to define magical realism in Latin American literature was Arturo Uslar-Pietri in 1948—he called it "a poetical divination or a poetical negation of reality.")[33]

Besides giving it unmistakable Latin American flavor, Carpentier's approach to magical realism is fundamental to my study because he continues Borges's fascination with transcendent and mystical themes. Carpentier's reading of magical realism, in fact, takes issue with Franz Roh's devaluation of the religious, mystical dimensions of reality. The key sentence in Roh's essay is the following: "With the word 'magic' as opposed to 'mystic,' I wish to indicate that the mystery does not descend to the represented world, but rather hides and palpitates behind it."[34] Putting aside Roh's weak understanding of mysticism (the sense of divine immanence is central to many of the classic Jewish and Christian mystics, so it is hard to understand what he means by the assumption here that mystery, for a mystic, does not reside and palpitate behind all of reality), it is clear that Roh intended to exclude a religious, transcendent dimension from the concept of magical realism.

As Roberto González Echevarría has shown, Roh's choice of the word "magic" reflected the popularity of this term in nineteenth- and twentieth-century ethnography. The term "magic" was preferred by many ethnographers to distance themselves (as scientists) from the ostensibly primitive rituals and beliefs they were studying. "Magic" describes the worldview and beliefs that the scientist does not and could not share for being too crude and superstitious. The language of magic served to distinguish Western claims to reality—certain and rational—from the myths and fictions of primitives. A Eurocentric prejudice is front and center.

To contest this portrait and use of the word "magic," Alejo Carpentier chooses another formulation for describing the wonders of the New World, *lo real maravilloso*. With the choice of *lo real maravilloso* in lieu of magical realism, Carpentier calls attention to the religious sympathies in

Latin American culture and literature. In the words of Echevarría, "The Latin American writer preferred to place himself on the far side of that borderline aesthetic described by Roh, on the side of the savage, of the believer. . . . Carpentier's concept of the marvelous or of magic rests on an onto-theological assumption: the existence of a peculiar Latin American consciousness devoid of self-reflexiveness and inclined to faith."[35]

In this key passage, Echevarría insists that there is a theological assumption in Carpentier's rendition of the marvelous and that it is grounded in this option in favor of the believer. Thus, even though there are clearly resemblances between Carpentier's rendition of the marvelous and Surrealistic view—in his first *Manifesto*, André Breton places the "marvelous" at the center of his aesthetics, and other Surrealistic themes like the cult of the irrational, the role of dreams and the unconscious, the fascination with primitive and archaic myths, the allure of fantasy and the uncanny all make their presence felt in magical realism—Carpentier is insistent about the differences, most glaring on the question of faith: "To begin with, the phenomenon of the marvelous presupposes faith. . . . There is no excuse for poets and artists who preach sadism without practicing it, who admire the supermacho because of their own impotence, invoke ghosts without believing that they answer to incantations . . . without being able to conceive of a valid mysticism or to abandon the most banal habits in order to bet their souls on the terrifying card of faith."[36]

Sounding a bit like Pascal, Carpentier describes the act of faith as a gamble fraught with risk and uncertainty, and won through long ordeals and trials—it's terrifying. Faith is synonymous with Latin American dreams and desires, groans and tears, and lo real maravilloso is full of faith in this way, sharing with faith these impossible hopes and passions. Carpentier wants his notion of the marvelous, therefore, to be informed by an understanding of faith inscribed with the blood of the people. He wants lo real maravilloso to follow in the footsteps of the colonized, oppressed folk of Latin America, down the terrifying *via dolorosa*.

Carpentier's impression of Surrealism is something else altogether: the marvels invoked by Surrealists are, in his partially unfair judgment, exotic pleasures for bored cultured elites. There is no experiential depth in their flirtations with marvels and wonders, only a superficial and hackneyed curiosity. As much as they sought to recover primitive and folk traditions, Surrealists could not feed the souls of a wide variety of people. Surrealism was for him elitist, a movement of a privileged few who found pleasure in the strange and refreshingly different cultures of non-Europeans, but always from a safe distance in Paris or New York, rarely willing or able to enter those cultures' worldviews or share their struggles. To see things from a distance, without engagement, devotion, and compassion, was, for Carpentier, pervasive among the Surrealists and is what he detested about them. They remained too objective, too scientific and dispassionate to risk intimacy with the poor of the Americas, and thus failed to understand the most vital fears and hopes of non-European peoples.[37]

In his famous essay on this topic—written as the prologue to his novel *The Kingdom of This World* in 1949—Carpentier brought the theme of spirituality to the forefront of his view of the marvelous. Whether the marvelous is manifest through Latin American popular culture, or whether it occurs in the lines and codes of a literary work, Carpentier describes the attentive observer/reader as achieving a kind of mystical clairvoyance: "The marvelous begins to be unmistakably marvelous when it arises from an unexpected alteration of reality [the miracle], from a privileged revelation of reality, an unaccustomed insight that is singularly favored by the unexpected richness of reality or an amplification of the scale and categories of reality, perceived with particular intensity by virtue of an exaltation of the spirit that leads it to a kind of extreme state."[38]

In this passage and others, echoes with theology get closer and closer, so that the experience of the marvelous begins to sound like the experience of mystical, divine revelation. Never under the control of the subject, never capable of being foreseen or predicted, never the accumulation of reason's efforts, revelation happens with a suddenness and surprise that startles and stuns, leaving one with the impression that something strange and marvelous has happened, something that has exalted the spirit and brought an unaccustomed insight to the reality of one's life, so that you feel bigger, enriched, grateful. Carpentier writes of the marvelous the way a theologian might speak of revelation.

With Carpentier, however, the marvelous is not circumscribed by the Bible or by Christian tradition. The unexpected amplification of reality that he speaks of may happen in a wide variety of contexts, and Carpentier would see the New World, in particular, as a special and unique setting for the marvelous, one in which the marvelous was present in concentrated and extreme abundance. In this light, New World cultures were a gift to the modern West, offering Europe and North America a new, surprising revelation, one that could break the stranglehold Eurocentric thought and culture had on reality. The marvels of the New World were iconoclastic, shattering and bursting the parochial barriers and prisons of European worldviews and, thus, extending and amplifying the representation of reality in the modern West. Reality suddenly became bigger, more expansive and heterogeneous.

In his estimation, then, Latin American cultures have something valuable that can educate Western reasoning in alternative visions of reality, more eccentric, more enchanting, something capable of exalting the spirit and indulging the senses. Carpentier may have learned from Surrealism on many of these themes—I repeat, more than he likes to admit—but he never tires of emphasizing its own Latin American identity. He claims that this approach to the marvelous in the Americas came to him on a trip to Haiti:

> After having felt the undeniable spell of the lands of Haiti, after having found magical warnings along the red roads of the Central Meseta, after having heard the drums of the Petro and the Rada, I was moved to set this recently experienced marvelous reality beside the tiresome pretension of creating the marvelous that has characterized certain European literatures over the past thirty years. . . .
>
> Because of the virginity of the land, our upbringing, our ontology, the Faustian presence of the Indian and the black man, the revelation constituted by its recent discovery, its fecund racial mixing [*mestizaje*], America is far from using up its wealth of mythologies. After all, what is the entire history of America if not a chronicle of the marvelous real?[39]

In contrast with the "tiresome pretensions" of Surrealism, Carpentier's direct contact with Haitian marvels—through traveling the red roads, hearing the drums beat in his chest, meeting the fecund diversity of cultures—cast a spell on him like no other and would lead him to sing of America's poetic and mythological potential. He recognizes the marvelous everywhere in his journeys through the Americas: the hybridity of cultures, the strange myths and symbols, the wild mixture of colors and spices, the zoology and botany. Carpentier's discovery of lo real maravilloso in Latin America is, thus, grounded in a kind of spiritual awakening that produced a determination in him to tell the enchanted story of its cultures, histories, and mythologies.

By the mid-1970s, Carpentier's eye was caught by another manifestation of the marvelous in the New World: the American Baroque. For Carpentier, Latin American culture would discover its soul mate in the art form known as the Baroque. As we learned earlier in my study, the art of the Baroque was embraced with enthusiasm by New World cultures, and both partners would be transformed by this relationship. Carpentier's famous essay on the Baroque, "The Baroque and the Marvelous Real" (1975), came much later than his prologue to *The Kingdom of This World*, but demonstrates well the nature of this transformation.

Extravagance and excess, plurality and mixture, ornamentation and sumptuous forms: when such features are present, Carpentier writes in this essay, you know you are close to the spirit of the Baroque. The Baroque detests empty spaces and shuns linear, harmonious lines. It is an iconic art, more visual than auditory. It is always in motion, transgressing and crossing borders: "It is art in motion, a pulsating art, an art that moves outward and away from the center, that somehow breaks through its own borders."[40] Baroque figures do not keep still, they dance and celebrate. When they settle down, it is in protean, ostentatious forms, like carnivalesque festivals, gyrating paintings, peripatetic theater, architecture that spins and whirls, ritual that dazzles.

Because it moves across borders like a citizen of all nations, the Baroque spirit does not observe restrictive laws and it does not fear contradictions or paradoxes. It casts rational rules aside and indulges in illogical mixtures, in symbiosis, mutations, mestizaje. If the Latin America Baroque prizes bombastic and intemperate art forms, it is for their ability to mirror the extravagant mixtures and spectacular hybridity of the people. These mixtures afford the Latin American with the "awareness of being Other, of being new, of being symbiotic, of being a *criollo*." Carpentier quotes Simon Rodriguez's taxonomy of the Latin American: "We have *huasos* [peasants], Chinamen and *barbaros* [barbarians], gauchos, *cholos* and *guachinangos* [people of mixed Indian and Spanish blood], blacks, browns and whites, mountain and sea-dwellers, Indians, tanned, mulattos, and *zambos* [black Indians], *blancos porfiados y patas amarillas* [stubborn whites and yellow shanks] and a world of crossbreeds: *tercerones*, quadroons, octaroons, and *saltatras* [throwbacks]."[41]

For Carpentier, these wild mixtures forced language to reinvent itself. New terms had to be created to account for this crazy diversity. Instead of clear, coherent, and logical statements, the linguistic confusion suggested by these "crossbreeds" called for formulations and terms as strange and marvelous as these new creatures. Before these mystifying identities—as unfathomable as the soul is for theologians—the mind stands in awe, silent and taciturn; or else, so that one can fully appreciate the silence and wonder, language turns profuse and exorbitant.

Like most Baroque artists, Carpentier is a devotee of aesthetics, allured and ravished by the manifold apparitions of beauty. When he considers the natural beauty of the Americas, he gushes about its anarchic and unruly forms of beauty, as if classic conceptions of beauty had come undone in the New World. In his novel *Explosion in a Cathedral*, the character Esteban marvels at the illogical and indefinable traits of nature and sea life in the Caribbean islands:

> Esteban marveled to realize how the language of these islands had made use of agglutination, verbal amalgams and metaphors to convey the formal ambiguity of things which participated in several essences at once. Just as certain trees were called "acacia-bracelets," "pineapple-porcelain," "wood-rib," . . . "iguana-stick," many marine creatures had received names which established verbal equivocations in order to describe them accurately. Thus a fantastic bestiary had arisen of dog-fish, oxen-fish, tiger-fish, snorers, blowers, flying fish; of striped, tattooed and tawny fish, fish with their mouths on top of their heads, or their gills in the middle of their stomachs. (*EC*, 178)

So much of Carpentier's vision of the marvelous resides in this description of the ambiguity of things, of things that participate in several essences at once, mestizaje in nature and culture both. The hyphen is a central and key signifier for him, a mediating element that sits on the border between two or more essences, becoming something totally other as a result, neither the one nor the other, neither this nor that.

Like the act of love—the supreme act of agglutination—the hyphen connects and combines two entities when they cannot stand alone, when reality is better captured by the lawless and unfettered union of different persons, places, and things. Baroque hyphens are wildly promiscuous in this sense, indiscriminate in their affections, haphazard in their love, a disordered mixture of various elements. The Baroque was shameless and impure when it came to its adoration of the hyphen. Like a heterodoxical icon, the Baroque hyphen indulges in deviant mixtures and fusions, joining what dogmatists fear, combinations that are immoderate and shocking. Carpentier noticed this everywhere in the New World, as if the lovesick Don Juan had affected everything with his disease, causing oxen and birds to mate with fish, iguana with trees, and, in the process, producing a fantastic bestiary that neither eye nor ear has witnessed before.

In Carpentier, then, "verbal equivocations" are necessary to account for these unprecedented and fabulous realities. When confronted with a reality so ambiguous, unclear, and indeterminate, only willful presumption insists on unequivocal language. The marvelous in Carpentier requires equivocation as mystery requires metaphor.

Later in his essay on the Baroque, Carpentier fixes his attention on another dimension of the marvelous to now include the sublime—something powerful and awe inspiring, neither beautiful nor ugly, that exceeds familiar norms: "The extraordinary is not necessarily lovely or beautiful. It is neither beautiful nor ugly; rather, it is amazing because it is strange. Everything strange, everything amazing, everything that eludes established norms is marvelous."[42]

The marvelous is not simply pleasurable or alluring, then; it can be repulsive and horrifying. The marvelous is a *mysterium tremendum et fascinans* and gathers in its grasp all that may be ugly, contorted, and chaotic in the human experience as much as the attractive and lovely. It includes so much of the wide world of human experience, sometimes painful and joyous, sometimes tragic and beautiful. The marvelous in Carpentier, in fact, resembles Nietzsche's portrait of tragic art, an elevating and affirming art, one that does not shrink before the gruesome and devastating faces of reality, one that ennobles the soul by gathering together all that is contradictory, bewildering, hard, ravishing.[43] Or else, as I've emphasized above, the marvelous includes the dark, foreboding coloring of the sublime, of an experience of wonder that has been darkened by overexposure to the black sun of exile.

While this dimension of the marvelous blossomed in the Baroque, Carpentier argued that the chroniclers and explorers were the progenitors of the marvelous, where everything is seen through a quixotic lens, filled with wonder and fantasy . . . and, no less, horror. Carlos Fuentes makes this point very well while discussing Carpentier:

> The novelty of Carpentier is that, paradoxically, he created a new language for the novel by going to the very sources of our prose: the chronicles of the conquest, the diaries of the explorers of the Americas. . . . This was a language that could just as effectively embrace the marvelous as the commonplace—mermaids swimming in the Antilles and miners mining in Potosi, the overthrow of empires and the cultivation of maize, Amazons with one breast and Leviathans with three. . . . Carpentier called it "lo real maravilloso," the "marvelous reality" of a land where the unusual is a daily occurrence.[44]

Fuentes follows Carpentier in tracing the lineage of magical realism back to the chroniclers of the New World. It is not surprising, thus, that Carpentier's final novel, *The Harp and the Shadow*, would return to the beginning of the Conquest, to the life of the Admiral, the one who wonders (*admirans*), as if he had to finish his own life and work with an account of the last days of Christopher Columbus. The novel places Columbus on his deathbed as he speaks to his confessor; and then the novel moves to the future, centuries later, as the ghost of Columbus awaits a tribunal's decision on his possible, though unlikely, beatification. There is plenty of shame and guilt in Columbus's faltering, moribund voice (the novel holds him responsible for launching the slave trade), but still flickers of pride are evident, especially as Columbus recounts his magnificent Discovery, comparing it to "an exploit full of marvels worthy of a chivalric song" (*HS*, 125). I love Carpentier's wonderful descriptions of Columbus's delight in language (and, of course, Carpentier's own delight) and of his capacity for wonder: "And so, having tried to substitute the flesh of the Indies for the gold of the Indies, seeing that I could obtain neither gold nor flesh to sell, I began—apprentice of a prodigious magician—to substitute, for gold and flesh, words. Great, beautiful, weighty, juicy, rich words, raised in the brilliant court of wise men, doctors, prophets and philosophers" (*HS*, 118). "Every gleaming, glistening, glittering, dizzying, dazzling, exciting, inviting image in the hallucinatory vision of a prophet came unbidden to my mouth as if impelled by a diabolical interior energy. Without my willing it, Hispaniola was transfigured by this inner music, so that it no longer resembled Castile and Andalusia, oh no! it grew, it swelled until it achieved the fabulous heights of Tarsus, of Ophir or Ophar, of the fabulous kingdom of Cipango" (*HS*, 102). "Each day I found more pleasure in studying the world and its wonders—and from so much study, I became convinced that I had opened secret doors to reveal marvels and mysteries unsuspected by most mortals" (*HS*, 42).

In Carpentier, Columbus is the first magical realist because he conjured words with fantastic, if diabolical, energy. When neither gold nor Indian flesh could be obtained, Columbus turned to words—juicy, dazzling words, words that opened secret mysteries. In Carpentier's reading, Columbus opened secret doors to new marvels, but in the process, he also opened Pandora's box, setting free maledictions and scourges that would plague the history of the New World. Columbus's descendants in "magical realists" would later testify to this ambiguous heritage, a marvelous one for being both amazing and disturbing.

The Marvelous in Asturias and Carpentier

Although García Márquez has dominated conversations on the topic of magical realism, Asturias and Carpentier are founding figures and have certain virtues, especially on the theme of religion, that distinguish them from García Márquez. Their significance runs deeper than the fact that their major works predate *One Hundred Years of Solitude* and that they played a key role in helping name this new style. It is far more significant that they established certain patterns of thought and expression that resonated with the religious traditions of Latin America, especially the mystical and prophetic inclinations of the New World. If there is magic at play in their works, it is for their ability to connect and join forms of thought and belief that were often severed and held apart (like the cut ropes of magic shows): myth and history, mysticism and prophecy, spirituality and politics, wonder and exile. Or else their magic is evident in their talent for suddenly making appear what was invisible to the naked eye, like the repressed and marginalized histories of the New World.

Miguel Ángel Asturias, the first Latin American novelist to win the Nobel Prize for Literature (in 1967), suggests an Indian source for these creative juxtapositions and odd marriages in magical realism. He tells us that the surprising combination of ideas or metaphors in magical realism is a lesson he learned from the study of American Indian poetry. "What I obtain from automatic writing," Asturias explains, "is the mating or juxtaposition of words which, as the Indians say, have never met before. Because that's how the Indian defines poetry. He says poetry is where words meet for the first time" (*MM*, 427). Poetry introduces words once alien and strange to one another, now suddenly joined in a new purpose. Poetry comes alive in juxtapositions of this sort, in combinations, aporias, and paradoxes that astonish for their unexpected fellowship. The location and place of poetry is always here, on the border regions, between words and elements once foreign to one another.

The extraordinary syncretism of Latin American Catholicism is pure poetry, in this regard: eclectic and polychromatic, miscegenetic and irrational. In Asturias's masterpiece, *Men of Maize*, the character Goyo Yic, a wanderer in search of his absent wife, observes syncretistic images of this kind as he comes upon a festival of the Holy Cross. Along with a crowd of Indian mothers and their babies, of men and women bent over by the weight of suffering, he turns in supplication before the cross: "The people, the color of hog-plum bark, motionless in front of those rigid timbers, seemed to plant their supplications in the holy sign of suffering with a whispering of leached ashes. . . . They looked up at the cross covered in river water, in volcanic lava, in chicken's blood, hen's feathers, maize silk, seeing it as something domestic, functional, solitary along the roads, valiant in the face of the storm, the devil and his thunderbolts, the hurricane, the plague and death" (*MM*, 121–22).

The people plant their supplications at the foot of the holy sign of suffering (Jesus in agony), as their own knees are calcified by kneeling and blood is everywhere, blood from chickens and blood from their own and God's wounds. Jesus on the cross is solitary and lonely like them, and yet valiant for enduring the storms and thunderbolts of a world so far from God. Goyo Yic is heard praying, "Festival of Santa Cruz de las Cruces! For the sake of the peasant who on your day becomes an exile from the earth and shins up your mastlike arms, your bloodied sails, to call on God" (*MM*, 131). In his anguish and desperation, amid a multitude of the poor, Goyo Yic calls on God the way all exiles have throughout the centuries. The scene of Goyo Yic before the procession and festival of the Holy Cross is replete with both Catholic and indigenous symbols. Neither the people nor Goyo Yic worries about the abundant mixtures and extravagant syncretism. They celebrate the points of intersection, the blurring of boundaries and crossing of borders. In this world, even the boundaries between humans and animals are permeable (*MM*, 220). The religious syncretism of this Catholic and indigenous world is a reflection of how Asturias describes poetry: the coming together of words and ideas that meet for the first time, in this case, the exotic wonders of Amerindian traditions with the agonizing sense of exile.

Both Asturias and Carpentier give us poetry of this kind, combining the marvels and myths of the Latin American imagination with the repressed voices of the Americas, Asturias on indigenous traditions, Carpentier on black history in the New World. And each of them knew personally the severe fate of exile. Asturias spent half of his life in exile and Carpentier was forced to flee to Europe during the Machado dictatorship in Cuba. The reality of exile helped shape and define these writers of the magical. Because they would endure and witness the political turbulence of the Americas, it is inconceivable for two of them to narrate the wonders and magic of being without attention to the dark histories of the Latin American people—the experiences of conquest and oppression, poverty and disease, war and injustice. Only in the intersection and borderlands of wonder and exile is "marvelous realism" able to fulfill the purpose established by

Asturias: to be the voice of the "most marginalized and despised peoples of the continent" (*MM*, 386).

Miguel Ángel Asturias

In the case of Asturias, the dictatorship of Estrada Cabrera in Guatemala (1898–1920) was a pivotal influence. He was raised during the reign of terror that Cabrera established in Guatemala in the early twentieth century. In his twenties, Asturias fled Guatemala—in part for fear of reprisal for his antimilitaristic articles in a weekly newspaper—and made his way to London and then to Paris. He would remain in Paris from 1924 to 1933, where he studied Amerindian ethnology at the Sorbonne and encountered many avant-garde movements, including Surrealism. It is hard to say, therefore, whether his fascination with dreams and myth comes from his contact with the avant-garde or from the indigenous cultures of his homeland. The truth is probably with both.

Regardless, one of his best-known works, *El Señor Presidente*, is a story of a ruthless and bloody dictator. The nightmarish atmosphere that suffuses the narrative is a reflection of the fear and intimidation, brute violence and injustice under the rule of tyranny. The text opens with a focus on the beggars and outcasts of this unnamed Latin American city. Asturias describes for us a community of the poor and crippled, the blind and lame, that could be found in any "third world" country. One of the characters, the Zany, is mad; another, a pregnant mute; there is a mulatto known as the Widower (who cries out at intervals, "Mother of mercy, our hope and salvation, may God preserve you, listen to us poor down-and-outs and idiots"); and many unnamed figures, joined by nothing except their common destitution.

Asturias's writing opens windows into the shacks and hovels where the poor huddle together and where the destitute seek shelter. The character of the Zany, for instance, is accused of a murder in *El Señor Presidente* and he flees for safety, ending up on a dunghill of garbage, fighting with buzzards for his life: "Above the dunghill was a spiders-web of dead trees, covered with turkey-buzzards; when they saw the Zany lying there motionless, the black birds of prey fixed him with their bluish eyes and settled on the ground beside him, hopping all around him in a macabre dance. . . . One of the boldest birds had fastened its beak in his upper lip piercing it right through to the teeth like a dart, while the other carnivores disputed as to which should have his eyes and his heart" (*SP*, 19). The Zany survives the attack and falls into a state of delirium: "As he sat beside a pool of water among the wild plants whose lovely flowers had been engendered by the filth of the town, the idiot's brain was brewing gigantic storms within its small compass. 'Eee, ee, ee, ee, ee.' The steel finger-nails of fever were clawing at his forehead. Disassociation of ideas. A fluctuating world seen in a mirror. Fantastic disproportion. Hurricane of delirium. Vertiginous flight, horizontal, vertical, oblique, newly-born and dead in a spiral" (*SP*, 20).

Asturias places the Zany where the biblical Job found himself after being dispossessed of everything precious to him, on the desolation and filth of a dunghill. His company is carnivorous buzzards that seek in the Zany nothing but a meal. In this place and others, Asturias's fragmented and delirious writing draws the reader into the mind of madness (as William Faulkner does with the character of Benjy in *The Sound and the Fury*).[45] In the case of the Zany, we see reality as he might: a confused, disordered, illusory, horrifying world. The atmosphere of the novel is saturated with this same madness, as if we are seeing reality through the eyes of beggars and the mad ("fantastic disproportion, hurricane of delirium"). Asturias writes in this condition—disassociation of ideas, illogical metaphors, fantastic images—foregoing realistic norms of reason and clarity. Asturias captures all that is unreasonable about the human experience. He chooses dream sequences, stream of consciousness, onomatopoeia, myth and magic, to interpret the nightmares and derangement of human life. In the case of the Zany, it is his vision—not a sane person's vision—that sees things as they truly are, that recognizes the insanity and horror of the dictator's reign, a wisdom born of suffering.

This representation of the madness of the world—where the innocent suffer and the wicked thrive—makes it obvious that things are not right in Asturias's universe, tragically wrong, in fact. Asturias presents us with an apocalyptic vision of a degraded and fallen world, like something out of a Goya painting. The perplexing opening to the book, "Boom, bloom, alum-bright, Lucifer of alunite," in the context of church bells summoning people to prayer, makes sense with this in mind. The world is given over to the diabolical. "Hell is emptied out. All the devils are here," as Shakespeare puts it (*The Tempest*, 1.2.214–15). There is no age of Enlightenment in Asturias's novels. The decayed world he describes—of the poor and exploited, of prostitutes, beggars, and the mad—is an age of darkness, not of light. The time is out of joint and he captures this sensibility by his disjointed, fragmented writing. Ariel Dorfman describes well Asturias's choice of writing form:

> Thus, the deformation of the world through language, the vortex of metaphors which press objects beyond all recognition, the grotesque mirror wherein time and the word come together in a monstrous copulation, is much more than a literary recourse or an influence of European surrealism. It expresses the desire to shape the horror caused by the loss of the magical, so that a demoniacal reality can be shown through the twisted, bestial lenses. . . . Magic still reigns in that world where the exiled wander without rest and with little hope, but it no longer shows any evidence of the primitive and beneficent power which sustained the dream of Gaspar Ilom [a mythical hero in *Men of Maize*].[46]

Caught in a web of horrors and political brutalities, Asturias's characters are terrified and fugitive souls on the run from the monsters in power. The efficacy of magic in this grotesque, exiled world has been irreparably damaged. The slaughter-bench that is history (Hegel) has forced myth into submission, not simply by discrediting it (an Enlightenment strategy), but by crushing and overpowering it. The world of magic is now reeling from the blows of history and the reader gets a taste of this not only by seeing reality through the twisted, bestial lenses he provides, but by attending to the words on the page that shriek and scream and come together in an unhappy, monstrous copulation.

Although there are clear Baroque precedents of Asturias's grotesque and monstrous world (I discussed these themes in earlier chapters), the loud cries for justice stretch further back in time to biblical, prophetic, and apocalyptic texts. In this, Asturias brings us close to biblical narratives, where the tears and laments of the Israelites are soothed by no magic, no balm or panacea (indeed, most of the Hebrew Bible is consistently hostile to magic). The apocalyptic tone of *El Señor Presidente* is, in fact, impossible to miss and collects the laments and complaints of the afflicted of the earth, surely echoing the voices of innocent sufferers in the Bible. One character, Nina Fedina, is unjustly incarcerated along with her infant child:

> The first night in a prison cell is a terrible thing. Nina Fedina began a hurried prayer: "Oh most merciful Virgin Mary, it is said that you never abandon anyone who has sought your aid, implored your help

and claimed your protection! So it is with confidence I turn to you, oh Virgin of Virgins, and throw myself at your feet, weeping for my sins." . . . The darkness was choking her. She could not pray any more. She slipped to the floor, stretching out her arms—they seemed very long, very long—to embrace the cold floor, all the cold floors of all the prisoners who were being persecuted in the name of justice, the dying and the homeless. She repeated the litany: *Ora pro nobis, Ora pro nobis, Ora pro nobis. (SP, 110)*

The injustices of the world described by Asturias are overwhelming, unspeakable (as they were to Las Casas). In the exiled world of *El Señor Presidente*, the world of magic and wonder is barely audible above the laments of the characters. The traces of it are hard to detect in these insane circumstances.

There are, however, a few surprising appearances of the marvelous throughout the novel. In this bleak and scorched world, Asturias interrupts the severity of the narrative with the appearance of angels. In one case, an angel comes to the assistance of the Zany as he is on the threshold of death. Along with a woodcutter, the angel aids the Zany, carrying him away from the garbage dump. The angel's comments to the woodcutter concern the Zany's helplessness and poverty: "It's obvious from his clothes that he's very poor. What a sad thing it is to be poor" (*SP*, 27). Later, when the Zany is shot and killed, a hand reached out to him and "gave him absolution and opened the door to the Kingdom of Heaven to him" (*SP*, 50). There is almost a gospel-like purity to this episode: the poor and mistreated will enter the kingdom of heaven. In the kingdom of man, ruled by the prince of darkness, the idiots of the world are scorned and abused; in the kingdom of God, they become the privileged, a radical reversal of the earthly state of affairs.

While the magical dimension is marginal in *El Señor Presidente*, the most obvious display of magical realism occurs in his masterpiece, *Men of Maize*, published in 1949, a few years after *El Señor Presidente*. The apocalyptic tone from *El Señor* continues in *Men of Maize*, but the primary focus becomes the recovery of the mythical world of the natives of Latin America. The novel captures the rhythmic beauty of the rituals and myths of indigenous communities even as it narrates the history of violence against Indian peoples. The words of the anthropologist John Murra on the novels of José María Arguedas are perfectly applicable to Asturias: the issue for Arguedas, he argues, is "how to transmit to the reader of Spanish not only compassion for the oppressed, but a sense that the latter also had a perception, a world view of their own, in which people, mountains, animals, the rain, truth, all had dimensions of their own, powerful, revealing and utterly unlike the Iberian ones."[47]

In the case of Asturias and Arguedas alike, literature is the modern translation of the ancient wisdom of indigenous cultures. Literature gathers the ruins and fragments of lost and marginal histories. Writing is an act of remembrance and resistance. Writing exposes the harsh truth of the continent, that the "wounds of the Conquest have still not healed."[48] Mario Vargas Llosa sums up well the literary achievement of *Men of Maize*: the book is rooted in "a lacerating experience, the history of the oppression and destruction of primitive cultures, from which it takes all its wisdom, myths, characters, poetry, and extravagance."[49]

Thus, the inspiration for *Men of Maize* comes from the poetry and myth of ancient texts like the Mayan *Popol Vuh*, the *Chilam Balam*, the *Legend of the Suns*, and other indigenous narratives. Asturias was thoroughly familiar with these texts from his studies of Amerindian ethnology at the Sorbonne (he helped translate the *Popol Vuh* into Spanish). Even the style of writing in *Men of Maize* is indebted to the poetry and myth of ancient Indian narratives. In numerous places—especially at the beginning, where Asturias brings us into the magical world of ancient Indian traditions—the language itself is evocative of myth and ritual. The cadences of the language, the presence of dreams, the depiction of an animistic world, the onomatopoetic expressions, all these elements transport the reader to a time and culture governed by myth and magic.

Reading Asturias, in fact, gives one the feeling of what it is like to read the *Popol Vuh* or any other ancient Indian narrative. The words and metaphors impart and evoke a feeling of the sacred. Read aloud, the words sound as if they belong to a ritual or ceremony. They have religious significance, as Asturias himself once explained in relation to *Men of Maize*: "In *Hombres de Maíz* the spoken word has a religious significance. The characters of the book are never alone, but always surrounded by the great voices of nature, the voices of the rivers, the mountains. . . . Words are fundamental, magic elements endowed not only with the powers of witchcraft and enchantment but also with miraculous healing powers."[50]

As case in point, the book begins with the prophetic calling of Gaspar Ilom, a Mayan chief. The earth summons Gaspar through a dream to rise up and resist the exploitive encroachment by outsiders onto their lands. At first, the earth accuses Gaspar of failure of nerve, the way the God of the Hebrew Bible accuses the prophets of faithlessness: "Gaspar Ilom lets them steal the sleep from the eyes of the land of Ilom. Gaspar Ilom lets them hack away the eyelids of the land of Ilom with axes. Gaspar Ilom lets them scorch the leafy eyelashes of the land of Ilom with fires that turn the moon to furious red" (*MM*, 7). The earth demands retribution but it speaks with the eloquence of a ritual: "The earth falls dreaming from the stars, but awakens in what once were green mountains, now the barren peaks of Ilom, where the guarda's song wails out across the ravines, the hawk swoops headlong, the great ants march, the dove sighs, and where sleeps, with his mat, his shadow, and his woman, he who should hack the eyelids of those who fell the trees, singe the eyelids of those who burn the forest, and chill the bodies of those who dam the waters of the river" (*MM*, 7). The earth calls Gaspar to punish those who are violating the earth, who make barren lands out of once verdant mountains, who burn the lands in order to plant corn for sale. These violators profane what is sacred, and they do violence to native peoples, people of maize.

Behind the magic of his poetry, Asturias describes with realistic detail the modernizing trends of many Latin American governments of the late nineteenth and twentieth centuries. Allied with scientific positivism, the ruling oligarchies were seeking to liberalize Latin American governments and economies by welcoming capitalist enterprise from "first world" countries. The interests and well-being of the indigenous were seldom if ever considered by these modernizing trends. Asturias shows us the ruinous effects of these efforts, the disruption and destruction of Indian lands and cultures by the modern forces of imperialism and capitalism.[51] As one of the characters comments, this version of progress advances "with the tread of the conqueror" (*MM*, 237).

But in Asturias's great novel, the native peoples are not passive and inactive in the face of these changes. They resist. Though initially the reluctant prophet, Gaspar Ilom eventually awakens and begins guerilla warfare against the government and, in this process, becomes a mythical hero, a man of maize, a seer and prophet:

> Gaspar is invincible, said the old folk of the town. The rabbits with maize-leaf ears protect Gaspar, and for the yellow rabbits with maize-leaf ears there are no secrets, no dangers, no distances. Gaspar's hide is mamey skin and gold his blood—"great is his strength," "great is his dance"—and his teeth, pumice stones when he laughs and flint stones when he bites or grinds them, are his heart in his mouth, as

his heelbone is his heart in his feet as he walks. . . . Gaspar walks for all who have walked, all who walk and all who will walk. Gaspar talks for all who have talked, all who talk and all who will talk. (*MM*, 12)

Gold is in his blood and it is the secret of his strength, the key to his invincibility like Samson with his hair. Gaspar walks for all exiled natives, dancing as he goes along, and he talks for them, like Asturias does, with a wizardly command of the tongue. In Gaspar's dance, in Gaspar's walk, we have the summation of all Indian long walks and displaced histories.

Like any biblical prophet, nonetheless, Gaspar turns out to be quite human: he will succumb to death after his enemies poison him. Following the death of Gaspar, all of creation itself cries out in a sequence of dirges: "After the death of Gaspar Ilom the firefly wizards went up onto the Mountain of the Deaf Ones and wept. Five days and nights they wept, with their tongues crossed through by spines, and on the sixth day, on the evening before the day of curses, they kept a silence of dried blood in their mouths, and on the seventh day they made the auguries" (*MM*, 27).

The failure of Gaspar the prophet brings the novel into an apocalyptic realm (when prophecy fails, apocalypticism takes over), where the forces of nature (hurricane and earthquake, owls and fireflies) become central characters in the justice sought on behalf of Gaspar and the native peoples. An apocalyptic curse is then invoked and visited on all who were responsible for the death of Gaspar Ilom and their progeny: "Light of the sons, light of the tribes, light of the progeny, before your countenance let it be said, here before you let it be said that the carriers of the white-root poison shall have the pixcoy bird to their left along the trails; that their sunflower seed shall be as dead earth in the bellies of their women and daughters; and their descendants shall embrace the spinebushes. . . . What's certain is that the woods will all be gone, turned to clouds of smoke and plains of ash" (*MM*, 27, 48).

The action in this part of the novel is perfectly apocalyptic because the agents that will bring this curse to fruition are supernatural forces, not humans. One of the government officials, Colonel Godoy, meets his death by being encircled by animals of the wild and then consumed in a spectacular display of nature's might, by an earthquake and fire (*MM*, 94–95). The historical persona Gaspar Ilom may have met his death by poison, but Gaspar the myth lives and his death is revenged by his beloved mother earth.

Following nature's vengeance against the destroyers of the earth and the killers of Gaspar, the novel moves to several other stories, particularly ones that narrate the experience of women who have left their husbands, parables of the aching "presence of absence" in the novel. The characters Goyo Yic, a blind peddler, and Señor Nicho, a postman, have been abandoned by their women and they spend the rest of their days as wanderers and nomads, searching to fill the void left by their absent wives (known as *tecunas*, runaway wives—a name originating from the wife of Goyo Yic, María Tecún).

Above all, these stories are about exile, about lost relationships with the earth and with Indian cultures. They are about a desperate longing for what we cannot possess. Nicho and Goyo Yic describe the pain of absence in this way:

> The longing, it thumps at my chest, I look on it with fear, because it beats on my head, closes my eyes, wrinkles my hands, dries out my mouth. . . .
>
> Rock of María Tecún, image of absence, love ever present and moving away, traveler always standing still, tall as the towers, opaque with forgetfulness, stone flute for the wind and, like the moon, with no light of its own. (*MM*, 194, 209)

Goyo Yic and Nicho are searchers, yearning for love, for communion with the earth, for cultural belonging, but it all eludes them. They have only traces of what they seek, like the memories of the lost María Tecún, memories filled with absence, like a love that is never still, forever moving away. Instead of completeness, emptiness is their only companion. It is an emptiness that thumps Nicho's chest and dries out his mouth: "There was another deepness inside him, dark, terribly dark since his companion abandoned him; but he only looked into that deep dark place when the weight of his sorrow grew heavy, when the pain he endured snapped the nape of his neck like the neck of a hanged man, and forced him, suspended in the void, to look down into his darkness, his awesome human darkness, until sleep stole up on him" (*MM*, 187).

The presence of this dark and terrible abyss—which makes Nicho feel like a hanged man—gives the novel a very modern quality. He is haunted by this deep black hole within him where no light escapes. Even the lights of the heavens are no longer reliable guides and beacons of light. Nature is an abyss, another face of absence. Mourning blackens the moon and stars and the sky itself is rent in two: "Those great golden dots we see lighting up the night aren't happy, I can assure you. On the contrary, when I stare at them and stare at them and become almost one of them through so much staring at them, I can tell they are lights of longing. The infinite vault is full of absences" (*MM*, 249).

In *Men of Maize*, Asturias is trying to cope with these manifestations of absence as much as Goyo Yic and Nicho are: the loss of a premodern, communal world; the loss of harmony and trust in the universe; the loss of myth and magic. In this regard, this great epic of the Guatemalan Indians is a modernist work, written in disjointed and fragmented lines both to capture Indian poetry and to describe the wastelands created by the modern world. As much as it seeks to recapture the wisdom and myth of an archaic culture, it does so in a modern, critical way. It is written with plenty of avant-garde traces and influences, none more obvious than this sense of absence in the universe or the haunting specter of exile that accompanies Goyo Yic and Nicho.

Nicho the postman learns, however, that his experience of aimless wandering, of desiring what we cannot possess (the text mentions Plato in this regard!), is not unique to him, but is a symptom and reality of the human condition (*MM*, 213). Human flesh is in exile. We, too, are runaway and restless creatures like a tecuna: "Man's flesh has tasted the drink of migration, a powder mixed with spider's crawl, and sooner or later it too migrates, like a shooting star, like a runaway wife, it escapes from the skeleton to which it stayed fixed for a life, it goes, it cannot stay: our flesh, too, is a tecuna" (*MM*, 274).

Migration, thus, is a symbol of the human condition—to understand it is to understand the tragic beauty of being alive. When this lesson is learned, as in Asturias's story of Nicho, portals are opened that shine light on the dark passageways of human life. In the case of Nicho, in particular, this flickering light comes to him in the darkness of a cave as he is being initiated into spiritual and shamanistic mysteries.

After Nicho's fruitless search for his beloved, he turns to spiritual paths much like Dante after the death of his beloved, Beatrice. In Nicho, though, his guide through the otherworld is no Virgil, but an animal, his *nahual*, a coyote. Nicho soon assumes the identity of his guide as he crosses the boundaries of animal and human life and takes the form of a coyote. In this form, he is directed by a mysterious man to enter a cave and his journey to the other world begins. He is stunned by the overwhelming beauty he witnesses (like Don Quixote in the Cave of Montesinos): water frozen in the likeness of diamonds, crystals, glittering gems, an underground lake, the fantastic sounds of birds singing. He then comes upon ghostly men and women wrapped in white blankets. One of them speaks:

I am one of the great firefly wizards, descendants of the great clashers of flint stones, who dwell in tents of virgin doeskin, who sow seeds of light in the black air of the night to be sure there will be guiding stars in the winter. . . . You have journeyed toward the West across lands full of wisdom and maizefields. . . . Brother to the postman is the horizon of the sea, lost to infinity when it delivers the correspondence of the parakeets and the flowers of the fields to the planets and the clouds. Brother to the postman, the meteors that fetch and carry the correspondence of the stars. . . . Brother to the postman the winds that fetch and carry the missives of the seasons. (*MM*, 272–73)

Nicho the postman journeys through these lands and learns that he is brother to the sea, brother to the vast universe. As he journeys across these lands of wisdom and maize, he finally comes to dwell in the darkness of a cave, where he is to meet his other self, his animal and spiritual self. In the process of this shamanistic journey, Nicho must face a variety of trials and tribulations: solitary days, abstinence from food and water, darkness and death: "Almost all those who get back alive return from their mysterious journey with their eyes hollowed round by deep black rings, their lips burned from smoking, their ankles weak with exhaustion, frozen, trembling. Have they been through a long illness? Have they been through a long dream?" (*MM*, 278).

When they emerge from the trials (again, like Dante's journey through hell), the mystical motif of incommunicability and ineffability is emphasized:

Life beyond the peaks that come together is as real as any other life. Not many men, however, have succeeded in going beyond the underground darkness to the luminous grottoes by way of fields of yellow minerals, enigmatic, phosphorescent, minerals of a fixed rainbow, cold motionless greens, blue jades, orange jades, indigo jades, and plants of sleepwalking watery majesty. And those who have succeeded in going beyond the subterranean darkness, when they return tell that they have seen nothing, and keep a constrained silence, letting it be known that they understand the secrets of the world hidden beneath the mountains. (*MM*, 277)

If Asturias can be construed as a "magical realist," it is because his understanding of reality ("life beyond the peaks") is infinitely more marvelous and mysterious than rival accounts of scientific realism or positivism, as this passage suggests. In *Men of Maize*, reality is reconfigured and distended in order to account for the truth-bearing power of religion and myth, magic and wonder, beyond the circumscribed borders of scientific positivism or, in literature, beyond realism. In the darkness of the cave—the womb of mother earth—Nicho discovers himself, a man with dark spaces and unfathomable spirits deep within his own soul. As the exact converse of Plato, Nicho goes into the darkness, instead of the light, in order to find wisdom (like Christian mystics such as Gregory of Nyssa, Pseudo-Dionysus, Eriugena, and John of the Cross).

The end of the novel leaves Nicho, in coyote form, along with the Curer-Deer of the Seven Fires, seeking instruction on the life of a seer: "You've got a long way to go to become a seer, my friend the coyote. A lot of walking, a lot of listening, a lot of looking. . . . A seer you become the moment you stand alone with the sun up above you" (*MM*, 304). Asturias's rendition of magical realism is determined through admonitions of this sort. Magical realism is the imaginative product of long trails and trials, of looking into the dark, of listening to what is almost inaudible. It is filled with ancient longings, both sacred and profane, and with dreams both fantastic and frightening. It is, for this reason, a mighty river with innumerable streams and eddies, some leading to the great ocean, others evaporating into puddles on barren and desolate ground. It is with this latter sentiment in mind that the novel ends, as it recalls for us the end of life in the dust of the earth (or it prefigures the last of the Buendías, as the child is eaten by ants): "Old folk, young folk, men and women, they all became ants after the harvest, to carry home the maize: ants, ants, ants, ants" (*MM*, 306).

Carpentier's Novels and the Marvelous

Under the spell of modern anthropology—like Asturias, Carpentier studied ethnology at the Sorbonne in the late 1920s and early 1930s—Carpentier would succumb to the allure that many avant-garde artists felt for archaic, non-European myths. As Asturias unearthed and retold a wide variety of indigenous myths, Carpentier was determined to tell the history of the African diaspora in the Americas.

His first major work, *Ecue-Yamba-O*, for instance, is an ethnological study of Cuban blacks, and the research he did for it would bear fruit in later fiction (the same can be said for his 1946 study *Music in Cuba*, which would reappear in many of his novels). His fiction is, in fact, congruent with his anthropology—it is searching for similar myths and dreams. As with all anthropologists, Carpentier wanted to play his part in establishing a science of origins, with a focus, of course, on the New World. He wanted to narrate the genesis of Latin American cultures, and do so with an accent on the refreshing otherness of these cultures in respect to the modern West. This is the 1920s and 1930s after all; he shared with a wide spectrum of artists and intellectuals the allure of foreign lands and foreign cultures, as if journeys of this sort could give them otherworldly experiences and provide them with alternatives to the meager and desiccate spiritual diet of their times. Coming of age between the world wars, and seeing so much of the modern West in a condition of rubble, they would look elsewhere for signs of life to withstand the dread and dismay. Liberal optimism had no chance of surviving unscathed.

Carpentier's fiction, his marvelous realism, has these contexts to explain it, then: the mystical and mythological search for origins and belonging, on the one hand, and the fragmented history of the modern age on the other. His novels take us on archaic journeys to mythical beginnings, but the point of departure is Carpentier's own unmoored and unhinged age. Carpentier's works stand there, longing for union with one part of his soul, while feeling the traumatic effects of modern history with the other. His soul, like his literature, is a house divided, rent in two, severed and ruptured, but it aches for wholeness. Because he knows this estrangement, he speaks with an accent, in a hyphenated and hybrid voice, part Cuban, part French, part black.

By the time that Carpentier returns to Havana in 1939, in fact, the overarching theme in Carpentier's reading of history is exile. It could hardly be any different for any attentive writer from the Caribbean. In speaking of Cuba, Fernando Ortiz has this to say: "This is one of the strange social features of Cuba, that since the sixteenth century all its classes, races, and cultures, coming in by will or by force, have all been exogenous and have all been torn from their places of origin, suffering the shock of this first uprooting and a harsh transplanting."[52]

So much of a Latin American literature, not only in the Caribbean, makes this principle (the shock of an uprooting) into the fundamental condition of Latin American culture. Latin American literature is the poetry of this trauma. It almost always returns to this fact as if it is circumambulating a profound abyss or void, the Kaaba of Latin American writers. The troubled tone of Latin American writers is the most obvious symptom of this disjunction and dislocation. Feeling like a Theseus who has lost Ariadne's thread, the way out of the American labyrinth of exile has become a desperate and painful search for these American writers. Whether lost in a labyrinth or exiled from the Garden of Eden, there is no doubt that Latin Americans inhabit a postlapsarian age.[53]

Of course, for most Latin American writers, the Fall marks not only the beginning of the human race, but also the source of the New World. Creation is coeval with the Fall, the birth of the New World with the violent uprooting of the Conquest. Carpentier's literary creations are interpretations of this gnostic mythology, attempts to write the genesis and apocalypse at once. Carpentier has both aims in mind, mystical communion with nature, culture, and God, on the one hand, and the beast of exile, on the other. In perfect Baroque fashion—contradictory, that is—his God is both transcendent and absent, like the gnostic God, and immanent and present, like the pantheist God.

Carpentier's short story about the Conquest of the New World, "The Highroad of St. James," is a good example of these ambivalent forces, though in this case, the gnostic position (divine absence) is the prevailing sentiment. The world, in this story, works out its salvation not only in fear and trembling, but also infinitely removed from the heavens altogether. Stronger forces, infernal and malevolent, are closer to home. The figure of Beelzebub appears only once, at the end of the story, but his presence is felt everywhere.

Set in the sixteenth century, the main character, Juan of Antwerp, finds the allure of wealth and adventure too much to resist and sets sail—after abandoning his pilgrimage to Santiago in Spain—for the New World. Carpentier's description of the circumstances of life in the Americas is a litany of sins. The cruel intolerance of the Inquisition only begins the list: "One man was denounced for having bought aphrodisiac herbs from a Negro witch doctor who had been whipped at Cartagena de Indias; the Town Crier was accused of committing the abominable sin; an Ecomendero of moving the boundaries of State property; the Precentor of debauchery; the Chief Gunner of drunkenness; and the Beadle of sodomy" (*WT*, 31). The Old and New Worlds alike are sites of iniquity:

> Here everything smelled of scorching flesh, burning *sambenitos*, the grilling of heretics . . . the shrieks of prisoners, the weeping of women buried alive, the tumult of slaughter, the terrible cries of denunciation issuing from unborn children pierced by swords in their mother's wombs. Some said that better days would emerge from all this blood

and tears; others cried that the Sixth Seal had been broken and that the sun would turn as black as a cilice, that the kings of the earth, princes, rich men, and leaders, all those in power, all slaves and free men, would take to the caves and mountains. (*WT*, 56)

At this point, Beelzebub enters, wearing a black hat on his horns and singing the following tune:

Then, take heart, good sirs,
Courage, poor gentlemen,
Good news for the poor
And joy for those in trouble!
For those who wish to go
And see this new marvel;
Ten ships will sail together
From Seville this year!
(*WT*, 57)

It is Beelzebub, after all, who entices Christian souls to the New World; Beelzebub is the sorcerer and wizard of New World marvels. In droves they come to see this new marvel, but the devil is waiting, turning their salvation into damnation.

This tragic sensibility—a world exiled from God—is also the dominant motif of Carpentier's first great novel, *The Kingdom of This World* (1949). The title itself makes it clear that the novel is about exile, about being wretchedly separated from the kingdom of God. For the epigraph, Carpentier chose a poem by Lope de Vega that dramatizes a conversation between the devil and providence. The devil identifies himself as the king of the West and proclaims himself the ruler of the New World. The inference is obvious and will be the reference by which he narrates the events of the novel: it is not God but the devil that rules the New World. The novel breathes apocalyptic air, then, inhaling with asthmatic breath, wheezing and panting for life in an environment polluted by sin.

The history that *The Kingdom of This World* narrates is based on actual events in Haiti, particularly the black slave revolts against French colonial rule and the regimes that followed.[54] Traces of goodness in the novel are eclipsed by the preponderance of greed and brutality, lust and horror, vanity and death. The lessons learned about history are tragic—if one can speak of progress at all, it is measured in inches not yards. In fact, in this world, even the most warranted forms of human struggle are inherently flawed and carry within them the seed of a potentially new harvest of evil. Thus the regimes of the blacks and mulattos that follow liberation from French colonial rule are described as extending, not eradicating, the outrageous forms of injustice that existed before the revolution. The new regimes imitate and perpetuate the same abuses of power once endured under French colonial rule. The web of sin and evil is so despotic and ubiquitous that it proves impossible to untangle. One of the main characters of the novel, a black slave named Ti Noel, makes these observations about the condition of life under the rule of the black king Henri Christophe:

> Ti Noel soon learned that this had been going on for more than twelve years [slavery under Henri Christophe] and that the entire population of the North had been drafted for this incredible task. Every protest had been silenced in blood. Walking, walking, up and down, down and up, the Negro began to think that the chamber-music orchestras of Sans Souci, the splendor of the uniforms, and the statues of naked white women soaking up the sun on their scrolled pedestals among the sculptured boxwood hedging the flowerbeds were all the product of a slavery as abominable as that he had known on the plantation of M. Lenormand de Mezy. (*KW*, 122)

Toward the end of the novel he expresses similar sentiments regarding the new rule of the mulattos: "Try as he would, Ti Noel could think of no way to help his subjects bowed once again beneath the whiplash. The old man began to lose heart at this endless return of chains, this rebirth of shackles, this proliferation of suffering, which the more resigned began to accept as proof of the uselessness of all revolt" (*KW*, 178).

As much as Ti Noel is tempted, however, he does not succumb to the indolent pleasures of despair and resignation. His tragic awareness of the human condition does not undermine the demands for action in history and society. And it does not sap his moral courage.

Ti Noel will discover a power of resistance through a link with his primitive ancestors and gods (the Orishas in the Yoruba tradition; also a great Cuban hip-hop group incidentally). His ancestors become his teachers and spiritual guides, and open up a world of unimaginable possibilities. He successfully channels their spiritual powers and eventually is able to metamorphose into diverse forms, first a bird, then a stallion, a wasp, and an ant, later a goose. None of these magical transformations proves satisfactory or

meaningful to him, however, until he undergoes a change of a more profound sort, body and soul together. Ti Noel now finds that the purpose
and authenticity of any magical conjuration is its ability to "help his subjects bowed once again beneath the whiplash." Without this dimension,
magic is bogus and spurious, the effort of a charlatan.

This is the lesson that Macandal (a black revolutionary and mythical
hero) had bequeathed to him: "Macandal had disguised himself as an animal for years to serve men, not to abjure the world of men" (*KW*, 184).
And in not abjuring the world of men, Macandal has the uncanny ability
to hear what others ignore, the supplications and laments of his people.
Carpentier cites this African chant of boundless suffering:

> *Yenvaló moin Papa!*
> *Moin pas mangé q'm bambo*
> *Yenvaló, Papa, yenvaló moin!*
> *Ou vlai moin lavé chaudier,*
> *Yenvaló moin?*

> "Will I have to go on washing the vats? Will I have to go on eating
> bamboos?" As though wrenched from their vitals, the questions trod
> one on the other, taking on, in chorus, the rending despair of peoples
> carried into captivity to build pyramids, towers, or endless walls.
> "Oh father, my father, how long is the road! Oh father, my father,
> how long the suffering!" (*KW*, 48)

For many long, hard years, the New World has been the home and witness to this kind of rending despair and religious longing. By attending to
the cries of his people, Ti Noel is then described as having a "supremely
lucid moment." He feels countless centuries old—not unlike the abrupt
aging of Gaspar Ilom in *Men of Maize*—and has a glimpse of all his remote
African ancestors and gods. This moment of epiphany brings him wisdom
and strength to love in the face of affliction and to embrace beauty in the
face of human misery: "For this reason, bowed down by suffering and
duties, beautiful in the midst of his misery, capable of loving in the face of
afflictions and trials, man finds his greatness, his fullest measure, only in
the Kingdom of This World" (*KW*, 185).

This revelation inspires him, old age and all, to declare war against the
new masters, "ordering his subjects to march in battle array against the
insolent works of the mulattos in power" (*KW*, 185). In short, Ti Noel

finds himself through his African gods—like Ogoun and Damballah—and through his devotion to his afflicted people. African religion proves redemptive in this way, and provides Ti Noel with hope in these desperate circumstances. Under the powerful and magical influence of the Orishas, and with the guidance of Macandal, Ti Noel grows in self-understanding until he emerges as a prophet and liberator himself, someone who has found his greatness in the kingdom of this world.

Ti Noel's epiphany speaks loudly of Carpentier's use of magic and religion in his work. Already in his first novel, it is quite clear that his version of magical realism is an incantation of justice. The ethical-political commitment is unambiguous in Carpentier, and we already know that whatever value there is to the idea of lo real maravilloso, it is about justice as much as wonder. And this commitment never wavers in Carpentier; indeed it is fundamental to his final work, mentioned earlier in this chapter, *The Harp and the Shadow*. As the judgment of Columbus's life is being weighed before a tribunal, to recall another moment of this novel, Las Casas is called to testify against the case for his beatification. Columbus sees Las Casas enter the courtroom and exclaims in fear and resignation, "I'm screwed, now I'm really screwed" (*HS*, 144). The shade of Las Casas, my point is, frequents and shadows all of Carpentier's work, as does justice. The specter of justice looms large in his novels, and it disturbs and troubles any version of magical realism that ignores it the way it disturbs Columbus as he awaits the judgment of his life.

To move again from the end to the beginning of Carpentier's career, back to *The Kingdom of This World*, we also learn that Carpentier will always remain interested and motivated, ironically given the title, by otherworldly concerns and desires. Religion will occupy his mind to the point of saturation, sometimes with African religion, sometimes with Catholicism, even with the Kabbalah, but most frequently with a Baroque mixture of all the above, as in this moment in the novel when Ti Noel stops to contemplate the paganism and syncretism of Spanish Catholic churches: "The Negro found in the Spanish churches a Voodoo warmth he had never encountered in the Sulpician churches of the Cap. The baroque golds, the human hair of the Christs, the mystery of the richly carved confessionals, the guardian dog of the Dominicans, the dragons crushed under saintly feet, the pig of St. Anthony, the dubious color of St. Benedict, the black Virgins, the St. Georges . . . all had an attraction, a power of seduction in presence, symbols, attributes and signs similar to those of the altars of the *houmforts* consecrated to Damballah, the Snake god" (*KW*, 86).

Ti Noel found this strange beauty warm and seductive, with the Christian images oddly related and commensurable with his own gods. The redemptive possibilities in *The Kingdom of This World* occur in moments like this, when beauty and love inspire tenacity in the face of misery and affliction, when one is suddenly dogged in the face of injustice because of the surprising pleasure found in this voluptuous Baroque spirituality. The fantastic sacramentality of New World Catholicism—with its strange and uncanny union with archaic religion—is for Carpentier a manifestation of the marvelous, a mutant sort of beauty patterned on ritual and liturgical time as an alternative to the chaos and disorder of Western history.[55]

Thus, what Carpentier achieves throughout his novels is a very capacious and bountiful logic that is inclusive of a Baroque, Catholic, mystical-aesthetic imagination as well as a Reformed, quasi-gnostic sensibility. By keeping these strands together with a hyphen, Carpentier rescues his novels from a bleak and hopeless vision. No one can accuse Carpentier of diluting the horror of history, but it would be equally careless and erroneous to accuse him of abandoning all hope. Lo real maravilloso is the death knell of optimism and idealism, for sure, but Carpentier preserves hope and dresses it in the vibrant colors and impossible dreams of Latin American cultures. The liturgical form of *The Kingdom of This World*, the invocation of magical events, the opulence of the language, even the terrifying, demonic history that is being narrated, all witness to the Baroque extravagance in his work that welcomes a wide variety of human experiences—African and American, Catholic and Protestant, pagan and Christian, secular and religious—to the spacious table of his fiction.

The conjuring of wonder continues in all of Carpentier's later fiction, but it takes a different path from the 1950s on, beginning with his masterpiece, *The Lost Steps*. Like many nineteenth- and twentieth-century explorers and travel writers, the novel ventures back in time, in search of the master code to evolution, to a place in the cosmos that is wild and raw, unspoiled by civilization. Romantic convictions are abundant in the novel, as they were for many scientific explorers with dreams of unraveling the secrets of nature. It is not surprising that the rhetoric of wonder and astonishment pervades the journals of such explorers, as Roberto González Echevarría notes: "The rhetorical strategy was the constant expression of wonder, of surprise, achieved through repeated comparisons between the European and colonial world."[56]

As is well-known, the novel also follows Carpentier's own journeys into the South American jungle, particularly his expeditions in the late 1940s while he was living in Venezuela. The novel tells the story of a bored and dissatisfied man, once a scholar of primitive music and now in a dead-end job. The decision to leave academic life is responsible for financial reasons but leaves him empty. The protagonist has lost all zeal for life. The mood from Ecclesiastes—vanity, vanity, vanity—captures the essence of his forlorn state of mind. By chance, however, he meets his former music teacher and is commissioned to travel from France, where the novel begins, to Latin America in search of both an aboriginal musical instrument and ancient beginnings. He suddenly is given a new lease on life.

As the novel unfolds, we soon become aware that this expedition to the New World is a journey back in time as much as it is travel to a new place. "I asked myself," the protagonist wonders, "whether in bygone days, men had longed for bygone days as I, this summer morning, longed for certain ways of life that man had lost forever" (*LS*, 36). This establishes the theme for the entire novel: the search for lost steps, for the beginning of time, for the beginning of the New World. With this purpose in mind, the protagonist describes his journey to the Americas as retracing the steps of the first Discoverers. At a celebration of the Catholic Mass, he suddenly feels contemporaneous with the events of the sixteenth century: "Time had been turned back four hundred years. This was the Mass of the Discoverers. . . . Perhaps this is the year of grace 1540" (*LS*, 176–77).

But his journey back in time does not stop there. He soon finds himself moving through the corridors of memory into an archaic world, at the beginning of all beginnings: "We are in the world of Genesis. If we go back a little farther, we will come to the terrible loneliness of the Creator, the sidereal sadness of the times without incense or songs of praise, when the earth was without order and empty, and darkness was upon the face of the deep" (*LS*, 187). His journey through memory's mysterious labyrinths brings him to the time before time, the empty void that preceded creation.

As much as the protagonist meditates on cosmic and cultural origins, however, it is clear that he is also narrating a discovery closer to home, his own autobiography: "As we emerged from the opalescent fog, which was turning green in the dawn, a phase of discovery began for me" (*LS*, 77). As he becomes familiar with the world of American cultures and jungles, he gradually begins to recognize himself beneath all the false and inauthentic roles that he had assumed in his previous life. He now finds a sense of purpose and significance that is a hint of light in the black hole of his previous life. He discovers something else within him, something stranger and more fantastic than anything he had known before. Suddenly, the fog recedes and he now sees things with the freshness of a child or a young man in love. This traveler of the New World perceives everything, including himself, with the surprise and wonder that is a natural companion of any lover's vision. The world around him pulses with life and somehow becomes a part of him, as though this new world is the answer to his deepest desires and dreams. The protagonist is effusive in his description of the mysteries he encounters. Wonder and awe are the most common adjectives: "We let ourselves succumb to the world of wonder, eager for still greater portents. There arose beside the hearth, conjured up by Montsalvatje, the medicine men who healed wounds with the magic incantation of Bogota, the Amazon Queen, Cicafiocohora, the amphibious men who slept at night in the bottoms of lakes, and those whose sole nourishment was the scent of flowers. . . . We all felt an impulse to rise, set out, and arrive before the dawn at the gateway of enchantment" (*LS*, 144–45).

Later in the narrative, they approach a village that leaves the narrator stunned and silenced by the majesty and grandeur of both nature and town:

> With aching limbs, I stepped out of the cabin, looked, and stood speechless, my mouth filled with exclamations that did nothing to relieve my amazement. . . . My memory had to recall the world of Bosch, the imaginary Babels of painters of the fantastic, the most hallucinated illustrators of the temptations of saints, to find anything like what I was seeing. . . . In the proportions of these Forms, ending in dizzying terraces, flanked by organ pipes, there was something not of this world . . . that the bewildered mind sought no interpretation of that disconcerting telluric architecture, accepting, without reasoning, its vertical, inexorable beauty. . . . Almost overwhelmed by so much grandeur, I brought my eyes back to my own level after a moment. (*LS*, 171–72)

The narrator here writes with mystical awe, overwhelmed by a vision of fantastic, Bosch-like beauty, and he is struck with such glory that he is forced to divert his eyes back to the level of the ordinary. His response is evocative of countless mystical accounts through the ages—think of Isaiah and Ezekiel covering their eyes and falling on their faces as they behold the glory of the Lord, or, closer in spirit to this Baroque scene, Sor Juana's dream-like vision of cosmic mysteries.

Carpentier was fascinated by mystical-aesthetic epiphanies like this, when the soul is undone by so much beauty, so much grandeur. The character Esteban in *Explosion in a Cathedral* has a similar moment on the shore of the Caribbean as he falls into a mystical-aesthetic stupor before the beauty around him:

> He had such an expression of joy on his face that he looked like some fortunate mystic, favored with an ineffable vision. . . . Amidst a growing economy of zoological forms, the coral forests preserved the earliest baroque of Creation, its first luxuriance and extravagance. . . . Contemplating a snail—a single snail—Esteban reflected on how, for millennium upon millennium, the spiral had been present to the everyday gaze of maritime races, who were still incapable of understanding it. . . . What sign, what message, what warning is there, in the curling leaves of the endive, the alphabet of moss, the geometry of the rose-apple? Contemplate a snail—a single snail. *Te Deum.* (*EC*, 175)

In Carpentier's vision, the Baroque is so spacious that it makes room for the opulence and splendor of creation itself. In other words, nature has Baroque bearings and it leaves the character Esteban stunned for all its mysteries, beginning with the enigma of a single snail. That such contemplative moments leave us silent and joyful is never more apparent than in the protagonist's love affair with Rosario in *The Lost Steps*. She is the incarnate figure of all the wonders of the Indies in a flesh-and-blood person and he cannot resist falling in love her. She is lo real maravilloso in feminine form. Her beauty is the summation of the Baroque New World: she is a wild mixture of cultures, "Indian in the hair and cheekbones, Mediterranean in brow and nose, Negro in the heavy shoulders and the breadth of hips. . . . There was no question but that this living sum of races had an aristocracy of her own" (*LS*, 81). For Carpentier, as for the protagonist of the novel, Rosario is a mystery of New World mestizaje. She is the wondrous product of the impurity of blood, a descendent of Cervantes's Zoraida.

In both of these episodes—concerning Rosario and Esteban's mystical experience in *Explosion in a Cathedral*—magical realism is expressed perfectly: the crazy mixtures of Rosario's blood, the luxuriousness of coral forests, the mystery of a single snail, all of this is marvelous. In most instances, Carpentier writes with abandon and aesthetical extravagance, combining an excess of language with a speech of unsaying (Pseudo-Dionysius is a theological analogue). His apophaticism picks up speed when he is searching for language to name the nameless. When mystified the most, Carpentier turns profuse with his tongue, piling together long sentences if only to deepen, not resolve, the perplexity of the reader. His writing follows arabesque patterns, spreading and filling all empty spaces with writing. In lieu of the walls of the Alhambra, he gives us books containing the markings and designs of intricate, obscure, immoderate poetry. With words imitating byzantine designs, he wants our attention to be jarred by the lavishness, for the reader to share the bewildering experience of seeing something entirely new and different, and if it is something familiar, to see it for the very first time and to approach with reverence instead of manipulation.

Carpentier's strategy in his fiction, thus, is consistent with Baroque motives: to surprise and astound, to shock us out of our complacent and lazy perceptions of reality. His kinship with a wide variety of mystical and gnostic spiritualities—in *Explosion in a Cathedral* there are numerous references to the occult and gnosticism, dream interpretation and automatic writing—works toward this end. In *Explosion*, Esteban is characterized as having a "taste for the imaginative and fantastic, and would day-dream for hours in front of pictures by modern artists representing monsters, spectral horses, or impossible scenes" (*EC*, 18). Esteban has Surrealistic taste.

Even the *Zohar* makes appearances in *Explosion*: the epigraph of the novel is a quote from the kabbalistic text, "Words do not fall into the void," which is to say, language is not wasted, not devoid of creative power. The art of words has magical power and partakes in the creation of the world ex nihilo.

The Spanish title of the work, *El siglo de las luces*, "The Century of Lights," is important in this regard, and refers both to the age of Enlightenment and to the kabbalistic notion of divine lights emanating from the Godhead. In the Lurianic Kabbalah, the lights of the divine emanate from the Godhead and are carried forth in vessels of the Sefirot (divine emanations). At some point in the history of the Godhead, catastrophe occurs and there is a "breaking of the vessels," a cleavage and fragmentation within the very nature of God. As a result, all of being is out of place, separated from its source and alienated from God. In the words of the *Zohar*: "Now that the Temple is destroyed and the *Shekinah* is with them in exile, no day passes without curses; the world is cursed and joy cannot be found."[57]

In the Kabbalah, therefore, Carpentier found a theological framework for understanding exile, and this discovery seems to have been as exciting for him as the protagonist's self-discovery in *The Lost Steps*. Carpentier found the Kabbalah's myths of brokenness and fragmentation to be oddly related to the Baroque, and even more so to his understanding of history in the New World, a history that suffers along with Israel the gravity and magnitude of the exile of the *Shekinah*.[58] As kabbalists would rise at midnight, smear ashes on their foreheads, and rub their eyes in the dust of the earth, all in reverence of the *Shekinah*, "the Beautiful One without Eyes," Carpentier displays a comparable emotion of mourning, if not blindness, from so many tears.[59] Like this midnight ritual—the *tikkun chatzot*—his novels are testimonies to the trails of tears in history, or to prayers that weep bitterly in the night, all for the desolation of Mother Zion.

The apocalyptic sensibilities in his fiction, then, are contained within a theology of fallenness and exile. The English title of the book, *Explosion in a Cathedral*, is a reference to a painting in the novel by an anonymous Neapolitan master, and it perfectly represents Carpentier's fragmented theology, the "apocalyptic immobilization of a catastrophe." The painting is a vision of great columns "shattering into fragments in mid-air," and for Esteban it encapsulates the disasters of his age (*EC*, 18):

> If, in accordance with the doctrines he had once been taught, the cathedral was a symbol—the ark and the tabernacle—for his own being, then an explosion had certainly occurred there. . . . If the cathedral was the Age, then a formidable explosion had indeed overthrown its most solid walls, and perhaps buried the very men who had built the infernal machine beneath an avalanche of debris. If the cathedral was the Christian Church, then Esteban noticed that a row of sturdy pillars remained intact, opposite those which were shattering and falling in this apocalyptic painting, as if to prophesy resilience, endurance and a reconstruction, after the days of destruction and of stars foretelling disasters had passed. (*EC*, 253)

Like most Baroque artists, Carpentier prefers fragments and ruins to represent the modern age. In this passage, he subjects everything to a process of decay and fragmentation: his own being, his epoch, Christianity. Though there is a clear hope for redemption—a prophesy of resilience and reconstruction, of *tikkun* or mending, as the Kabbalah has it—nothing will return to original glory. The steps are lost and Adam and Eve's expulsion is final.

If we consider Carpentier's attraction to ruins in light of Esteban's epoch—the Century of Lights—then we can appreciate another purpose in these pages, a severe and unforgiving criticism of the modern age. Carpentier is now assessing the heritage of the Enlightenment from the perspective of the colonized populations in the Caribbean and Latin America. From this vantage point, it is hard to see any traces of light when so much darkness floods our vision. If there are sparks imprisoned by broken shards, they are hard to detect if you are one of the millions in Europe's colonies imprisoned, enslaved, and massacred. "If one takes a look around, this famous age of Enlightenment," writes Carpentier, "it was an awful Age. . . . On the one hand, the Enlightenment did in fact arrive for the philosophers, for the French encyclopedists; on the other, it remained dark for millions in the colonies, massacred and enslaved."[60]

El siglo de las luces exposes the barbarity and brutality of this age of light. Apocalyptic images and symbols of ruin and fragmentation collect in Carpentier's novel to illustrate the extent of the damage and the horror that has silenced so many lives. Esteban confesses that so much of his age has been a nightmare:

> As the days of the voyage slipped by, what he had lived through came to seem like a long nightmare—a nightmare of fire, persecution and chastisement, as foreseen by Cazotte, with his camels vomiting up greyhounds, and by all the other augurs of the End of the World who had so proliferated during this century. . . . He saw what he had left behind him in terms of darkness and tumult, drums and death agonies, shouts and executions, and he associated it in his mind with the idea of an earthquake, a collective convulsion or a ritual fury. (*EC*, 248)

Not an age of lights, but of darkness, an age that has the same blighted and disfigured look as a village laid to waste and ravaged by an earthquake (or like Mother Zion in the book of Lamentations, a distraught and lonely widow). In *Explosion in a Cathedral*, Carpentier stands on the ruins of the modern age, meditating on Western history from the viewpoint of the enslaved and oppressed, from the perspective of blacks in the Caribbean and Latin America. He rewrites the history of the Enlightenment from a colonized perspective. The prophetic and apocalyptic themes of Carpentier's fiction are the bursts of sound and booming blows—drums and death agonies—that disturb and frighten normative accounts of European evolution, those that leave out the colonized and silence their laments. Throughout *Explosion*, in this regard, there is consideration of black experience on its own merit, without appealing to Western Enlightenment standards. In recalling the many black revolts long before the French Revolution, for instance, Carpentier is making his case for understanding New World history through the eyes of the colonized without needing the example of European models. "All the French Revolution has achieved in America is to legalize the Great Escape which has been going on since the sixteenth century. The blacks didn't wait for you, they've proclaimed themselves free a countless number of times" (*EC*, 231).

The extent of the ruins is even more appalling when one considers modern history in light of the Holocaust, as the protagonist of *The Lost Steps* does as he recalls his personal experience as a military interpreter at the scenes of the genocide: "This entire symphony in ruins. . . . Were the routes of the Apocalypse, winding between walls so shattered that they seemed the letters of an unknown alphabet? . . . I could have never have conceived such total bankruptcy of Western man as that to which that residue of horror bore witness" (*LS*, 94).

Carpentier causes the reader to gasp here, not only for being out of breath but also for having to come to terms with these new and unprecedented ministries of horrors. If lo real maravilloso is for Carpentier the delight in beauty and the capacity for wonder, and it certainly is, it is also the unintelligible script of human tragedy, "an unknown alphabet" that makes us shudder when we consider the depth and degree of human carnage and cruelty. Carpentier's brand of marvelous realism is, indeed, meant to be an explosion, a bomb thrown in the camp of cultured peoples who ignore the smoke palls emerging from scorched communities. It is a bomb that blasts to pieces the triumphalist and congratulatory versions of Western, modern history. His fiction is about the bankruptcy of modern man told from the perspective of the margins of modern civilization, from the wayside of history where the poor and oppressed dwell. The "breaking of the vessels" in the doctrine of the Kabbalah is, for Carpentier, a perfect image of cosmic fragmentation that leaves everything—including modern Western history—in tatters. The location of his fiction amid ruins and exile reminds us that his Baroque mystical-aesthetic extravagance is always interrupted by a history of suffering and by a history of failure. Indeed, a central metaphor in Carpentier's novels has to be failure: the failure of the modern age, the failure of union, the failure of return.

As I have yet to explain, for instance, the journey of the main protagonist in *The Lost Steps* ends in precisely this way—failed. After spending time with Rosario in this mystical world of beauty and wonder, he returns to the West in order to publish the journal of his experiences. He intends on making a return journey to be reunited with his beloved, but never finds the gateway for this return. The source is lost. He fails and his mystical union is disrupted and shattered by the reality of separation. According to Echevarría, "The failure of the protagonist's intended marriage with Rosario, her inability to unite with him once he had reached the Valley Where Time Had Stopped, is the most clear formulation of the protagonist's failure at reintegration within the Romantic symbolism that the novel mobilizes."[61]

The failure of the protagonist's longing for union (with nature, American culture, Rosario, his own being) makes obvious that he belongs to the domain of a fallen history of decay, ruins, and death. He is a wanderer as much as Goyo Yic or Nicho the postman. His life is torn asunder and the path to mystical oneness is lost. Rosario is now dead to him. He is a confused and disillusioned sojourner of the labyrinthine paths of history. As much as the mystical and Romantic drive for unity permeates his work, *The Lost Steps* is about exile.

As I have been suggesting, this sense of failure in the protagonist's spiritual search has great significance for Carpentier's depiction of lo real maravilloso. By the 1950s when Carpentier wrote *The Lost Steps*, he began to supplement his notion of the "American marvelous real" with an interest in the Baroque, as we saw earlier. Carpentier's growing fascination with the Baroque was salutary in my opinion because it expanded his understanding of the marvelous to include a broader brush stroke of different, universal sources (avoiding cultural essentialisms and nationalisms). In light of his meditations on the Baroque, his version of magical realism became larger and more magnanimous, now digesting and encompassing a wider spectrum of world spiritualities and cultures. It was now the product of a world traveler and someone wise to the spectacular extravagance and diversity of human cultures.

Where does this leave us with the idea of magical or marvelous realism? In the present study, I have suggested that magical realism in Latin American literature is somewhere between wonder and exile, mystical and prophetic thought. Carpentier's writing creates conciliatory, even conjugal relationships between competing schools of thought and experience. It is a citizen of the border. When the dark and nightmarish histories that Carpentier narrates threaten to eclipse all traces of hope, Carpentier gives us beauty and love, he gives us a catholic, sacramental, Baroque, mystical-aesthetic imagination that sustains shimmers of hope, small flickers of light in an otherwise malevolent history. I read Carpentier's fiction as a gathering of the fragments, as a Baroque attempt to piece together diverse and wild mixtures. Carpentier ties together—in a provisional, open-ended way, mind you—the small lights still sparkling in the broken shards of his universe: the wonder and beauty of nature, the rhythms of music and art, the mysticism of love and sexuality, the strange and fantastic forms of spirituality and religion.

For sure, literature, too, has become one of those lights for Carpentier, a vessel of marvelous beauty, and specifically, a modern vessel that transmits ancient myths and rituals. Literature has become for Carpentier a lot more than just storytelling. It encapsulates a mystical, esoteric wisdom or arcane gnosis. Like mystical texts, Carpentier's literature both reveals and conceals. It reveals truths and pieces of wisdom accessible only to the few able to decipher the codes and spiritual clues. It is akin to a musical performance or a religious ritual. "*El siglo de las luces* also demonstrates that American narrative is never merely storytelling, or history retelling," explains Echevarría, "but an activity that is akin both to philosophical meditation and religio-cultural ritual."[62] For those not attuned to the spiritual ciphers of Latin American literature, the message remains concealed, inaccessible.

And yet, we would be mistaken to push the elitist framework of gnostic, literary initiation too far, because in Carpentier's fiction, mystical ecstasy is encompassing and democratic, for the lettered and unlettered. In *Explosion in a Cathedral*, Sophia is a prime example of this wisdom. As her name suggests, there is mystical significance to her being, a wisdom that is ancient and arcane. As Sophia falls in love, wisdom blossoms within her and connects her to the rhythms and cycles of nature. It integrates her, like a ritual would, into the symphony of creation:

> The language of the two lovers went back to the roots of language itself, to the bare word, to the stammered single word which lay behind all poetry—a word of thanksgiving for the heat of the sun, for the river overflowing on to the newly-turned soil. . . . Sofia felt supremely in command of herself. Her flesh satisfied, she turned back to people, books and things with a quiet mind, marveling at the intelligence of physical love. She had heard that some Eastern sects thought that physical satisfaction was a necessary step on the upward path to Transcendence, and she could believe that now, as she became aware that an unsuspected capacity for understanding was flowering within her. (*EC*, 314)

Sophia experiences wisdom flowering within her, the product of love's intelligence. She and her lover are perfectly attuned to the rhythms of creation and they take delight in the heat of the sun, the warmth of love, the rain, plants, rivers. Her gratitude is the same as reverence, her joy and serenity the same as transcendence. She is a mystic of the flesh and never feels more alive than at this moment in love with creation's erotic beauty. Sophia is the incarnation of the medieval conception of faith, knowledge born of love.

Thus, Sophia clearly incarnates a mystical transcendence that reunites her body with the body of creation (her body now a microcosm of the whole). In sexual ecstasy, Sophia experiences a respite from separateness, as she experiences oneness and achieves spiritual harmony and repose. Her mystical experience returns us again to the secret, religious desire evident in Latin American literature, the return to the source of being, the desire for union with the All. Even when the final outcome is failure, Carpentier's fiction offers us glimpses of redemption—however partial, however incomplete—that are testimonies to the ecstasies of beauty, love, and wonder.

Conclusion

The lesson imparted by the wise bookseller in *One Hundred Years*, the Catalan character, would find widespread agreement among Asturias and Carpentier, even with certain qualifications in mind: "Upset by two nostalgias facing each other like two mirrors, he lost his marvelous sense of unreality and he ended up recommending to all of them that they leave Macondo, that they forget everything he had taught them about the world and the human heart, that they shit on Horace, and that wherever they might be they always remember that the past was a lie, that memory has no return, that every spring gone by could never be recovered, and that the wildest and most tenacious love was an ephemeral truth in the end" (*OHYS*, 433).

This surely is the lesson of Carpentier in *The Lost Steps* and Asturias in *Men of Maize*, but with one major qualification: the fictions of Asturias, Carpentier, and García Márquez never, in fact, lose a "marvelous sense of unreality." Their narratives are not as despairing and fatalistic as the bookseller suggests. They are, for sure, tragic, but with redemptive fragments scattered throughout. Their rendition of magical realism seeks to salvage something from the wreckage of the modern world, to rescue from oblivion the myths and narratives that have fallen victim to the colonizing and imperial forces of the modern West. Their fiction searches for wisdom and truth in the ruins of time, in what has been named irrational and primitive by "enlightened" Western man. In this sense, magical realism in their fiction is more like the character of José Arcadio Segundo than like the Catalan bookseller. It follows José Arcadio Segundo's compassion for dispossessed and exploited workers, his refusal to forget the horrors of history, as well as his search for an arcane, mystical wisdom that might provide—if not wholeness and happiness—perhaps an ephemeral glimpse of the All. With the strong sense of exile that runs throughout their writing, they warn us that mystical knowledge can never be more than hints and guesses, lacking in certainty and absoluteness. It opens windows of infinity, not totality.[63] There can be no premodern return to the place of origins. As Carpentier insisted, the portals have vanished. If magical realism salvages primitive, non-European traditions—indigenous, African, Spanish, and folk cultures—it does so at a post-critical, post-modern level.

With this fact in mind, magical realists have been spiritual guides for many twentieth-century readers, seeking in their writings hints and clues of a mystical beauty that can be trusted in the aftermath of modern experiences of desolation and agony. The fiction of Asturias, Carpentier, and García Márquez fills our minds with marvels and wonders, opens doors to enchanted and fantastic worlds, and makes us more soulful, even as it records and testifies to the acts of violence and injustice that have polluted modern history. The success of their magical realism owes much to their luminous abilities to represent the voices and narratives of forgotten and oppressed histories, and to take us on journeys to strange and impossible worlds. In this regard, Mario Vargas Llosa saw in the journeys of Ulysses the beginning of magical realism: "Among the many things that Ulysses has been, there is one constant in Western literature: the fascination with human beings that do away with limits, who, instead of bowing to the servitude of what is possible, endeavor, against all logic, to seek the impossible."[64]

CONCLUSION

In my concluding remarks, I want to return to the beginning of my study, where I mentioned my upbringing on the border of the U.S. Southwest (Tucson, Arizona). My family has deep roots in this part of the United States, once the territory of Spain and Mexico. Previous generations of mine would cross the U.S.-Mexico border (in both directions) with regularity and without the same risk and danger that accompanies the journey today. Today's generation of immigrants face a different border, one that is a land mine of threatening terrain and aggressive laws. With the militarization of the urban areas of the border, immigrants—at least the poorest of them— are forced to try to cross in the most remote and desolate of border territory, hence the escalating number of deaths among illegal immigrants. And still they come and see in the magnificent Saguaro cacti of these regions what European immigrants see in the Statue of Liberty—hope for tired and poor peoples.

As I've tried to show in this study, I see the trials of today's immigrants and refugees as echoing throughout the history of the New World. I see their journeys filled with the same risks, dangers, and dreams as pioneering explorers of the Americas. So, in meditating on the history of the New World, I have embraced literary voices—voices of the dispossessed—that would capture the hardships and possibilities of migration, that would give expression to wonder and exile. In our own age of global displacements and international diasporas, we would do well to recover and remember these voices, not for antiquarian purposes, but to inspire similar acts of love and justice.

I want to believe, therefore, that my intellectual life follows in spirit, if not in desperate actuality, the desert trails of migrants. In the book before the reader, I have tried to follow this spirit of border-crossers, from mystics and prophets to poets and novelists, and tried to show how their ideas and lives illuminate the dark and indefinite spaces between disparate and contrasting propositions. David Tracy's work has been a silent partner of this journey. His own wide-ranging engagement with the hyphens and conjunctions of philosophical and theological ideas—like the hyphen connecting mystical-prophetic traditions—appears in my own work in this book, with a focus on the border territory between wonder and exile in the New World.

In light of Tracy's concern with these border spaces, then, I began my study with mystics and prophets in order to see what they can teach us about the history of wonder and exile long before 1492. With this theological background, we were in a better position to understand how wonder and exile can be construed as languages of dispossession. Though mystics and prophets can teach us a lot in this regard, the epoch-making discovery of the New World gives us, or so my study argues following Stephen Greenblatt, a special opportunity to understand wonder and exile.[1] As a language of first encounters, wonder saturated the minds and tongues of many European conquerors and explorers when first setting foot on this peculiar New World. And then exile, too: exile flooded the age like a typhoon and left everything in ruins. Las Casas and Cabeza de Vaca were witnesses of this.

Subsequent to these formative figures, I explored the transformations of wonder in the age of the Baroque. Under the impact of exile, or so my book argues, the wonders of the Baroque turned frightening and monstrous like the wonders of apocalyptic texts, like the wonders that appear in the works of avant-garde artists and the mad, or like the wonders of "magical realists."

In chapter 2, we saw how Cabeza de Vaca and Las Casas were thoroughly familiar with the language of wonder and exile and how they arrived, through their long sojourns, at a destination that was tolerant and pluralistic for knowing firsthand the curious diversity of human beings in this wide world. Their capacity for wonder gave their theological understanding a modesty and tentativeness when they spoke of God, and their prophetic spirit a fierceness when they spoke of the indigenous people they had come to know and defend. In chapter 3, I introduced the tragic motifs of the Baroque and argued that "wonder" underwent a grave change that was an effect of the apocalyptic signs of the times—in particular, the withdrawal and hiddenness of God. Exile came to define the spiritual condition of the age: a feeling of estrangement from God, or in some cases, exile within God. With all the irony that was precious to the Baroque, however, this sense of the divine hiddenness produced a spirituality that was nothing like the atheism of the European Enlightenment. The Baroque did not retreat from religious forms and representations, but gathered the threats of nothingness within its arms and produced a tragic Christian vision, a spirituality of suffering. Like the excessive monsoon rains in desert terrain, it responded to the threat of desolation and nothingness with a profusion and abundance of faith. The result was a new vision of faith, broken and fragmented, distressingly familiar with the agony of the times, a wounded faith.

The Baroque artists, Cervantes and Sor Juana, are examples of this kind of wounded faith, and I read them—in chapter 4—as Catholic intellectuals who gave us an alternative modernity outside the European paradigm of Enlightenment. Out of his own experiences of loss, imprisonment, and exile, Cervantes invents the modern genre of the novel and fills it with a prodigious account of the wonders and fantasies of the human imagination, and how they can go tragically wrong, whether in the mind of his debased hero, Don Quixote, or in the madness of Spain's imperial project. Cervantes gives us a Baroque portrait of the strange drama and tragic actors of this age: the misfits and criminals, the mad and imprisoned, the exiled and defeated, the dead and dying. With a similar madness as the book-intoxicated Don Quixote, Sor Juana embraced wisdom as her sweet Dulcinea and paid the heavy price of persecution, punishment, and envy for her devotion to book learning. Instead of the novel, Sor Juana recorded her soaring imagination in diverse forms, from poetry, philosophy, and drama to music, theology, and liturgy. In all these cases, the experience of loss, death, and disillusionment that haunts Cervantes's great novel is abundantly clear, but Sor Juana adds her own unique signature, both as a woman who knew that her gender was enough to disenfranchise her and as a voice of the cultures of the New World, including the Indians of her Mexican homeland.

By the time we reach the twentieth century with the emergence of "magical realism," the world has changed but Latin Americans remain partial to metaphors of wonder and exile. With the so-called Latin American boom, magical realists explode onto the literary scene and introduce New World Baroque motifs to a universal audience. By seeking to preserve premodern resources and traditions in a post-critical way, they would challenge many of the binary oppositions and separations that modernity fostered: reason and emotion, form and content, theory and practice, materialism and spirituality, aesthetics and ethics, mysticism and prophecy. Indeed, in the last case noted here, magical realists have many points of affinity with the mystics of old, one being the emphasis, to quote Carlos Fuentes, on "nonrational and intuitive forms of knowing."[2] In following this path of human knowledge, magical realists have opened doors to different dimensions of reality and have discovered wonders and beauties in unexpected places, especially in the folk traditions and popular religion of Latin America. Throughout all this, they have tried to remain faithful to Las Casas in being voices of the dispossessed.

In the book before the reader, I have read the New World Baroque in this way, as a voice from the Americas crying out in the desert, speaking on behalf of colonized peoples. In this study, I am following a long line of intellectuals—ones that Lois Parkinson Zamora has done exceptional work in recovering—that have argued for the explosive and subversive potential of the European and New World Baroques. Under various names—Counter-Modernity, Neo-Baroque, Counter-Conquest—intellectuals like José Lezama Lima, Irlemar Chiampi, Severo Sarduy, and Enrico Mario Santí have interpreted the New World Baroque as subverting the sterile structures of Enlightenment rationality, the way the European Baroque once challenged classical norms of reason and order.[3] As an alternative to the suffocating and parochial versions of the Enlightenment, Latin America embraced the Baroque because, to quote Zamora, "it seemed to offer structures large enough to encompass its multiple histories, cultures, and discourses, including those of the *indigenista* movements developing throughout the continent at the time."[4] The Baroque, in other words, proved itself to be magnanimous enough to embrace the wild and eccentric wonders of New World cultures and to be serious enough to testify to the ruin that colonization and forced exile has left on the Latin American soul. The language of wonder in the New World became expansive and open-ended in this way, a shape-shifter that would adopt the colors and contours of its environment and become thoroughly American in the process.

In this embrace of change, hybridity, and wonder, the New World Baroque would give us many things that can enrich our present circumstances, but one, in my view, is the abundant spirituality that the Enlightenment had tried to contain and circumscribe, if not eradicate altogether. From the time of the Conquest to the twentieth century, Latin America gave us a motley collection of mystics, prophets, poets, dissenters, and avant-garde artists, and their voices continue to echo and reverberate into our own time and context. They gave us cultural fragments that open windows of infinity not totality, fragments that are "alive with the memory of suffering and hope," to quote David Tracy.[5] They gave us a spirituality that is enduring and attractive perhaps because it came at a time when it was contested the most. In a passage noted by Zamora, Gilles Deleuze sums up the spirituality of the Baroque in this manner: "That is where the Baroque assumes its position: Is there some way of saving the old theological ideal at a moment when it is being contested on all sides, and when the world cannot stop accumulating its 'proofs' against it?"[6]

The position of theology has not changed all that much, still being contested on all sides, and yet it, too, along with the Baroque, has had a strange resilience. The question of God remains one of the great wonders of our age, sometimes an alluring and fascinating wonder, sometimes terrifying, but still present, present by being absent. And it couldn't be any different given the tragic histories of the modern era—war and imperialism, poverty and injustice, the massive displacements and expulsions of millions of people. The naming of God in our age has to rise from the ruins and ashes of these circumstances. When it faces these realities with clarity and creativity, the question of God can engender the kind of dreams that are synonymous with hope, with a hope that is realistic and magical at once. It can engender the kind of wonders that are manifestations of what we cannot possess or control, of an otherness and difference that we can understand only if it is received with hospitality, gratitude, love. Wonders of this sort have not ceased in our troubled age, but they are as dark and fragmented as Baroque wonders. When we become capable of peering into the darkness of unknowing, of venturing into undiscovered regions of the world, perhaps then, only then, will the darkness become the light and the stillness the dancing.[7]

NOTES

INTRODUCTION

1. For an excellent discussion of the sublime in "postmodern" thinkers—especially in Kant, Jean-Francois Lyotard, Gilles Deleuze, Nietzsche, and Jean-Luc Nancy—see David Bentley Hart, *The Beauty of the Infinite: The Aesthetics of Christian Truth* (Cambridge: William B. Eerdmans, 2003), 43–93. Hart shows well how Kant's idea of the sublime changes and develops in the hands of later intellectuals.

2. Rudolph Otto, *The Idea of the Holy* (Oxford: Oxford University Press, 1958).

3. I am indebted to Diana de Armas Wilson for her excellent reading of Cervantes in light of the New World. See her *Cervantes, the Novel, and the New World* (Oxford: Oxford University Press, 2000). See also her essay "Cervantes and the New World," in *The Cambridge Companion to Cervantes*, ed. Anthony Cascardi (Cambridge: Cambridge University Press, 2002).

4. Tzvetan Todorov described Columbus's quixotic traits in this manner: "a credulous and overtaxed imagination; a great fondness for the ceremonies of naming; an alertness to the appearances of enchantment; an ideology based on prescience rather than experience; a tendency to adjust the data, as well as challenge the humanity, of informants bearing unwelcome intelligence; a penchant for imposing oaths on other people; and finally, a kind of injudicious bookishness." Quoted by Diana de Armas Wilson, "Cervantes and the New World," 211.

5. Ibid., 213.

6. See Walter Mignolo, *The Darker Side of the Renaissance: Literacy, Territoriality, and Colonization* (Ann Arbor: University of Michigan, 2003), 1.

7. J. H. Elliott, *The Old World and the New, 1492–1650* (Cambridge: Cambridge University Press, 1970), 7.

8. Cornel West, *The Cornel West Reader* (New York: Basic Civitas Books, 1999), 378.

9. See Friedrich Nietzsche, *On the Advantage and Disadvantage of History for Life*, trans. Peter Preuss (Indianapolis: Hackett, 1980).

10. Ibid., 7.

11. Carlos Fuentes, "Don Quixote; or, The Critique of Reading," *Wilson Quarterly* 1, no. 5 (1977): 189.

12. Stephen Greenblatt, *Marvelous Possessions: The Wonder of the New World* (Chicago: University of Chicago Press, 1991), 24.

13. Homi Bhabha, *The Location of Culture* (London: Routledge, 1994), 4–5.

14. For the role of the apocalyptic imagination in American literary traditions, see Lois Parkinson Zamora, *Writing the Apocalypse: Historical Vision in Contemporary U.S. and Latin American Fiction* (Cambridge: Cambridge University Press, 1993).

15. See José Lezama Lima, "Baroque Curiosity," in *Baroque New Worlds: Representation, Transculturation, Counterconquest*, ed. Lois Parkinson Zamora and Monika Kaup (Durham: Duke University Press, 2010).

16. Herman Melville, *Moby Dick; or, The Whale* (New York: Penguin, 1992), 196.

17. Ibid., 579.

CHAPTER I

1. See Gerald Martin, *Gabriel García Márquez: A Life* (New York: Knopf, 2009), 296.

2. See Roberto González Echevarría, *Alejo Carpentier: The Pilgrim at Home* (Ithaca: Cornell University Press, 1977), 120.

3. See René Descartes, *The Passions of the Soul,* in *The Philosophical Writings of Descartes,* trans. John Cottingham, Robert Stoothoff, and Dugald Murdoch (Cambridge: Cambridge University Press, 1985), 1:353.

4. Greenblatt, *Marvelous Possessions,* 20.

5. See Descartes, *Passions of the Soul,* 354. See also Jean-Luc Marion, *The Visible and the Revealed,* trans. Christina Gschwandtner (New York: Fordham University Press, 2008), 35.

6. Descartes, *Passions of the Soul,* 354.

7. Ibid., 355.

8. Descartes, *The Meditations,* in *The Philosophical Writings of Descartes,* trans. John Cottingham, Robert Stoothoff, and Dugald Murdoch (Cambridge: Cambridge University Press, 1984), 2:32. See also see Marion, *The Visible and the Revealed,* 46.

9. Descartes, *The Meditations,* 82. See also Marion, *The Visible and the Revealed,* 46.

10. Descartes, *The Meditations,* 36. See also Marion, *The Visible and the Revealed,* 46.

11. Marion, *The Visible and the Revealed,* 36–37.

12. Ibid., 35.

13. Ibid., 44.

14. Denys Turner, *The Darkness of God: Negativity in Christian Mysticism* (Cambridge: Cambridge University Press, 1995), 19–20. See also Michael Sells, *Mystical Languages of Unsaying* (Chicago: University of Chicago Press, 1994), 3, 7.

15. Quoted in Jacques Derrida, "How to Avoid Speaking: Denials," in *Derrida and Negative Theology,* ed. Harold Coward and Toby Foshay (Albany: SUNY Press, 1992), 78.

16. Quoted in Jean-Luc Marion, "Introduction," in *Mystics: Presence and Aporia,* ed. Michael Kessler and Christian Sheppard (Chicago: University of Chicago Press, 2003), 4.

17. See Jean-Luc Marion, "In the Name," in *God, the Gift, and Postmodernism,* ed. John Caputo and Michael Scanlon (Bloomington: Indiana University Press, 1999), 25.

18. Fernando Pessoa, *The Book of Disquiet,* trans. Richard Zenith (London: Penguin, 2001), 387–88.

19. Jacques Derrida, *On the Name,* ed. Thomas Dutoit (Stanford: Stanford University Press, 1995), 36, 43. See also Kevin Hart, *The Trespass of the Sign: Deconstruction, Theology, and Philosophy* (New York: Fordham University Press, 2000), 283.

20. Derrida, *On the Name,* 55–56.

21. Ibid., 85.

22. Dante Alighieri, *The Divine Comedy, Volume III: Paradise* (San Francisco: Chronicle Books, 2005), Canto VI, 139–41.

23. Ibid., Canto XVII, 19–24, 46–48.

24. See R. W. B. Lewis, *Dante* (London: Penguin, 2002), 96.

25. Giuseppe Mazzotta, *Dante, Poet of the Desert: History and Allegory in the Divine Comedy* (Princeton: Princeton University Press, 1979), 12, 7.

26. Bernard McGinn, *The Foundations of Mysticism* (New York: Crossroad, 1991), xviii.

27. Marion, "In the Name," 27, 30, 37.

28. Quoted in Bernard McGinn, "Ocean and Desert as Symbols of Mystical Absorption in the Christian Tradition," *Journal of Religion* 74, no. 2 (April 1994): 162.

29. Consider Orhan Pamuk's wonderful description of Islamic calligraphy: "Before the art of illumination there was blackness and afterward there will also be blackness. Through our colors, paints, art and love, we remember that Allah had commanded us to 'See'! . . . Thus painting

is remembering the blackness. The great masters, who shared a love of painting and perceived that color and sight arose from darkness, longed to return to Allah's blackness by means of color. Artists without memory neither remember Allah nor his blackness. All great masters, in their work, seek that profound void within color and outside time." In this sense, mystical theology, like this description of Islamic calligraphy, is in remembrance of the blackness of Allah. The greatest of these spiritual masters are never more illuminating than when they signify the blackness from which we come and to which we return. See Orhan Pamuk, *My Name Is Red*, trans. Erdag M. Goknar (New York: Vintage Books, 2001), 76.

30. Marguerite of Porete, *Mirror of Simple Souls*, in *Marguerite of Porete: Mirror of Simple Souls*, trans. Ellen Babinsky (New York: Paulist Press, 1993), 172.

31. Plotinus, *The Enneads*, trans. Stephen Mackenna (London: Penguin, 1991), 245.

32. Though I have learned and benefited from Edward Said's reflections on exile, I find his total neglect of the Jewish tradition of exile (in both biblical traditions and later history) to be shortsighted and thoughtless. His inability to pay greater attention to Judaism, or to religion in general for that matter, severely restricts his otherwise illuminating insights about exile. See his *Reflections on Exile, and Other Essays* (Cambridge: Harvard University Press, 2002).

33. In Rulfo's novel, Comala is haunted by traces of absence—tormented spirits, empty and abandoned houses, ruined and sterile soil, deserted roads, infernal heat, deadening silences. Rulfo's speech is, thus, prophetic and has a brown hue to it, nothing like the green of garden spaces. See Susan Sontag's "Foreword," in *Pedro Páramo*, trans. Margaret Sayers Peden (New York: Grove Press, 1994), viii.

34. Quoted in the epilogue to Pablo Neruda, *The Poetry of Pablo Neruda*, ed. Ilan Stavans (New York: Farrar, Straus and Giroux, 2003), 20.

35. Jacques Derrida, *Memoirs of the Blind*, trans. Pascale-Anne Brault and Michael Naas (Chicago: University of Chicago Press, 1993), 122, 126.

36. Octavio Paz, *The Labyrinth of Solitude*, trans. Lysander Kemp (New York: Grove Press, 1985), 57.

37. Quoted in Enrico Mario Santi, *Pablo Neruda: The Poetics of Prophecy* (Ithaca: Cornell University Press, 1982), 216.

38. Maurice Blanchot describes prophetic speech in these terms: When speech becomes prophetic, it is not the future that is given, it is the present that is taken away, and with it any possibility of a firm, stable, lasting presence. Even the Eternal City and the indestructible Temple are all of a sudden—unbelievably—destroyed. It is once again like the desert, and speech also is desertlike, this voice that needs the desert to cry out and that endlessly awakens in us the terror, understanding, and memory of the desert. See *The Book to Come*, trans. Charlotte Mandell (Stanford: Stanford University Press, 2003), 79.

39. María Rosa Menocal, *Shards of Love: Exile and the Origins of the Lyric* (Durham: Duke University Press, 1994), 3–4.

40. Michel de Certeau, "Mystic Speech," in *The Certeau Reader*, ed. Graham Ward (Oxford: Blackwell, 2000), 193.

41. Søren Kierkegaard, *Fear and Trembling/Repetition*, trans. Edna Hong and Howard Hong (Princeton: Princeton University Press, 1983), 198.

CHAPTER 2

1. See my book *The Mystical and Prophetic Thought of Simone Weil and Gustavo Gutiérrez* (Albany: SUNY Press, 2002).

2. Bhabha, *Location of Culture*, 71.

3. No one else in Shakespeare's play speaks as Othello does. His language is exotic and rhetorically dazzling. He enchants Desdemona by poetry of this sort and by the stirring tales of his distant travels and encounters with anthropophagi, with "men whose heads do grow beneath their shoulders," and other strange beings (*Othello*, 1.3.143–45). Desdemona, Othello tells us, devoured his discourse on such matters.

4. Greenblatt, *Marvelous Possessions*, 73.

5. Inga Clendinnen, "Fierce and Unnatural Cruelty: Cortes and the Conquest of Mexico," in *New World Encounters*, ed. Stephen Greenblatt (Berkeley: University of California Press, 1993), 23.

6. Carlos Fuentes, *The Buried Mirror: Reflections on Spain and the New World* (New York: Houghton Mifflin, 1992), 139–40.

7. See Anthony Pagden, *European Encounters with the New World* (New Haven: Yale University Press, 1994), 19.

8. Fuentes, *Buried Mirror*, 126.

9. Quoted in Anne Carson, *Eros: The Bittersweet* (New York: Dalkey Archive Press, 1986), 20.

10. See José Enrique Rodó, *Ariel*, trans. Margaret Sayers Peden (Austin: University of Texas Press, 1988).

11. Bhabha, *Location of Culture*, 75.

12. Greenblatt, *Marvelous Possession*, 81.

13. Ibid.

14. Billie Holiday, "Strange Fruit" (Commodore Records, 1939).

15. Besides the figures of Cabeza de Vaca and Las Casas, there is another fascinating case of this ethic of dispossession in the writings of Pedro de Quiroga, a secular priest and author of *Colloquies of Truth* (1555). This work is a scathing and bitter portrait of the age of the Conquest. One of the key characters, Barchilon, is a longtime resident of Cuzco whose fate has voluntarily changed from that of a rich man to a destitute wanderer. Because he sees so much misery and cruelty in the New World—parallels with the work of Las Casas are evident here—he takes up the life of a penitent and dresses in sackcloth and ashes. Barchilon wanders the land, despised by all "for favoring the natives of this kingdom" (PQ, 43). And at a key moment in the dialogue, Barchilon advocates an ethic of dispossession, of ideas and possessions at once. He instructs a young man who has recently arrived from Spain in search of wealth and power, Justino, that he first must *unlearn* everything he once knew: "If you are to stay, you must forget everything you thought you knew at home" (PQ, 52). Then comes Barchilon's plea for silence: "Learn how to be silent if you want to learn how to talk. . . . Do not deal with matters of this land before you understand them because they are foreign matters and other languages that experience alone can demonstrate to you" (PQ, 52). Barchilon pleads with Justino to unlearn the preconceptions, prejudices, and fantasies that he has brought with him from Castile, to learn how to be silent. Barchilon advocates the route of ignorance, into the cloud of unknowing. He will discover a new world and a new self only through disinheritance. In the process of wandering in the New World, Barchilon unlearns much of his previous Spanish identity and metamorphoses into something else, an American. He is no longer quite Spanish, nor quite Indian, but something in between, an exile, criollo, or mestizo.

16. Greenblatt, *Marvelous Possessions*, 135.

17. Quoted in ibid., 81.

18. Ibid., 20.

19. Recall that More's *Utopia* is set in the New World and the protagonist, Raphael Hythloday, is an explorer. Indeed, More suggests that Raphael was one of the twenty-four men that Vespucci, in his *Four Voyages of 1507*, left for six months in Cabo Frio, Brazil. From here, Raphael travels farther to discover the island of Utopia, where he spends five years studying the customs of the natives. See Thomas More, *Utopia* (London: Penguin, 2003).

20. Greenblatt, *Marvelous Possessions*, 48.

21. Ibid., 74.

22. Ibid., 127.

23. See Anthony Pagden, "Text and Experience in the Writings of Bartolomé de Las Casas," in Greenblatt, *New World Encounters*, 88.

24. See Rolena Adorno, "The Negotiation of Fear in Cabeza de Vaca's *Naufragios*," in Greenblatt, *New World Encounters*.

25. Quoted in Paul Schneider, *Brutal Journey: Cabeza de Vaca and the Epic First Crossing of North America* (New York: Owl Books, 2007), 220.

26. Ibid., 206.

27. Ilan Stavans, "Introduction," in CV, xviii.

28. Quoted in Rolena Adorno, *The Polemics of Possession in Spanish American Narrative* (New Haven: Yale University Press, 2007), 229.

29. Ibid., 234.

30. William Pilkington, "Epilogue," in Álvar Núñez Cabeza de Vaca, *Adventures in the Unknown Interior of America*, ed. and trans. Cyclone Covey (Albuquerque: University of New Mexico Press, 1993), 149.

31. This passage is reminiscent of one placed in the mouth of the Indians by the Franciscan friar Motolinia. Brought before one of the governing councils or tribunals in the Indies (the Audiencia), a group of Indians tells them why they favor the Franciscans: "When the president of the second Audience asked them the reason why they liked these friars better than the others, the Indians answered 'because these go about poorly dressed and barefoot just like us; they eat what we eat, they settle among us, and their intercourse with us is gentle.'" See Motolinia, *History of the Indies of New Spain*, quoted in Tzvetan Todorov, *The Conquest of America*, trans. Richard Howard (Norman: University of Oklahoma Press, 1999), 200.

32. Richard Rodriguez, *Brown: The Last Discovery of America* (New York: Viking Books, 2002), xi.

33. Quoted in Gustavo Gutiérrez, *Las Casas: In Search of the Poor of Jesus Christ*, trans. Robert Barr (Maryknoll, N.Y.: Orbis Books, 1993), 46.

34. Las Casas describes their ascetical way of life in the following way: "For the sick, one could beg from door to door. So it fell out that on Easter day they had nothing to eat except some boiled cabbage, no oil, garnished only with axi and salt. They kept to this life of austerity for many years." See LC, *HI*, 136.

35. See Gutiérrez, *Las Casas*, 39.

36. Ibid., 51.

37. Adorno, *Polemics of Possession in Spanish American Narrative*, 43.

38. See Gutiérrez, *Las Casas*, 378.

39. See Momme Brodersen, *Walter Benjamin: A Biography* (New York: Verso, 1996), 262.

40. Pagden, *European Encounters with the New World*, 78.

41. Quoted in Gutiérrez, *Las Casas*, 55.

42. See Lewis Hanke, *The Spanish Struggle for Justice in the Conquest of America* (Dallas: Southern Methodist University Press, 2002), 81.

43. Quoted in Gutiérrez, *Las Casas*, 305.

44. Ibid., 62.

45. Quoted in Greenblatt, *Marvelous Possessions*, 150.

46. Quoted in Pagden, *European Encounters with the New World*, 79.

47. Arthur Cohen, *The Tremendum: A Theological Interpretation of the Holocaust* (New York: Continuum, 1993), 1.

48. Quoted in Gutiérrez, *Las Casas*, 91.

49. See Hanke, *Spanish Struggle for Justice in the Conquest of the Americas*, 89.

50. Quoted in Pagden, *European Encounters in the New World*, 126.

51. Quoted in Todorov, *Conquest of America*, 190–91.

52. Quoted in Tom Conley, "The Essays and the New World," in *The Cambridge Companion to Montaigne*, ed. Ullrich Langer (Cambridge: Cambridge University Press, 2005), 80.s

53. Quoted in Gutiérrez, *Las Casas*, 87.

54. Adorno, *Polemics of Possession in Spanish American Narrative*, 96, 268.

55. Quoted in Gutiérrez, *Las Casas*, 204.

CHAPTER 3

1. Hamlet speaks in this fashion when he refers to wounded wonders, a sentiment that captures this age that bleeds with so much confusion and grief, uncertainty and crisis (*Hamlet*, 5.1.244–47).

2. T. S. Eliot, *The Wasteland, and Other Poems* (New York: Harcourt Brace Jovanovich, 1934).

3. Mignolo, *Darker Side of the Renaissance*.

4. David Tracy, *Dialogue with the Other* (Louvain: Peeters Press, 1990), 121.

5. Michelangelo, *Michelangelo: Poems and Letters*, trans. Anthony Mortimer (London: Penguin, 2007), 18.

6. Louis Dupré, *Passage to Modernity* (New Haven: Yale University Press, 1993), 244.

7. George Steiner makes a similar point, arguing that the tragic sense broadened with the decline of hope and the darkening of the spirit in the generations after the early Renaissance. See *The Death of Tragedy* (New Haven: Yale University Press, 1980), 16.

8. Jacques Derrida, *The Gift of Death*, trans. David Wills (Chicago: University of Chicago Press, 2007), 89.

9. Heiko Oberman, *The Dawn of the Reformation* (Edinburgh: T. and T. Clark, 1986), 132.

10. Lucien Goldmann, *The Hidden God: A Study of Tragic Vision in the Pensées of Pascal and the Tragedies of Racine* (London: Routledge and Kegan Paul, 1977), 36.

11. On the theme of exile, see Pascal's *Pensées*, 219.

12. David Tracy, "The Hidden God: The Divine Other of Liberation," *Cross Currents: The Journal of the Association of Religion and Intellectual Life* 46, no. 1 (1996): 9.

13. Ibid., 10.

14. See Steiner, *Death of Tragedy*, 6.

15. Carlos Fuentes, "The Novel as Tragedy: William Faulkner," in Zamora and Kaup, *Baroque New Worlds*, 543.

16. Quoted in Michel de Certeau, *The Mystic Fable*, vol. 1, trans. Michael Smith (Chicago: University of Chicago Press, 1992), 140.

17. Ibid., 77.

18. Roberto González Echevarría, "Góngora's and Lezama's Appetites," in Zamora and Kaup, *Baroque New Worlds*, 564.

19. Christine Buci-Glucksmann, *Baroque Reason: The Aesthetics of Modernity* (London: Sage, 1994).

20. Peter Brown, *Augustine of Hippo: A Biography* (Berkeley: University of California Press, 2000), 260.

21. Roberto González Echevarría, *Love and the Law in Cervantes* (New Haven: Yale University Press, 2005), 57.

22. Wu-Tang Clan, "Triumph," in *Wu-Tang Forever* (Loud/RCA Records, 1997).

23. José Antonio Maravall, *Culture of the Baroque: Analysis of a Historical Structure* (Minneapolis: University of Minnesota Press, 1986), 149.

24. In Toledo, a Jesuit describes a mob of common people, "saying they wanted to kill those governing the city because there was no bread to be found." See ibid., 45.

25. Ibid., 47.

26. Ibid., 52.

27. Dupré, *Passage to Modernity*, 245.

28. Quoted in Maravall, *Culture of the Baroque*, 150.

29. Juergen Hahn, *On the Origins of the Baroque Concept of Peregrinatio* (Chapel Hill: University of North Carolina Press, 1973).

30. Baltasar Gracián, *El Criticón*, quoted in ibid., 169.

31. Like Gracián, Comenius sketches the travel experience of a pilgrim who sets off to experience the world and ends up disillusioned and troubled by the reign of false appearances and disorders. And the writer Saavedra Fajardo adds to this tragic portrait of the dismayed and homeless pilgrim: Fajardo tells us, in fact, that he composed his *Empresas* "writing in the inns about what I had rambled upon on the road." See Maravall, *Culture of the Baroque*, 188.

32. Quoted in ibid., 186.

33. While this sentiment may be as ancient as Adam and Eve's expulsion from the Garden, the history of exile in the memory of Spain is, at least, as old as the first great ruler of al-Andalus, Abd al-Rahman, "the Falcon." Abd al-Rahman was the sole survivor of the Abbasid massacre of the Umayyads in 750. After fleeing his homeland in Damascus, the capital of the Umayyad caliphate, he followed the trail of his mother's Berber ancestry in North Africa, but now ventures farther into what Rome called Hispania or Iberia. As a political refugee and stranger in Iberia, this Umayyad exile brings with him to Spain the palm and citrus trees that will later become defining traits of southern Spain. He put to the pen this touching line about his own and the palm tree's exile: "How like me you are far away and in exile. In long separation from family and friends. You have sprung from soil in which you are a stranger; and I, like you, am far from home." See David Levering Lewis, *God's Crucible: Islam and the Making of Europe* (New York: Norton, 2008), 195. See also María Rosa Menocal, *The Ornament of the World* (New York: Little, Brown, 2002), 6, 53–65.

34. Pascal, *Pensées*, 64.

35. See Roberto González Echevarría, *Celestina's Brood: Continuities of the Baroque in Spanish and Latin American Literature* (Durham: Duke University Press, 1993), 90.

36. Ibid., 87.

37. Paul O. Kristeller, *Renaissance Thought* (New York: HarperCollins, 1961).

38. Buci-Glucksmann, *Baroque Reason*, 55–56.

39. See Louis A. Ruprecht, *Tragic Posture and Tragic Vision* (New York: Continuum, 1994). See also P. E. Easterling, ed., *The Cambridge Companion to Greek Tragedy* (Cambridge: Cambridge University Press, 1997).

40. In this regard, Benjamin makes another point important to my study: that Calderón's genius when handling the question of tragic fate had a lot to do with his "pagan-cum-Catholic" vision (*T*, 130). It is in the drama of Spain, Benjamin remarks, "a land of Catholic culture in which the baroque features unfold more brilliantly, clearly, and successfully," that the pagan conception of fate could be represented and enacted in a Christian world (*T*, 81). On the contrary, the German Baroque *Trauerspiel*, influenced by Lutheran antipathy to anything pagan (Lutheran not Luther!), "is characterized by an extreme paucity of non-Christian notions. For this reason— and one is almost tempted to say for this reason alone—it was not able to develop the drama of fate" (*T*, 130).

41. Maravall, *Culture of the Baroque*, 213.

42. Fuentes, *Buried Mirror*, 196.

43. Alejo Carpentier, *Baroque Concerto* (New York: André Deutsch, 1991).

44. Quoted in Iris Zavala, "One Hundred Years of Solitude as Chronicle of the Indies," in *Gabriel García Márquez's "One Hundred Years of Solitude": A Casebook*, ed. Gene Bell-Villada (Oxford: Oxford University Press, 2002), 113.

45. Ibid., 110.

46. Echevarría, *Celestina's Brood*, 158.

47. Leszek Kolakowski, *Modernity on Endless Trial* (Chicago: University of Chicago Press, 1990), 58.

48. "Pues los europeos creen que los estudios de los hombres del nuevo mundo son bárbaros." Juan Espinosa de Medrano, *Apologético en favor de Don Luis de Góngora*, ed. Luis Jaime Cisneros (Lima: Universidad de San Martín de Porres, 2005), 13. See also Echevarría, *Celestina's Brood*, 154.

49. "Si al Duque mi señor y Mecenas deste papel no desagradare esta ofrenda humilde, tenme por animado a mayores empresas. Ocios son éstos que me permiten estudios más severos: pero qué puede haber que contente a los europeos, que desta suerte dudan? Sátiros nos juzgan, tritones nos presumen, que brutos de alma, en vano se alientan a desmentirnos máscaras de humanidad. . . . Mucho valdría Papagayo que tanto parlase." Medrano, *Apologético*, 127. See also Echevarría, *Celestina's Brood*, 156.

50. In speaking of Africans, Hume writes, "'Tis likely that he is admired for very slender accomplishments, like a parrot, who speaks a few words plainly." See "Of National Characters," in *Essays: Moral, Political, and Literary*, ed. T. H. Green and T. H. Grose (London: Longmans, 1895), 105.

51. See Henry Louis Gates, *The Signifying Monkey: A Theory of African-American Literary Criticism* (Oxford: Oxford University Press, 1988), 113.

52. Echevarría, *Celestina's Brood*, 154.

53. Quoted in ibid., 158.

54. "Una pluma del orbe indiano." Medrano, *Apologético*, 125.

55. "Vivimos muy lejos los criollos y, si no traen las alas del interés, perezosamente nos visitan las cosas de España." Ibid., 127.

56. Echevarría, *Celestina's Brood*, 165.

57. Henry Louis Gates defines "signifying" as the language of trickery, in which a set of words arrives at direction through indirection. It is a verbal strategy in which the apparent significance of a message is different from its real significance. Unlike the case of Lunarejo, however, the African American tradition of "signification" often involves a game of insults and boasts. This element, it seems to me, is lacking in Lunarejo. For the meaning of "signification" in the African American tradition, see Gates, *Signifying Monkey*, 74.

58. Quoted in Mariano Picón-Salas, *A Cultural History of Spanish America* (Berkeley: University of California Press, 1962), 100.

59. Lois Parkinson Zamora, *The Inordinate Eye: New World Baroque and Latin American Fiction* (Chicago: University of Chicago Press, 2006), 17. Jorge Luis Borges was an unmistakable heir of this tradition and would sketch similar features of moon and mirrors, but with an added intensity of terror. In his poem titled "Mirrors," he explains his fear as follows: "Now, after so many troubling years of wandering beneath the wavering moon, I ask myself what accident of fortune handed to me this terror of all mirrors. . . . They extenuate this vain and dubious world within the web of their own vertigo. . . . God has created nights well-populated with dreams, crowded with mirror images, so that man may feel that he is nothing more than vain reflection. That's what frightens us." We can answer Borges's query about the origin of his fear of mirrors, therefore: the clue is in the Baroque. Mirrors terrify Borges because they remind him of the falsity of appearances, the impermanence of reality, and the uncertainty of everything save the severe power of death. In the mark of the moon on Lunarejo's face, we have traces of Borges's own modern insecurities and fears, or that of García Márquez (in a dream of José Arcadio

Buendía, Macondo is a city of frozen mirrors—i.e., unreal reflections and shadows). See Jorge Luis Borges, *Selected Poems*, ed. Alexander Coleman (London: Penguin, 1999), 106–7.

60. See Echevarría, *Celestina's Brood*, 5.

61. Quoted in Zamora, *Inordinate Eye*, 146.

62. Fuentes, *Buried Mirror*, 196.

63. Echevarría, *Celestina's Brood*, 164.

64. Picón-Salas, *Cultural History of the Baroque*, 91.

65. Ibid., 96.

66. The fine collection *Baroque New Worlds*, edited by Lois Parkinson Zamora and Monika Kamp, gathers evidence of this transgressive potential of the New World Baroque, how it went from a colonizing instrument to a subtle and cunning decolonizing strategy. Although there are many figures in Spain and Latin America that were resuscitating the Baroque (Federico García Lorca, Dámaso Alonso, Alejo Carpentier, Alfonso Reyes, et al.), the Argentinian Ángel Guido in 1936, then José Lezama Lima in 1957, made the argument explicit that the New World Baroque is a counter-conquest force and, as such, a subversive, anticolonial alternative to Enlightenment versions of modernity.

67. José Lezama Lima's classic essay "Baroque Curiosity," in Zamora and Kamp, *Baroque New Worlds*, speaks of the family pact between native and African artists and those of the Baroque.

68. Gonzalo Celorio, "From the Baroque to the Neobaroque," in Zamora and Kamp, *Baroque New Worlds*, 496.

69. See Fuentes, "Novel as Tragedy," 544.

70. Quoted in Zamora, *Inordinate Eye*, 178.

71. Ibid., 201.

72. Picón-Salas, *Cultural History of the Baroque*, 117.

73. See Nava, *Mystical and Prophetic Thought of Simone Weil and Gustavo Gutiérrez*, 143–44.

74. Fuentes, *Buried Mirror*, 146.

75. The differences between Liberation theology and the Baroque are equally important even if beyond the scope of this chapter. One glaring difference concerns the heritage of the Enlightenment. Liberation theology is most certainly a child of the Enlightenment (especially in the affection for Marx, Hegel, and Kant), and thus is committed to modern achievements in philosophy, the arts, and social sciences.

76. See Gustavo Gutiérrez, *On Job: God-Talk and the Suffering of the Innocent*, trans. Matthew O'Connell (Maryknoll, N.Y.: Orbis Books, 1987). This is certainly also true for African American theology. See James Cone, *The Spirituals and the Blues* (Maryknoll, N.Y.: Orbis Books, 1992); West, *Cornel West Reader*, 55–86.

77. In addition to emphasizing the image of the suffering Christ among Hispanic traditions of North America, Goizueta's book includes very insightful reflections on the relationship between aesthetics and an ethics of justice in these traditions. See *Caminemos con Jesus* (Maryknoll, N.Y.: Orbis Books, 1995).

78. Fuentes, *Buried Mirror*, 125.

CHAPTER 4

1. Michel Foucault, *The Order of Things: An Archaeology of the Human Sciences* (New York: Vintage Books, 1994), 46.

2. Carlos Fuentes draws this connection between *locura* and *lectura*. See his "Don Quixote."

3. As mentioned in my introduction, I am following Diana de Armas Wilson in highlighting the impact of the New World on the life and art of Cervantes. In her words, "I believe that

238   NOTES TO PAGES 116–136

Cervantes's novels were stimulated by the geographical excitement of a new world. The rise of the early modern novel came on the heels of the incorporation of the Indies into European maps and legal documents." See *Cervantes, the Novel, and the New World*, 3.

4. See Carlos Fuentes, *Don Quixote; or, The Critique of Reading* (Austin: University of Texas Press, 1976), 9. See also Diana de Armas Wilson's discussion of the Latin American reception of *Don Quixote* in *Cervantes, the Novel, and the New World*, 28–30, 39–43.

5. María Antonia Garcés's book *Cervantes in Algiers: A Captive's Tale* (Nashville: Vanderbilt University Press, 2002) narrates well the influence of this captivity on the life and writing of Cervantes.

6. Quoted in ibid., 25.

7. Foucault, *Order of Things*, 47–49.

8. The priest, for instance, refers to a Miguel de Cervantes as author of *La Galatea*, and during the Captive's Tale there is a mention of the Spanish soldier Saavedra held captive in Algiers (*DQ*, part 1, 6, 40).

9. Mikhail Bakhtin, *Problems of Dostoevsky's Poetics*, trans. Caryl Emerson (Minneapolis: University of Minnesota Press, 1984), 128.

10. Quoted in Zamora, *Inordinate Eye*, 266.

11. György Lukács, *Theory of the Novel*, trans. Anna Bostock (Cambridge: MIT Press, 1971), 103–4.

12. See Benjamin Lazier, *God Interrupted: Heresy and the European Imagination Between the World Wars* (Princeton: Princeton University Press, 2008), for a discussion of this motif of divine nothingness in the study of the Kabbalah.

13. Henry Kamen, *The Disinherited: Exile and the Making of Spanish Culture* (New York: HarperCollins, 2007), 136.

14. Quoted in ibid., 56.

15. *Trato*, 1.1–9, quoted in Garcés, *Cervantes in Algiers*, 137.

16. *Trato*, 1.21–24, quoted in ibid., 143.

17. *Trato*, 4.1974–91, quoted in ibid., 157.

18. *Trato*, 4.2548–601, quoted in ibid., 176.

19. *Los baños*, 2.1922–25, quoted in ibid., 215.

20. Alighieri, *Divine Comedy*, Canto XXIX, 79–88.

21. Erich Auerbach, *Dante: Poet of the Secular World*, trans. Ralph Manheim (New York: New York Review of Books, 2007), 34.

22. Garcés, *Cervantes in Algiers*, 219.

23. Leo Spitzer, "Linguistic Perspectivism," in *Cervantes' "Don Quixote": A Casebook*, ed. Roberto González Echevarría (Oxford: Oxford University Press, 2005), 188–89.

24. *Trato*, 1.396–403, quoted in Garcés, *Cervantes in Algiers*, 175.

25. Bruce Wardropper, "Don Quixote: Story or History?" in Echevarría, *Cervantes' Don Quixote*, 146.

26. Echevarría, *Love and the Law in Cervantes*, 124.

27. Buci-Glucksmann, *Baroque Reason*, 85.

28. Echevarría, *Love and the Law in Cervantes*, 159.

29. Anthony Cascardi, "Introduction," in Cascardi, *Cambridge Companion to Cervantes*, 6–7.

30. "Two discursive domains intersect here: chivalry, the feudal institution whose available and automatic language Don Quixote aims to revive, and imperialism, the more contemporaneous, and more American, institution to which his exploits often allude." Wilson, *Cervantes, the Novel, and the New World*, 114.

31. Ibid., 135.

32. Echevarría, *Love and the Law in Cervantes*, 242.

33. See also Echevarría, *Love and the Law in Cervantes*, 242.

34. Frederick de Armas, "Cervantes and the Italian Renaissance," in Cascardi, *Cambridge Companion to Cervantes*, 46.

35. Frances Yates, *Giordano Bruno and the Hermetic Tradition* (Chicago: University of Chicago Press, 1964), 259–61.

36. Karen Silvia de Leon-Jones, *Giordano Bruno and the Kabbalah* (Lincoln: University of Nebraska Press, 2004), 118–19.

37. See Yates, *Giordano Bruno and the Hermetic Tradition*, 260. Both Bruno and Agrippa, furthermore, were fascinated by the story of Balaam's ass in the book of Numbers. In the Bible, Balaam's ass recognizes an angel of the Lord standing in the roadway as a warning, while Balaam himself cannot see it. Out of fear, the ass turns away from the angel and Balaam angrily whips it three times. In response, the ass suddenly speaks to him to protest Balaam's abuse. For many Renaissance Neo-Platonists, the story is about Balaam's failure—specifically, his inability to recognize prophecy in strange and uncanny places. Equipped only with scientific logic, Balaam could not imagine anything beyond the stretch of reason. See Leon-Jones, *Giordano Bruno and the Kabbalah*, 129.

38. In the late Middle Ages, this sensibility was furthered by mystical voices of the laity and ordinary folk. Jean Gerson spoke of young girls and simple people (*idiotae*) as being competent in the area of mystical theology. Meister Eckhart protested the confinement of God to circumscribed and restricted parts of the world (churches, monasteries, introspective prayer): "Because truly, when people think that they are acquiring God more in inwardness, in devotion, in sweetness and in various approaches than they do by the fireside or in the stable, you are acting just as if you took God and muffled his head up in a cloak and pushed him under a bench." Meister Eckhart, *Meister Eckhart: The Essential Sermons, Commentaries, Treatises, and Defense*, trans. Edmund Colledge and Bernard McGinn (New York: Paulist Press, 1981), 183.

39. Erich Auerbach, "The Enchanted Dulcinea," in Echevarría, *Cervantes' Don Quixote*, 53.

40. Cervantes, "The Dogs Colloquy," in *Exemplary Stories*, trans. C. A. Jones (London: Penguin, 1972), 224.

41. Stephen Toulmin, *Cosmopolis: The Hidden Agenda of Modernity* (Chicago: University of Chicago Press, 1990), 33.

42. Walt Whitman, *Leaves of Grass, 1855 Edition*, ed. Malcolm Cowley (New York: Penguin, 1959), 48.

43. Quoted in Echevarría, *Love and the Law in Cervantes*, 118.

44. I agree with Frederick de Armas that there are parallels with Apuleius's work *The Golden Ass* in the conversion of Don Quixote. In Apuleius's work, the main character Lucius is transformed into an ass because of his excessive curiosity (desire to learn witchcraft). Don Quixote's eagerness to learn the ways of knight-errantry parallels Lucius's unconstrained zeal for the magic and wonders of witchcraft. They both become asses in the process. In the *Golden Ass,* it is the vision of the goddess of the Moon, Isis, who brings about the salvation and subsequent transformation of Lucius back into human form. With Don Quixote, his experience of the Moon (in this case, his defeat at the hands of the Knight of the Moon) also initiates the process of his salvation, but now it is not the Moon goddess Isis, but the Christian Mother of God, Mary (often represented with the image of the moon). See de Armas, "Cervantes and the Italian Renaissance," 53.

45. See Eric Ziolkowski, *The Sanctification of Don Quixote: From Hidalgo to Priest* (University Park: Pennsylvania State University Press, 1991).

46. Ramón Menéndez Pidal, "The Genesis of Don Quixote," in Echevarría, *Cervantes' Don Quixote*, 83–84.

47. Simone Weil defines "justice" in terms of dispossession. Justice is the renunciation of power in the interests of the powerless. See Nava, *Mystical and Prophetic Thought of Simone Weil and Gustavo Gutiérrez.*

48. Don Quixote is clearly guided by this kind of faith in things unseen. Consider, for instance, the famous incident when he demands of the merchants encountered on the road that they confess the peerless beauty of Dulcinea without ever seeing her, for "the important thing is that without ever having seen her you should believe, confess, swear, and defend it." I am suggesting that this confession of faith is at the heart of the biblical understanding of faith as foolishness. For a discussion of this episode, see Fuentes, "Don Quixote," 196.

49. In the words of Pascal, "As men could not make might obey right, they have made right obey might. As they could not fortify justice, they have justified force." *Pensées*, 51.

50. Richard Kagan, *Lawsuits and Litigants in Castile, 1500–1700* (Chapel Hill: University of North Carolina Press, 1981). See also Echevarría, *Love and the Law in Cervantes*, 66.

51. Friedrich Nietzsche, "Attempt at Self-Criticism," in *The Birth of Tragedy*, ed. Michael Tanner and Shaun Whiteside (New York: Penguin, 1994), 12.

52. See Georgina Sabat-Rivers, "A Feminist's Re-reading of Sor Juana's Dream," in *Feminist Perspectives on Sor Juana Inés de la Cruz*, ed. Stephanie Merrim (Detroit: Wayne State University Press, 1991), 144.

53. I am grateful to Michelle Gonzalez's book for the reference to this poem. See *Sor Juana: Beauty and Justice in the Americas* (New York: Orbis Books, 2003), 36.

54. Pamela Kirk, *Sor Juana Inés de la Cruz: Religion, Art, and Feminism* (New York: Continuum, 1998), 74.

55. Ibid.

56. Luis de Góngora, "First Solitude," in Góngora, *Selected Poems by Luis de Góngora*, ed. and trans. John Dent-Young (Chicago: University of Chicago Press, 2007), 35.

57. Lois Parkinson Zamora sees this dialectic between presence and absence as a hermeneutical key in understanding the Baroque spirit. *Inordinate Eye*, 260.

58. Góngora, "Soneto (1582)," in *Selected Poems of Luis de Góngora*, 25.

59. Hermes Trismegistus is a mythical figure associated with Egyptian wisdom, philosophy, and magic, although the Renaissance considered him a historical person, an Egyptian priest who lived and taught before the time of Plato. He was often identified with the Egyptian god Thoth, responsible for the laws and letters of Egypt. The Jesuit Kircher considered Hermes to be one of the greatest gentile prophets. He dated Hermes to the time of Abraham and believed that he was the fount of all pagan wisdom and learning. If Socrates professed belief in God as the One and the Good, he derived this wisdom from more ancient Egyptian sources. "And this Trismegistus," Kircher writes, "was the first who in his *Pimander* and *Asclepius* asserted that God is One and Good." See Yates, *Giordano Bruno and the Hermetic*, 418.

60. See ibid., 23, 239.

61. For many Renaissance thinkers, including Kircher, Pico della Mirandola, and Ficino, Christian mysticism represented a hidden and esoteric wisdom that could also be found in other religions, especially among the schools of Hermeticism, Neoplatonism, and the Kabbalah. Marsilio Ficino had, in fact, translated Pseudo-Dionysius's *The Divine Names* and saw affinities between the apophatic naming of God in Pseudo-Dionysius (the Good beyond Being) and that of Hermeticism. In the words of Ficino, "These mysterious sayings of Dionysius are confirmed by Hermes . . . who says that God is nothing and yet that God is all. That God has no name, yet God has every name." Pico della Mirandola made similar claims, but with a focus on synthesizing Hermeticism and the Kabbalah. In his mind, these ancient traditions of wisdom could be traced back to Moses (in the case of the Kabbalah) and to the Egyptian Moses, Hermes Trismegistus (in the case of the *Corpus Hermeticum*). Pico's attempt to synthesize various philosophies on a mystical basis will have a long life far removed from the Renaissance. See ibid., 125.

62. Nicholas of Cusa, *Nicholas of Cusa: Selected Spiritual Writings*, trans. H. Lawrence Bond (New York: Paulist Press, 1997), 32.

63. Quoted in Edward Hirsch, *How to Read a Poem and Fall in Love with Poetry* (New York: Harvest Books, 1999), 257.

64. Nicholas of Cusa, *Selected Spiritual Writings*, 43.

65. Ibid., 127.

66. Ibid., 17.

67. Karsten Harries, *Infinity and Perspective* (Cambridge: MIT Press, 2001), 47–49.

68. For a nice discussion of this theme in early modern lyric, see Roland Greene, *Unrequited Conquests: Love and Empire in the Colonial Americas* (Chicago: University of Chicago Press, 1999), 14.

69. There is a wonderful poem of Petrarch that expresses this perfectly: "A rain of tears, a fog of disdain drenches and loosens the already tired ropes which are made of error entwined with ignorance. Hidden are my two usual sweet stars: reason and art, dead among the waves, such that I am beginning to despair of the port." Quoted in ibid., 142.

70. Lawrence Bond, "Introduction," in Nicholas of Cusa, *Selected Spiritual Writings*, 17.

71. Hans Blumenberg, *The Legitimacy of the Modern Age*, trans. Robert Wallace (Cambridge: MIT Press, 1985), 490.

72. See sections 1 and 3 of SJ, *SW*.

73. Foucault opened up new vistas on the question of philosophy in his growing preoccupation with the meditative and spiritual disciplines of the ancient Greeks and Romans (this has been well studied by James Miller, Arnold Davidson, and David Tracy). Sparked by Pierre Hadot's work on the spiritual exercises of the ancients, Foucault increasingly viewed the art of philosophy as a spiritual discipline to reshape and reform the human self. Philosophy is concerned with the manipulation of human bodies and souls the way a sculptor creates beauty out of an amorphous block of stone. Only in the process of living differently would one be able to think differently. Foucault gave us, in his own words, "a critical ontology of ourselves that has to be considered not, certainly, as a theory, a doctrine, nor even a permanent body of knowledge that is accumulating; it has to be conceived as an attitude, an ethos, a philosophical life in which the critique of what we are is at one and the same time the historical analysis of the limits that are imposed on us and the ordeal of their possible transcendence." Quoted in James Miller, *The Passion of Michel Foucault* (Cambridge: Harvard University Press, 2000), 279.

CHAPTER 5

1. Mario Vargas Llosa, "García Márquez: From Aracataca to Macondo," in *Gabriel García Márquez*, ed. Harold Bloom (New York: Chelsea House, 1989), 17.

2. Angel Flores, "Magical Realism in Spanish American Fiction," in *Magical Realism: Theory, History, Community*, ed. Lois Parkinson Zamora and Wendy B. Faris (Durham: Duke University Press, 1995), 114.

3. Llosa, "García Márquez," 17.

4. Zamora and Faris, "Introduction," in *Magical Realism*, 5–6.

5. Said, *Reflections on Exile*, 185–86.

6. Quoted in Menocal, *Ornament of the World*, 10–11.

7. Echevarría, *Alejo Carpentier*, 125.

8. Ibid.

9. Octavio Paz, *Convergences: Essays on Art and Literature*, trans. Helen Lane (New York: Mariner Books, 1991), 89.

10. Cathy Jrade, *Modernismo: Modernity and the Development of Spanish American Literature* (Austin: University of Texas Press, 1998), 78.

11. James Joyce, *A Portrait of an Artist as a Young Man*, ed. Chester Anderson (New York: Penguin, 1968), 221.

12. For an excellent description of the Neoplatonism of the Renaissance, see Dupré, *Passage to Modernity*, 42–64.

13. Paz, *Labyrinth of Solitude*, 20.

14. T. S. Eliot, "Burnt Norton," in *The Four Quartets* (New York: Harcourt Brace and Company, 1943), 15.

15. Friedrich Nietzsche, *Thus Spoke Zarathustra*, edited and translated by Walter Kaufmann (New York: Penguin, 1954), 334.

16. Paz, *Convergences*, 74.

17. Ibid., 45, 76.

18. Jrade, *Modernismo*, 88–89.

19. Ibid., 115.

20. David Tracy, *The Analogical Imagination* (New York: Crossroad, 1991), 209.

21. See especially *Epistle to the Romans*, trans. Edwin Hoskyns (Oxford: Oxford University Press, 1933).

22. Franz Roh, "Magical Realism: Post-expressionism," in Zamora and Faris, *Magical Realism*, 20.

23. Quoted in Seymour Menton, *Magical Realism Rediscovered* (New York: Art Alliance Press, 1982), 40.

24. Quoted in ibid.

25. Quoted in ibid., 47.

26. Irene Guenther, "Magical Realism, New Objectivity, and the Arts During the Weimar Republic," in Zamora and Faris, *Magical Realism*, 35.

27. Edwin Williamson, *Borges: A Life* (New York: Viking Press, 2004), 176.

28. Jorge Luis Borges, *Labyrinths*, ed. Donald Yates and James Irby (New York: New Directions, 1964), 10.

29. Ibid., 92.

30. Ibid., 164.

31. Quoted in Williamson, *Borges*, 179.

32. Ibid., 208.

33. Quoted in Guenther, "Magical Realism, New Objectivity, and the Arts," 61.

34. Roh, "Magical Realism," 16.

35. Echevarría, *Alejo Carpentier*, 116, 125.

36. Alejo Carpentier, "On the Marvelous Real in America," in Zamora and Faris, *Magical Realism*, 86.

37. Carpentier's fondness for folk culture and premodern, non-European forms of understanding parallels, more than he acknowledged, trends in the culture he professes to despise, the modern West. Consider Peter Gay's comment about Freud's *Interpretation of Dreams*: "As Freud pointed out in his first, still most astonishing masterpiece, *The Interpretation of Dreams*, in arguing that dreams have meanings that can be understood and interpreted, he was taking the side of the unlettered and the superstitious against blind philosophers and obtuse psychologists." This is precisely what was happening not only in the mind of Carpentier but also in many avant-garde movements of the late nineteenth and early twentieth centuries. They wished to take the side of the unlettered and primitive against the prosaic crowd of European intellectuals. The fascination with dreams and the irrational, with archaic and non-Western cultures and religions, or with the phenomenon of faith reflected an instinctual desire, Dionysian-like, to explore unknown regions beyond the borders of Western thought and culture. Carpentier found the concept of the marvelous vis-à-vis the Americas as working toward that end. See Sigmund Freud, *The Freud Reader*, ed. Peter Gay (New York: Norton, 1989), xvi.

38. Carpentier, "On the Marvelous Real in America," 86.

39. Ibid., 84, 88.

40. Ibid., 93.

41. Ibid., 93, 101.

42. Ibid., 101.

43. See Nietzsche, *Birth of Tragedy*.

44. Carlos Fuentes, foreword to Carpentier, *Baroque Concerto*, 15–16.

45. It is well-known that William Faulkner influenced many Latin American writers. Carlos Fuentes explains this influence in the following way: "This is why we Latin Americans feel the work of William Faulkner lies so close to us. In North American literature, only Faulkner stands apart from that closed world of optimism and success and offers us instead a vision shared by both the United States and Latin America: the image of defeat, separation, doubt—the image of tragedy." See "Novel as Tragedy," 543.

46. Ariel Dorfman, "*Men of Maize*: Myth as Time and Language," in *MM*, 407.

47. Quoted in Roberto González Echevarría, *Myth and Archive: A Theory of Latin American Narrative* (Durham: Duke University Press, 1998), 160.

48. Ibid.

49. Mario Vargas Llosa, "A New Reading of *Men of Maize*," in *MM*, 451.

50. Quoted in Luis Harss and Barbara Dohmann, "The Land Where the Flowers Bloom," in *MM*, 426–27.

51. Gerald Martin, "Introduction to *Men of Maize*," in *MM*, xvii.

52. Quoted in Echevarría, *Alejo Carpentier*, 26.

53. Ibid., 147.

54. In this case, Carpentier steers a careful path between two major narratives about the Haitian Revolution: one that emphasizes the unspeakable acts of violence by African slaves against white people; and the story of an oppressed people who took revolt and revolution in their own hands against the horrors of slavery. For studies of the Haitian Revolution, see Matthew Clavin, *Toussaint Louverture and the American Civil War* (Philadelphia: University of Pennsylvania Press, 2011); and Laurent Dubois, *Avengers of the New World: The Story of the Haitian Revolution* (Cambridge: Harvard University Press, 2005).

55. Echevarría, *Alejo Carpentier*, 84.

56. Echevarría, *Myth and Archive*, 108.

57. *The Zohar*, trans. Daniel Matt (Stanford: Stanford University Press, 2006), 245.

58. See Walter Benjamin, *The Trauerspiel: On the Origins of German Tragic Drama*, trans. George Steiner (New York: Verso, 1992).

59. See Gershom Scholem, *On the Kabbalah and Its Symbolism* (New York: Schocken Books, 1996), 149–50.

60. Quoted in the introduction to *EC* by Timothy Brennan.

61. Echevarría, *Alejo Carpentier*, 167–68.

62. Echevarría, *Celestina's Brood*, 193.

63. See Emmanuel Levinas, *Totality and Infinity: An Essay on Exteriority* (New York: Springer, 1980).

64. Quoted in Alberto Manguel, *Homer's The Iliad and The Odyssey: A Biography* (New York: Grove Press, 2007), 200.

CONCLUSION

1. Greenblatt, *Marvelous Possessions*.

2. Quoted in Zamora, *Inordinate Eye*, 297.

3. See the edited collection by Zamora and Kaup, *Baroque New Worlds*.

4. Zamora, *Inordinate Eye*, 286. Zamora prefers the term "Neobaroque" because, in her estimation, it preserves and salvages the cultural past and its products. Postmodernity, in her reading, cuts its ties with the past in a "discontinuous" way. Also, her preference for "Neobaroque" implies a "possibility of meaning" that she sees as lacking in many postmodern thinkers (294–95). I actually agree with her version of the "Neobaroque," but I take issue with her working definition of postmodernity. I'm following, instead, David Tracy here. In Tracy's reading, postmodernity has a liberating potential, one that can recover the fragments of the past in a post-critical way.

5. David Tracy, "Fragments: The Spiritual Situation of Our Times," in *God, the Gift, and Postmodernism*, ed. John Caputo and Michael Scanlon (Bloomington: Indiana University Press, 1999), 179.

6. Quoted in Zamora, *Inordinate Eye*, 297.

7. T. S. Eliot, "East Coker," in *Four Quartets*.

BIBLIOGRAPHY

Adorno, Rolena. "The Negotiation of Fear in Cabeza de Vaca's *Naufragios*." In Greenblatt, *New World Encounters*.

———. *The Polemics of Possession in Spanish American Narrative*. New Haven: Yale University Press, 2007.

Alighieri, Dante. *The Divine Comedy*. Vol. 3, *Paradise*. San Francisco: Chronicle Books, 2005.

Armas, Frederick de. "Cervantes and the Italian Renaissance." In Cascardi, *The Cambridge Companion to Cervantes*.

Asturias, Miguel Ángel. *Men of Maize*. Translated by Gerald Martin. Pittsburgh: University of Pittsburgh Press, 1995.

———. *El Señor Presidente*. Translated by Frances Partridge. New York: Waveland Press, 1997.

Auerbach, Erich. *Dante: Poet of the Secular World*. Translated by Ralph Manheim. New York: New York Review of Books, 2007.

———. "The Enchanted Dulcinea." In Echevarría, *Cervantes' "Don Quixote."*

Bakhtin, Mikhail. *Problems of Dostoevsky's Poetics*. Translated by Caryl Emerson. Minneapolis: University of Minnesota Press, 1984.

Barth, Karl. *Epistle to the Romans*. Translated by Edwin Hoskyns. Oxford: Oxford University Press, 1933.

Benjamin, Walter. *The Trauerspiel: On the Origins of German Tragic Drama*. Translated by John Osborne. New York: Verso, 1992.

Bhabha, Homi. *The Location of Culture*. London: Routledge, 1994.

Blanchot, Maurice. *The Book to Come*. Translated by Charlotte Mandell. Stanford: Stanford University Press, 2003.

Blumenberg, Hans. *The Legitimacy of the Modern Age*. Translated by Robert Wallace. Cambridge: MIT Press, 1985.

Bond, Lawrence. "Introduction." In *Nicholas of Cusa: Selected Spiritual Writings*. Translated by H. Lawrence Bond. New York: Paulist Press, 1997.

Borges, Jorge Luis. *Labyrinths*. Edited by Donald Yates and James Irby. New York: New Directions, 1964.

———. *Selected Poems*. Edited by Alexander Coleman. London: Penguin, 1999.

Brodersen, Momme. *Walter Benjamin: A Biography*. New York: Verso, 1996.

Brown, Peter. *Augustine of Hippo: A Biography*. Berkeley: University of California Press, 2000.

Buci-Glucksmann, Christine. *Baroque Reason: The Aesthetics of Modernity*. London: Sage, 1994.

Cabeza de Vaca, Álvar Núñez. *Chronicle of the Narvaez Expedition*. Translated by Harold Augenbraum. New York: Penguin, 2002.

Calderón de la Barca, Pedro. *Life Is a Dream*. Translated by Gregary Racz. New York: Penguin, 2006.

Carpentier, Alejo. *Baroque Concerto*. New York: André Deutsch, 1991.

———. *Explosion in a Cathedral*. Translated by Harriet de Onis. Minneapolis: University of Minnesota Press, 2001.

———. *The Harp and the Shadow*. Translated by Thomas Christensen and Carol Christensen. New York: Mercury House, 2007.

————. *The Kingdom of This World*. Translated by Harriet de Onis. New York: Farrar, Straus and Giroux, 2006.

————. *The Lost Steps*. Translated by Harriet de Onis. Minneapolis: University of Minnesota Press, 2001.

————. "On the Marvelous Real in America." In Zamora and Faris, *Magical Realism*.

————. *War of Time*. New York: Knopf, 1970.

Carson, Anne. *Eros: The Bittersweet*. New York: Dalkey Archive Press, 1986.

Cascardi, Anthony, ed. *The Cambridge Companion to Cervantes*. Cambridge: Cambridge University Press, 2002.

————. "Introduction." In Cascardi, *The Cambridge Companion to Cervantes*.

Celorio, Gonzalo. "From the Baroque to the Neobaroque." In Zamora and Kaup, *Baroque New Worlds*.

Certeau, Michel de. *The Mystic Fable*. Vol. 1. Translated by Michael Smith. Chicago: University of Chicago Press, 1992.

————. "Mystic Speech." In *The Certeau Reader*, edited by Graham Ward. Oxford: Blackwell, 2000.

————. "Travel Narratives of the French to Brazil: Sixteenth to Eighteenth Centuries." In Greenblatt, *New World Encounters*.

Cervantes, Miguel de. "The Dogs Colloquy." In *Exemplary Stories*. Translated by C. A. Jones. London: Penguin, 1972.

————. *Don Quixote*. Translated by John Rutherford. New York: Penguin, 2003.

————. *Los trabajos de Persiles y Sigismunda*. Edited by Carlos Romero. Madrid: Cátedra, 2004.

Clavin, Matthew. *Toussaint Louverture and the American Civil War*. Philadelphia: University of Pennsylvania Press, 2011.

Clendinnen, Inga. "Fierce and Unnatural Cruelty: Cortes and the Conquest of Mexico." In Greenblatt, *New World Encounters*.

Cohen, Arthur. *The Tremendum: A Theological Interpretation of the Holocaust*. New York: Continuum, 1993.

Columbus, Christopher. *The Four Voyages*. Translated by J. M. Cohen. New York: Penguin, 1969.

Cone, James. *The Spirituals and the Blues*. Maryknoll, N.Y.: Orbis Books, 1992.

Conley, Tom. "The Essays and the New World." In *The Cambridge Companion to Montaigne*, edited by Ullrich Langer. Cambridge: Cambridge University Press, 2005.

Derrida, Jacques. *The Gift of Death*. Translated by David Wills. Chicago: University of Chicago Press, 2007.

————. "How to Avoid Speaking in Denials." In *Derrida and Negative Theology*, edited by Harold Coward and Toby Foshay. Albany: SUNY Press, 1992.

————. *Memoirs of the Blind*. Translated by Pascale-Anne Brault and Michael Naas. Chicago: University of Chicago Press, 1993.

————. *On the Name*. Edited by Thomas Dutoit. Stanford: Stanford University Press, 1995.

Descartes, René. *The Meditations*. In *Philosophical Writings of Descartes*, vol. 2. Translated by John Cottingham, Robert Stoothoff, and Dugald Murdoch. Cambridge: Cambridge University Press, 1984.

————. *The Passions of the Soul*. In *Philosophical Writings of Descartes*, vol. 1. Translated by John Cottingham, Robert Stoothoff, and Dugald Murdoch. Cambridge: Cambridge University Press, 1985.

Dorfman, Ariel. "*Men of Maize*: Myth as Time and Language." In Asturias, *Men of Maize*.

Dubois, Laurent. *Avengers of the New World: The Story of the Haitian Revolution*. Cambridge: Harvard University Press, 2005.

Dupré, Louis. *Passage to Modernity.* New Haven: Yale University Press, 1993.

Easterling, P. E., ed. *The Cambridge Companion to Greek Tragedy.* Cambridge: Cambridge University Press, 1997.

Echevarría, Roberto González. *Alejo Carpentier: The Pilgrim at Home.* Ithaca: Cornell University Press, 1977.

———. *Celestina's Brood: Continuities of the Baroque in Spanish and Latin America.* Durham: Duke University Press, 1993.

———, ed. *Cervantes' "Don Quixote": A Casebook.* Oxford: Oxford University Press, 2005.

———. "Góngora's and Lezama's Appetites." In Zamora and Kaup, *Baroque New Worlds.*

———. *Love and the Law in Cervantes.* New Haven: Yale University Press, 2005.

———. *Myth and Archive: A Theory of Latin American Narrative.* Durham: Duke University Press, 1998.

Eckhart, Meister. *Meister Eckhart: The Essential Sermons, Commentaries, Treatises, and Defense.* Translated by Edmund Colledge and Bernard McGinn. New York: Paulist Press, 1981.

Eliot, T. S. *The Four Quartets.* New York: Harcourt Brace and Company, 1943.

———. *The Wasteland, and Other Poems.* New York: Harcourt Brace Jovanovich, 1934.

Elliot, J. H. *The Old World and the New, 1492–1650.* Cambridge: Cambridge University Press, 1970.

Emerson, Ralph Waldo. *Nature and Selected Essays.* New York: Penguin, 2003.

Flores, Angel. "Magical Realism in Spanish American Fiction." In Zamora and Faris, *Magical Realism.*

Foucault, Michel. *Madness and Civilization.* Translated by Richard Howard. New York: Vintage Books, 1988.

———. *The Order of Things: An Archaeology of the Human Sciences.* New York: Vintage Books, 1994.

Freud, Sigmund. *The Freud Reader.* Edited by Peter Gay. New York: Norton, 1989.

Fuentes, Carlos. *The Buried Mirror: Reflections on Spain and the New World.* New York: Houghton Mifflin, 1992.

———. *Don Quixote; or, The Critique of Reading.* Austin: University of Texas Press, 1976.

———. "Don Quixote; or, The Critique of Reading." *Wilson Quarterly* 1, no. 5 (1977).

———. Foreword to *Baroque Concerto,* by Alejo Carpentier. London: André Deutsch, 1988.

———. "The Novel as Tragedy: William Faulkner." In Zamora and Kaup, *Baroque New Worlds.*

Garcés, María Antonia. *Cervantes in Algiers: A Captive's Tale.* Nashville: Vanderbilt University Press, 2002.

Gates, Henry Louis. *The Signifying Monkey: A Theory of African-American Literary Criticism.* Oxford: Oxford University Press, 1988.

Goizueta, Roberto. *Caminemos con Jesus.* Maryknoll, N.Y.: Orbis Books, 1995.

Goldmann, Lucien. *The Hidden God: A Study of Tragic Vision in the Pensées of Pascal and the Tragedies of Racine.* London: Routledge and Kegan Paul, 1977.

Góngora, Luis de. *Selected Poems by Luis de Góngora.* Edited and translated by John Dent-Young. Chicago: University of Chicago Press, 2007.

Gonzalez, Michelle. *Sor Juana: Beauty and Justice in the Americas.* Maryknoll, N.Y.: Orbis Books, 2003.

Greenblatt, Stephen. *Marvelous Possessions: The Wonder of the New World.* Chicago: University of Chicago Press, 1991.

———, ed. *New World Encounters.* Berkeley: University of California Press, 1993.

Greene, Roland. *Unrequited Conquests: Love and Empire in the Colonial Americas.* Chicago: University of Chicago Press, 1999.

Gutiérrez, Gustavo. *Las Casas: In Search of the Poor of Jesus Christ.* Translated by Robert R. Barr. Maryknoll, N.Y.: Orbis Books, 1993.

———. *On Job: God-Talk and the Suffering of the Innocent.* Translated by Matthew O'Connell. Maryknoll, N.Y.: Orbis Books, 1987.

Hahn, Juergen. *The Origins of the Baroque Concept of Peregrinatio.* Chapel Hill: University of North Carolina Press, 1973.

Hall, Stuart. "Negotiating Caribbean Identities." In *New Currents in Caribbean Thoughts,* edited by Brian Meeks and Folke Lindahl. Jamaica: University of West Indies Press, 2001.

Hanke, Lewis. *The Spanish Struggle for Justice in the Conquest of America.* Dallas: Southern Methodist University Press, 2002.

Harries, Karsten. *Infinity and Perspective.* Cambridge: MIT Press, 2001.

Harss, Luis, and Barbara Dohmann. "The Land Where the Flowers Bloom." In Asturias, *Men of Maize.*

Hart, Kevin. *The Beauty of the Infinite: The Aesthetics of Christian Truth.* Cambridge: William B. Eerdmans, 2003.

———. *The Trespass of the Sign: Deconstruction, Theology, and Philosophy.* New York: Fordham University Press, 2000.

Hirsch, Edward. *How to Read a Poem and Fall in Love with Poetry.* New York: Harvest Books, 1999.

Holiday, Billie. "Strange Fruit." Commodore Records, 1939.

Hume, David. "Of National Characters." In *Essays: Moral, Political, and Literary,* edited by T. H. Greena and T. H. Grose. London: Longmans, 1895.

Inés de la Cruz, Sor Juana. *Poems, Protest, and a Dream.* Translated by Margaret Sayers Peden. New York: Penguin, 1997.

———. *Selected Writings.* Translated and edited by Pamela Kirk Rappaport. New York: Paulist Press, 2005.

Joyce, James. *A Portrait of an Artist as a Young Man.* Edited by Chester Anderson. New York: Penguin, 1968.

———. *Ulysses.* New York: Vintage Books, 1990.

Jrade, Cathy. *Modernismo: Modernity and the Development of Spanish American Literature.* Austin: University of Texas Press, 1998.

Kagan, Richard. *Lawsuits and Litigants in Castile, 1500–1700.* Chapel Hill: University of North Carolina Press, 1981.

Kamen, Henry. *The Disinherited: Exile and the Making of Spanish Culture.* New York: Harper-Collins, 2007.

Kiberd, Declan. *Ulysses and Us.* New York: Norton, 2009.

Kierkegaard, Søren. *Fear and Trembling/Repetition.* Translated by Edna Hong and Howard Hong. Princeton: Princeton University Press, 1983.

Kirk, Pamela. *Sor Juana Inés de la Cruz: Religion, Art, and Feminism.* New York: Continuum, 1988.

Kolakowski, Leszek. *Modernity on Endless Trial.* Chicago: University of Chicago Press, 1990.

Kristeller, Paul O. *Renaissance Thought.* New York: HarperCollins, 1961.

Las Casas, Bartolomé de. *Apologia.* In Sullivan, *Indian Freedom.*

———. *History of the Indies.* In Sullivan, *Indian Freedom.*

———. *A Short Account of the Destruction of the Indies.* Translated by Nigel Griffin. New York: Penguin, 1992.

Lazier, Benjamin. *God Interrupted: Heresy and the European Imagination between the World Wars.* Princeton: Princeton University Press, 2008.

Leon-Jones, Karen Silvia de. *Giordano Bruno and the Kabbalah.* Lincoln: University of Nebraska Press, 2004.

Levinas, Emmanuel. *Totality and Infinity: An Essay on Exteriority.* New York: Springer, 1980.

Lewis, David Levering. *God's Crucible: Islam and the Making of Europe.* New York: Norton, 2008.

Lewis, R. W. B. *Dante*. London: Penguin, 2002.

Lima, José Lezama. "Baroque Curiosity." In Zamora and Kaup, *Baroque New Worlds*.

Llosa, Mario Vargas. "García Márquez: From Aracataca to Macondo." In *Gabriel García Márquez*, edited by Harold Bloom. New York: Chelsea House, 1989.

———. "A New Reading of *Men of Maize*." In Asturias, *Men of Maize*.

Lukács, György. *Theory of the Novel*. Translated by Anna Bostock. Cambridge: MIT Press, 1971.

Mandeville, Sir John. *The Travels of Sir John Mandeville*. Translated by C. W. R. D. Moseley. New York: Penguin, 2005.

Manguel, Alberto. *Homer's The Iliad and The Odyssey: A Biography*. New York: Grove Press, 2007.

Maravall, José Antonio. *Culture of the Baroque: Analysis of a Historical Structure*. Minneapolis: University of Minnesota Press, 1986.

Marion, Jean-Luc. "In the Name: How to Avoid Speaking of 'Negative Theology.'" In *God, the Gift, and Postmodernism*, edited by John Caputo and Michael Scanlon. Bloomington: Indiana University Press, 1999.

———. "Introduction." In *Mystics: Presence and Aporia*, edited by Michael Kessler and Christian Sheppard. Chicago: University of Chicago Press, 2003.

———. *The Visible and the Revealed*. Translated by Christina Gschwandtner. New York: Fordham University Press, 2008.

Márquez, Gabriel García. *One Hundred Years of Solitude*. Translated by Gregory Rabassa. New York: Harper and Row, 1970.

Martin, Gerald. *Gabriel García Márquez: A Life*. New York: Knopf, 2009.

———. "Introduction to *Men of Maize*." In Asturias, *Men of Maize*.

Mazzotta, Giuseppe. *Dante, Poet of the Desert: History and Allegory in the Divine Comedy*. Princeton: Princeton University Press, 1979.

McGinn, Bernard. *The Foundations of Mysticism*. New York: Crossroad, 1991.

———. "Ocean and Desert as Symbols of Mystical Absorption in the Christian Tradition." *Journal of Religion* 74, no. 2 (April).

Medrano, Juan Espinosa de. *Apologético en favor de Don Luis de Góngora*, edited by Luis Jaime Cisneros. Lima: Universidad de San Martín de Porres, 2005.

Melville, Herman. *Moby Dick; or, The Whale*. New York: Penguin, 1992.

Menocal, María Rosa. *The Ornament of the World*. New York: Little, Brown, 2002.

———. *Shards of Love: Exile and the Origins of the Lyric*. Durham: Duke University Press, 1994.

Menton, Seymour. *Magical Realism Rediscovered*. New York: Art Alliance Press, 1982.

Michelangelo. *Michelangelo: Poems and Letters*. Translated by Anthony Mortimer. London: Penguin, 2007.

Mignolo, Walter. *The Darker Side of the Renaissance: Literacy, Territoriality, and Colonization*. Ann Arbor: University of Michigan Press, 2003.

Miller, James. *The Passion of Michel Foucault*. Cambridge: Harvard University Press, 2000.

More, Thomas. *Utopia*. London: Penguin, 2003.

Nava, Alexander. *The Mystical and Prophetic Thought of Simone Weil and Gustavo Gutiérrez*. Albany: SUNY Press, 2002.

Neruda, Pablo. *The Poetry of Pablo Neruda*. Edited by Ilan Stavans. New York: Farrar, Straus and Giroux, 2003.

Nicholas of Cusa. *Nicholas of Cusa: Selected Spiritual Writings*. Translated by H. Lawrence Bond. New York: Paulist Press, 1997.

Nietzsche, Friedrich. *The Birth of Tragedy*. Edited by Michael Tanner and Shaun Whiteside. New York: Penguin, 1994.

———. *On the Advantage and Disadvantage of History for Life*. Translated by Peter Preuss. Indianapolis: Hackett, 1980.

————. *Thus Spoke Zarathustra.* Edited and translated by Walter Kaufmann. New York: Penguin, 1954.

Oberman, Heiko. *The Dawn of the Reformation.* Edinburgh: T. and T. Clark, 1986.

Otto, Rudolph. *The Idea of the Holy.* Oxford: Oxford University Press, 1958.

Pagden, Anthony. *European Encounters with the New World.* New Haven: Yale University Press, 1994.

————. "Text and Experience in the Writing of Bartolomé de Las Casas." In Greenblatt, *New World Encounters.*

Pamuk, Orhan. *My Name Is Red.* Translated by Erdag M. Goknar. New York: Vintage Books, 2001.

Pascal, Blaise. *Pensées.* Translated by A. J. Krailsheimer. London: Penguin, 1966.

Paz, Octavio. *Convergences: Essays on Art and Literature.* Translated by Helen Lane. New York: Mariner Books, 1991.

————. *The Labyrinth of Solitude.* Translated by Lysander Kemp. New York: Grove Press, 1985.

————. *Sor Juana; or, The Traps of Faith.* Translated by Margaret Sayers Peden. Cambridge: Harvard University Press, 1990.

Pessoa, Fernando. *The Book of Disquiet.* Translated by Richard Zenith. London: Penguin, 2001.

Picón-Salas, Mariano. *A Cultural History of Spanish America.* Berkeley: University of California Press, 1962.

Pidal, Ramón Menéndez. "The Genesis of Don Quixote." In Echevarría, *Cervantes' Don Quixote.*

Pilkington, William. "Epilogue." In Álvar Núñez Cabeza de Vaca, *Adventures in the Unknown Interior of America,* edited and translated by Cyclone Covey. Albuquerque: University of New Mexico Press, 1993.

Plotinus. *The Enneads.* Translated by Stephen Mackenna. London: Penguin, 1991.

Porete, Marguerite. *Marguerite of Porete: Mirror of Simple Souls.* Translated by Ellen Babinsky. New York: Paulist Press, 1993.

Quiroga, Pedro. *Coloquios de la Verdad.* Seville: Tip. Zarzuela, 1922.

Rodó, José Enrique. *Ariel.* Translated by Margaret Sayers Peden. Austin: University of Texas Press, 1988.

Rodriguez, Richard. *Brown: The Last Discovery of America.* New York: Viking Books, 2002.

Roh, Franz. "Magical Realism: Post-expressionism." In Zamora and Faris, *Magical Realism.*

Ruprecht, Louis A. *Tragic Posture and Tragic Vision.* New York: Continuum, 1994.

Sabat-Rivers, Georgina. "A Feminist's Re-reading of Sor Juana's Dream." In *Feminist Perspectives on Sor Juana Inés de la Cruz,* edited by Stephanie Merrim. Detroit: Wayne State University Press, 1991.

Said, Edward. *Reflections on Exile, and Other Essays.* Cambridge: Harvard University Press, 2002.

Santi, Enrico Mario. *Pablo Neruda: The Poetics of Prophecy.* Ithaca: Cornell University Press, 1982.

Schneider, Paul. *Brutal Journey: Cabeza de Vaca and the Epic First Crossing of North America.* New York: Owl Books, 2007.

Scholem, Gershom. *On the Kabbalah and Its Symbolism.* New York: Schocken Books, 1996.

Sells, Michael. *Mystical Languages of Unsaying.* Chicago: University of Chicago Press, 1994.

Sontag, Susan. "Foreword." In *Pedro Páramo.* Translated by Margaret Sayers Peden. New York: Grove Press, 1994.

Spitzer, Leo. "Linguistic Perspectivism in the *Don Quijote.*" In Echevarría, *Cervantes' Don Quixote.*

Stavans, Ilan. *The Hispanic Condition: Reflections on Culture and Identity in America.* New York: HarperCollins, 1995.

————. "Introduction." In Cabeza de Vaca, *Chronicle of the Narvaez Expedition.*

Steiner, George. *The Death of Tragedy.* New Haven: Yale University Press, 1980.

Sullivan, Frances Patrick, trans. *Indian Freedom: The Cause of Bartolomé de Las Casas, 1484–1566: A Reader*. Kansas City, Mo.: Sheed and Ward, 1995.

Todorov, Tzvetan. *The Conquest of America*. Translated by Richard Howard. Norman: University of Oklahoma Press, 1999.

Toulmin, Stephen. *Cosmopolis: The Hidden Agenda of Modernity*. Chicago: University of Chicago Press, 1990.

Tracy, David. *The Analogical Imagination*. New York: Crossroad, 1991.

———. *Dialogue with the Other*. Louvain: Peeters Press, 1990.

———. "Fragments: The Spiritual Situation of Our Times." In *God, the Gift, and Postmodernism*, edited by John Caputo and Michael Scanlon. Bloomington: Indiana University Press, 1999.

———. "The Hidden God: The Divine Other of Liberation." In *Cross Currents: The Journal of the Association of Religion and Intellectual Life* 46, no. 1 (1996).

Turner, Denys. *The Darkness of God: Negativity in Christian Mysticism*. Cambridge: Cambridge University Press, 1995.

Wardropper, Bruce. "Don Quixote: Story or History?" In Echevarría, *Cervantes' Don Quixote*.

West, Cornel. *The Cornel West Reader*. New York: Basic Civitas Books, 1999.

Whitman, Walt. *Leaves of Grass, 1855 Edition*. Edited by Malcolm Cowley. New York: Penguin, 1959.

Williamson, Edwin. *Borges: A Life*. New York: Viking Press, 2004.

Wilson, Diana de Armas. "Cervantes and the New World." In Cascardi, *The Cambridge Companion to Cervantes*.

———. *Cervantes, the Novel, and the New World*. Oxford: Oxford University Press, 2000.

Wu-Tang Clan. "Triumph." In *Wu-Tang Forever*. Loud/RCA Records, 1997.

Yates, Frances. *Giordano Bruno and the Hermetic Tradition*. Chicago: University of Chicago Press, 1964.

Zamora, Lois Parkinson. *The Inordinate Eye: New World Baroque and Latin American Fiction*. Chicago: University of Chicago Press, 2006.

———. *Writing the Apocalypse: Historical Vision in Contemporary U.S. and Latin American Fiction*. Cambridge: Cambridge University Press, 1993.

Zamora, Lois Parkinson, and Wendy B. Faris, eds. *Magical Realism: Theory, History, Community*. Durham: Duke University Press, 1995.

Zamora, Lois Parkinson, and Monika Kaup, eds. In *Baroque New Worlds: Representation, Transculturation, Counterconquest*. Durham: Duke University Press, 2010.

Zavala, Iris. "*One Hundred Years of Solitude* as Chronicle of the Indies." In *Gabriel García Márquez's "One Hundred Years of Solitude": A Casebook*, edited by Gene Bell-Villada. Oxford: Oxford University Press, 2002.

Ziolkowski, Eric. *The Sanctification of Don Quixote: From Hidalgo to Priest*. University Park: Pennsylvania State University Press, 1991.

The Zohar. Translated by Daniel Matt. Stanford: Stanford University Press, 2006.

INDEX

Abd al-Rahman, 235 n. 33
Abraham, 42, 148
absence, 20
  Baroque and, 77, 100, 152, 162
  God and, 33, 76–77, 123
  presence and, 21, 77–78, 152, 154, 162
  wonder and exile and, 8, 30
Adam and Eve, 42, 43, 216
Adorno, Rolena, 5, 50, 69
Agrippa, Cornelius, 138, 239 n. 37
Aguiar y Seijas, Francisco de, 116
Albert the Great, 44
Alegría, Fernando, 173
Alexander the Great, 46, 47
alienation, 79, 146, 178, 180–81
  Baroque and, 100, 168
  Medrano and, 103, 104
allegory, 81–82, 83, 84, 109
alterity, 29–30, 44
  wonder and, 8, 15, 68
amazement, 15, 20–21, 44, 179
analogy, 176, 177, 178
apocalypse, 95, 134, 196–97, 200
Apologético (Medrano), 102
apophasis, 16
Apuleius, 239 n. 44
Aquinas. *See* Thomas Aquinas
Arguedas, José María, 111, 197–98
Ariel (Rodó), 38–39
Aristotle, 40, 165
Armas, Frederick de, 137, 239 n. 44
Asturias, Miguel Ángel, 194–204
  and exile, 172, 194, 201, 222
  and magical realism, 197–98, 203–4, 221–22
  works: *Men of Maize*, 192–94, 197–204;
    El Señor Presidente, 194–95, 196–97
atheism, 123, 162, 225
Auerbach, Eric, 139
Augustine, St., 84, 157
avant-garde, 177–79, 181

Bakhtin, Mikhail, 119
Balbuena, Bernardo de, 107
barbarism, 67–68, 134–35

Baroque, 87, 137, 189
  absence and presence in, 77, 100, 152, 162
  allegory in, 81–82, 83, 84, 99
  ambiguity of, 93, 141
  anxiety and melancholy in, 122, 151
  Carpentier and, 187–88, 190, 214, 215, 216, 219
  Cervantes and, 120, 131, 141, 144
  conservative vs. revolutionary elements in, 107, 237 n. 66
  death and fiesta motifs in, 112–13
  despair and disillusionment in, 94, 99, 141
  emotionalism and sentimentalism in, 109
  Enlightenment and, 108, 226
  exile and, 73, 89, 90, 168
  hiddenness of God theme in, 73, 79, 81, 90, 98, 109–13, 123
  irony and, 224
  madness motif in, 88–89, 122, 134
  magical realism and, 170
  monsters and, 91–92
  New World flourishing of, 73, 85–91, 105–6, 187–88
  poetry and, 104, 107, 163
  polycentrism of in New World, 106, 107–8
  reality and, 93, 104, 129
  religion and theology in, 80, 107, 112, 225
  Renaissance and, 74–76, 161
  restless mobility of, 90
  tragic spirit of, 74–75, 76, 78, 81–85, 108, 224
  wonder and, 3, 73, 74, 89, 92, 112
  "world upside-down" motif in, 88
Barrionuevo, Jerónimo de, 89
Barth, Karl, 180–81
beauty, 93, 176
  Carpentier on, 100, 189, 219, 220
  wonder and, 23
Benjamin, Walter, 61, 235 n. 40
  on Baroque, 77, 81–82, 83, 94, 99
Bhabha, Homi, 8, 35
Bible, 23–24, 63, 239 n. 37
  Hebrew, 25, 196
  New Testament gospels, 138

Cuba, 205
Cuneo, Michele de, 40

dance, 176
Dante Alighieri, 19, 183–84
Darío, Rubén, 178–79
darkness, 78–79
death, 24, 97, 155–56
    Baroque and, 82, 112–13
    exile and, 24–25, 62
    madness and, 133–34
Deleuze, Gilles, 227
Derrida, Jacques, 17–18, 23–24
Descartes, René, 13–15, 140
desert image, 9, 33, 130
    exile and, 18–19, 176
    prophets and, 22–23
Díaz del Castillo, Bernal, 53
Dickinson, Emily, 163–64
Diego de Jesus, 82–83
dispossession, 56, 62
    exile and, 8, 30, 224
    justice and, 143, 239 n. 44
    of populations, 205–6
    wonder and, 8, 30, 224
diversity and pluralism, 45, 50, 126, 181
    New World Baroque and, 106, 107–8
    travel and, 139–40
    wonder and, 43
The Divine Comedy (Dante), 19
The Divine Narcissus (Sor Juana), 148, 152–53
Dominicans, 58, 59, 233 n. 34
donkey image, 137–38, 239 n. 37
Don Quixote (Cervantes), 121, 138–39, 141, 143
    Baroque nature of, 120, 144
    Captive's Tale in, 125–26, 127
    Cervantes as character in, 119–20
    exile as theme in, 118, 139
    Foucault on, 118–19
    historical elements in, 128–30, 134, 135, 136–37, 140–41
    Sancho Panza in, 7, 119, 122, 128, 129–30, 135, 138, 144
    as satire, 5, 131–32
    theatrical motif in, 119–20
    as tragedy, 128, 136–37
Don Quixote (character), 88, 128–29
    as antihero, 137
    and books, 114, 116
    chivalrous dreams of, 4, 118
    Christ affinities with, 142–43
    conversion of, 141–42, 239 n. 44
    disillusionment and defeat of, 137, 141, 156

madness of, 7, 88, 120, 121–22, 135, 139, 225
    passion for justice of, 143–44
    as *picaro*, 133
    wandering of, 115, 120
    wisdom of, 120, 121–22, 139
Dorfman, Ariel, 196
Dupré, Louis, 76, 88
Dussel, Enrique, 5

Ecclesiastes, 94
Echevarría, Roberto González, 5, 83, 86–87, 173
    on Carpentier, 136, 185, 211, 219
    on *Don Quixote*, 129, 131, 136
    on Medrano, 101, 103
    on Roh, 184, 185
Eckhart, Meister, 17, 43, 239 n. 38
"Ecstatic Journey to the Heavens" (Kircher), 156
Eliot, T. S., 29, 151
Elliott, J. H., 5
Enlightenment, 13, 15, 108, 217–18, 226
Eriugena, John the Scott, 17, 20, 43, 79, 204
eros, 174
Estrada Cabrera, Manuel, 194
evil, 65, 74, 80, 208
    Liberation theology on, 111
exile, 225, 235 n. 33
    Asturias and, 172, 194, 201, 222
    Baroque and, 73, 89, 90, 168
    Cabeza de Vaca and, 24, 32
    Carpentier and, 172, 193, 205, 216, 222
    Cervantes and, 116–17, 118, 121, 122, 123–29, 139
    death and, 24–25, 62
    desert image and, 18–19, 176
    dispossession and, 8, 30, 224
    Las Casas and, 32, 66, 224
    madness and, 132–33
    magical realism and, 171–73, 175–76, 225
    Medrano on, 101–2, 103
    in New World, 26–28, 100
    prophetic literature and, 22–26
    Sor Juana and, 117, 118, 168
    wonder and, 3, 32–33, 118, 180, 193, 224
Explosion in a Cathedral (Carpentier), 214–15, 216, 217–18, 220
Ezekiel, 24

faith, 143, 185, 240 n. 48. *See also* religion
fantasy, 35, 36, 41
Faris, Wendy, 172